How to use this book

Use the features in this book to focus your revision, track your progress through the topics and practise your exam skills.

② Features to help you revise

Scan the **QR codes** to visit the BBC Bitesize website. It will link straight through to more revision resources on that subject.

Each bite-sized chunk has a **timer** to indicate how long it will take. Use them to plan your revision sessions.

Complete **worked examples** demonstrate how to approach exam-style questions.

Tick boxes allow you to track the sections you've revised. Revisit each page to embed your knowledge.

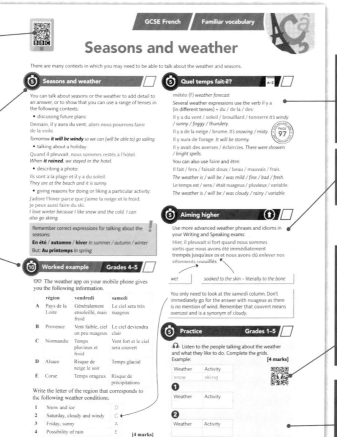

Key words and phrases are translated for each topic. Stamps refer you to the relevant **vocabulary** and **grammar** sections.

Aiming higher boxes give you tips for getting the best grades.

Scan the **audio QR codes** for the listening activities. You can also access these from your ActiveBook or by visiting **www. pearsonschools.co.uk/ BBCBitesizeLinks.**

Test yourself with exam-style practice at the end of each page and check your answers at the back of the book.

② Exam focus features

The *About your exam* section at the start of the book gives you all the key information about your exams, as well as showing you how to identify the different questions.

You will also find green *Exam skills* and red *Strategies* pages. These work through extended exam-style questions and provide techniques for approaching each exam paper.

② ActiveBook and app

This Revision Guide comes with a **free online edition**. Follow the instructions from inside the front cover to access your ActiveBook.

You can also download the **free BBC Bitesize app** to access revision flash cards and quizzes.

If you do not have a QR code scanner, you can access all the links in this book from your ActiveBook or visit **www.pearsonschools.co.uk/BBCBitesizeLinks.**

Your French GCSE

Your GCSE French exam tests your knowledge of French and your ability to communicate in speech and writing across a range of contexts.

 ## About the exam papers

You will have to take **four papers** as part of your GCSE French qualification. Each paper is equally weighted and worth 25% of the total marks.

Paper 1
Listening
Questions in English and French

Paper 2
Speaking
Role-play, photo card and conversation

Paper 3
Reading
Questions in English and French, translation into English

Paper 4
Writing
Writing tasks and translation into French

 ## What you need to know

The papers cover three themes. You need to understand and use vocabulary from all of them.

Theme 1: Identity and culture
Topic 1: Me, my family and friends
Topic 2: Technology in everyday life
Topic 3: Free-time activities
Topic 4: Customs and festivals in Francophone countries

Theme 2: Local, national, international and global areas of interest
Topic 1: Home, town, neighbourhood and region
Topic 2: Social issues
Topic 3: Global issues
Topic 4: Travel and tourism

Theme 3: Current and future study and employment
Topic 1: My studies
Topic 2: Life at school / college
Topic 3: Education post-16
Topic 4: Jobs, career choices and ambitions

Foundation and Higher tier

There are two tiers for each paper: Foundation and Higher.

You can sit either Foundation or Higher, as long as all four skills are the same tier. You must sit all four papers in the same exam series.

Foundation tier papers cover grades 1–5. Higher tier papers cover grades 4–9.

Revising for your exam

- ☑ Get into the habit of revising some vocabulary every day.
- ☑ Make a revision plan and make sure that you allow yourself enough time to cover everything you need to know.

- ☑ Listen to spoken French on a regular basis.
- ☑ Practise speaking on your own or with a friend.
- ☑ When you revise nouns, don't forget to learn the gender.
- ☑ Use the revision guide to see how words are used in context.

Your exam dates

Find out the date and time of each of your GCSE French papers and write them in this table.

	Date	AM or PM?
Paper 1		
Paper 2		
Paper 3		
Paper 4		

Paper 1: Listening

Paper 1 tests your ability to understand spoken French and to respond to questions in both French and English.

 Listening exam key facts

In the listening paper, you will be expected to understand and respond to different types of spoken French.

Duration: 35 minutes (45 minutes Higher tier)

Number of marks: 40 marks (50 marks Higher tier)

Percentage of exam: 25%

The exam includes 5 minutes' reading time of the paper before the audio is played.

The questions are in two sections:

Section A – questions in English to be answered in English.

Section B – questions in French to be answered in French.

 In the exam

- You will hear different extracts of spoken French and will need to respond to questions about each extract.
- Each extract will be played twice.
- You can make notes at any time.
- Each question will have a theme or topic, such as 'News reports' or 'Le mariage'.
- You will need to identify the gist or main points of what is said, including specific details and the speakers' opinions .
- For all of Section A you will be expected to answer in **English**. All of Section B will be in **French**. Read the question carefully to be sure which language to use.

 Exam explainer

Some questions are multiple choice. You need to select the correct option.

During your 5 minutes' reading time, and the pauses before the audio is played, try to predict what words you might hear for each scenario.

Write your response in the answer box.

Special occasions in France

You listen to a podcast sent to you by a French exchange student.

In this extract, you hear about special occasions and events in France. Write the correct letter to describe what it said.

The speaker is describing a...

   A   religious event.

   B   musical event.

   C   sporting event.

☐

[1 mark]

The heading sets the context for the audio clip and tells you what kind of language to expect.

For this task, you need to understand the overall gist of what you have heard. You will not need to understand every word.

In your exam, the invigilator will play each audio clip. In this book, you can scan the QR codes to play them or go to www.pearsonschools.co.uk/BBCBitesizeLinks.

In this question you need to give details from the extract you hear. You can make notes as you listen to the audio clips to help you answer.

Recycling

You overhear some French people discussing the advantages and disadvantages of recycling.

Write down in **English one** advantage and **one** disadvantage of recycling, according to each speaker.

1) Michelle

   Advantage: _____

   Disadvantage: _____

[2 marks]

Almost all the questions are worth one mark, so you only need to give a simple answer for each one.

Paper 2: Speaking

In your speaking exam, you will be expected to communicate effectively for a variety of purposes.

 Speaking exam key facts

Duration: 7–9 minutes (10–12 minutes Higher tier)

Number of marks: 60 marks

Percentage of exam: 25%

The speaking exam will be conducted by your teacher. It will be recorded and marked by an AQA examiner. There are three parts to the speaking exam:

- role-play (15 marks)
- photo card (15 marks)
- general conversation (30 marks).

 Preparation time

- You will be given a role-play card and a photo card. You will have 12 minutes to prepare them, and you will be supervised during this time.
- You are allowed to make notes and can take these into the exam with you.
- You will have to hand these notes to your teacher before the start of the general conversation.
- You are not allowed to use a dictionary.

 Part 1: Role-play

Vous parlez avec un(e) employé(e) dans un hôtel en France.

- Réservation hier et votre nom.
- !
- Arrivée en retard – une raison.
- Problème avec votre chambre (un détail).
- ? Piscine.

You will be given a card with five prompts to prepare for a role-play scenario. The role-play will last approximately 2 minutes.

You will be awarded up to 2 marks per task for successfully conveying the message.

Up to 5 further marks are awarded for knowledge and creative use of language.

! means you will have to answer an unprepared question.

? means you need to ask a question.

 Part 2: Photo card

Look at the photo and make notes. You will be asked questions about the photo and topics related to **me, my family and friends.**

You will be asked these questions and two more that you have not prepared:

- Qu'est-ce qu'il y a sur la photo?
- Que penses-tu des familles nombreuses?
- Qu'est-ce que tu as fait en famille le weekend dernier?

You will be given a photo card to prepare and you will be asked five questions, three of which are printed on the card so you can prepare your answers. This will last 2 minutes for Foundation tier and 3 minutes for Higher tier.

Your responses are assessed for communication only, and you can be awarded up to 15 marks.

You will be asked at least one question where you will need to give and explain your opinion.

For the first question, you will need to describe what you can see in the photo.

 Part 3: General conversation

The general conversation will be on the two themes not covered by the photo card. You will choose the first theme. You must ask a question at some point during the general conversation. General conversation will last for 3–5 minutes at Foundation Tier and 5–7 minutes at Higher Tier. Marks are awarded for:

- communication: 10 marks
- range and accuracy of language: 10 marks
- pronunciation and intonation: 5 marks
- spontaneity and fluency: 5 marks.

Paper 3: Reading

Paper 3 tests your ability to understand and respond to written French.

 Reading exam key facts

Duration: 45 minutes (1 hour Higher tier)

Number of marks: 60 marks

Percentage of exam: 25%

The questions are in three sections:

- **Section A** – questions in English to be answered in English or non-verbally.
- **Section B** – questions in French to be answered in French or non-verbally.
- **Section C** – translation from French into English (a minimum of 35 words for Foundation tier and 50 words for Higher tier).

Section C is worth 15% of the total marks for Paper 3 (i.e. 9 marks at both Foundation and Higher tier).

> You may be asked to read a short passage of French and answer in English.

> For questions only worth one or 2 marks you will need to give short and concise answers.

 **Exam explainer**

Read this extract from the novel *Le Journal d'une femme de chambre* by Octave Mirbeau, in which Célestine describes her new employment.

Aujourd'hui, 14 septembre, à trois heures de l'après-midi, par un temps doux, gris et pluvieux, je suis entrée dans ma nouvelle place. C'est la douzième en deux ans. Bien entendu, je ne parle pas des places que j'ai faites durant les années précédentes. Il me serait impossible de les compter (…)

L'affaire s'est traitée par l'intermédiaire des Petites Annonces du *Figaro* et sans que je voie Madame. Nous nous sommes écrit des lettres, ça'a été tout (…) Les lettres de Madame sont bien écrites (…) elles révèlent un caractère méticuleux.

(a) What was the weather like the day she started her new job? Give two details. **[2 marks]**

(b) Where did Célestine find out about her new job? **[1 mark]**

> You only need to give two details.

> The exam will include extracts of varying lengths from a range of sources, including authentic sources such as tweets, text messages, emails, websites, instructions, public notices, advertisements, brochures, guides, letters, newspapers, reports and magazines. There will also be extracts from literary sources.

 Exam explainer

Votre ami(e) français(e) vous a montré les tweets suivants au sujet de la musique.

> **@theo_s** Mon copain dit que la musique rock est ennuyeuse et je suis totalement d'accord. Je trouve ça terrible!

> **@Caro_K** Écouter la musique classique ne me dit rien. C'est monotone! Mais c'est tout de même vrai que les musiciens ont beaucoup de talent.

> **@JeSuisSophie** Le jazz est ma musique préférée. Je peux l'écouter pendant toute la journée!

Quelles sont leurs opinions sur la musique? Écrivez pour chaque personne **P** (pour positif), **N** (pour négatif) ou **P/N** (pour positif et négatif).

@theo_s	
@Caro_K	
@JeSuisSophie	

 Exam focus

- You will be expected to identify the gist of a text, as well as details and points of view.
- You will be expected to work out the meaning of some unfamiliar language, using your knowledge of the context, language and grammar.
- You will be expected to make inferences (read between the lines) for some texts and to draw conclusions.
- There will only be an example answer if this is necessary to help you understand how to answer a particular question.
- You are not allowed to use a dictionary.

 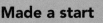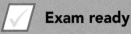

Paper 4: Writing (Foundation)

Paper 4 tests your ability to communicate in written French. This page explains the requirements for the Foundation tier.

 Writing exam key facts

Duration: 1 hour
Number of marks: 50 marks
Percentage of exam: 25%
You are not allowed to use a dictionary.

The Foundation paper has four questions

You must answer all of the questions. Questions 1, 2 and 4 are in French and you must answer in French.
For Question 3, you must translate an English text into French. The translation into French is worth 20% of the total marks for Writing (10 marks at Foundation tier).

 Exam explainer – Writing (Foundation) **Grades 1–5**

1 In question 1, you will see: Qu'est-ce qu'il y a sur la photo? Écrivez **quatre** phrases en **français**. This requires you to respond to a photo. You are expected to write four sentences, which are assessed for communication, 2 marks per sentence: **Total 8 marks.**

2 Vous êtes dans un restaurant et envoyez un texto à votre ami(e) français(e).
Mentionnez:
- où vous êtes
- le repas
- votre serveur(euse)
- vos activités pour le reste de la journée.

Écrivez environ **40** mots en **français**.
[16 marks]

> In Question 2, you will be given a scenario, such as a short message, and several bullet points to include.

> You have to respond in French and write around 40 words.

> You will be assessed on the content of your answer (10 marks) and its quality (6 marks).

3 Translate the following sentences into **French**.
(a) My sister is small.
_____
(b) At school I hate science and PE.
_____
...
(e) I played video games at my house with my friends.
_____ **[10 marks]**

> You will be given five sentences in English to translate into French. Each sentence is worth two marks.

> The marks are awarded for conveying the key message of the text (5 marks) and applying accurate grammatical knowledge and structures (5 marks).

4 Vous décrivez votre vie scolaire pour votre blog.
Décrivez:
- votre collège et ses élèves
- les aspects positifs et négatifs de votre collège
- un échange scolaire récent
- où vous voulez étudier à l'avenir.

Écrivez environ **90** mots en **français**. Répondez à chaque aspect de la question. **[16 marks]**

> In Question 4, you will have a choice of two tasks. Each task will give you a different scenario and four bullet points. You should write about each of the bullet points.

> You are expected to write approximately 90 words.

> You will be assessed on the content of your answer (10 marks) and the quality of the language used (6 marks).

  Made a start **Feeling confident** **Exam ready**

Paper 4: Writing (Higher)

Paper 4 tests your ability to communicate in written French. This page explains the requirements for the Higher tier.

Writing exam key facts

Duration: 1 hour 15 minutes

Number of marks: 60 marks

Percentage of exam: 25%

The Higher paper has three questions. Question 4 on the Foundation paper and Question 1 on the Higher paper are the same.

You must answer all of the questions. Questions 1 and 2 are in French and you must answer in French. For Question 3, you must translate an English text into French. The translation into French is worth 20% of the total marks for Writing (12 marks at Higher tier).

You are not allowed to use a dictionary.

Aiming higher

For the highest marks, your response to the task should be relevant, detailed and cover each element of the task.

You should use a wide range of vocabulary and grammatical structures, including more complex structures, such as relative clauses and **après avoir** + past participle. Your response should include the past, present and future tenses and you must make sure that what you're writing is accurate in terms of spelling and grammar.

Exam explainer – Writing (Higher)   Grades 4–9

In Question 1, you will be given a scenario and four bullet points. You should write about each of the bullet points.

1 Vous décrivez votre vie scolaire pour votre blog.

Décrivez:
- votre collège et ses élèves
- les aspects positifs et négatifs de votre collège
- un échange scolaire récent à votre collège
- où vous voulez étudier à l'avenir.

You are expected to write approximately 90 words.

Écrivez environ **90** mots en **français**. Répondez à chaque aspect de la question.   **[16 marks]**

You will be assessed on the content of your answer (10 marks) and the quality of the language used (6 marks).

2 Vous écrivez un article sur le sport pour un magazine français.

Décrivez:
- l'importance du sport
- un événement sportif mémorable.

You will need to write approximately 150 words.

Écrivez environ **150** mots en **français**. Répondez aux deux aspects de la question.   **[32 marks]**

Question 2 is an open-ended writing task. You might be asked to write a report, an article, an email, a blog post or a letter and will be expected to cover two compulsory bullet points.

Your answer will be assessed for content (15 marks), range of language (12 marks) and accuracy (5 marks).

In Question 3 you will need to translate a passage of English into French. It will be about 50 words long.

3 Translate the following passage into **French**.

To celebrate Christmas, all my family came to my house. My parents prepared a special meal and we watched films. I received a new book. It is useful for my homework. Next week, for New Year's Eve, I would like to go to a party in the town centre. I think it will be exciting!   **[12 marks]**

Your answer is assessed for your ability to convey the key messages (6 marks) and your ability to apply grammatical knowledge and structures (6 marks).

 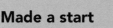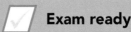

Understanding rubrics

Revise the French instructions you will find on your exam papers.

 ② About rubrics

The 'rubrics' are the instructions that are given for tasks on the exam papers. Always read them carefully and make sure you understand what you have to do. Occasionally, there may also be an example to help you understand what to do.

The rubrics will be in French on the writing paper and in part B of your listening and reading exams.

⑤ Following instructions

Question types

Choisissez (deux) phrases qui sont vraies. *Choose (two) correct sentences.*

Choisissez la réponse correcte / la bonne réponse. *Choose the correct answer.*

Complétez... en français / la grille / le texte suivant avec les mots de la liste ci-dessous.

Complete... in French / the grid / the following text with words from the list below.

Écoutez ce passage / cette conversation / cette interview / ce reportage... *Listen to this passage / this conversation / this interview / this report.*

Answering

Écrivez P (pour positif), N (pour négatif) ou P/N (pour positif et négatif).

Write P (for positive), N (for negative) or P/N (for positive and negative).

Décidez si c'est Vrai (V), Faux (F) ou Pas Mentionné (PM). Écrivez V, F ou PM.

Decide if it's True (T), False (F) or Not Mentioned (NM). Write T, F or NM.

Donnez (deux) détails. *Give (two) details.*

Répondez à ces questions. *Answer these questions*

Répondez (aux questions) en français.

Answer (the questions) in French.

Il n'est pas nécessaire d'écrire des phrases complètes.

It is not necessary to write in full sentences.

C'est quelle personne? Écrivez le nom de la bonne personne.

Which person is it? Write the name of the correct person.

② Instructions on the Writing paper

Écrivez environ 90 mots en français. Répondez à chaque aspect de la question. *Write approximately 90 words in French. Write something about each bullet point.*

Écrivez quatre phrases en français à propos de la photo. *Write four sentences in French about the photo.*

⑤ Vocabulary A–Z

aspect (m) *aspect*
positif *positive*
négatif *negative*
avantage (m) *advantage*
inconvénient (m) *disadvantage*
détail (m) *detail*
vrai *true*
faux *false*
nom (m) *name*
pas mentionné *not mentioned*
blanc (m) *blank*
case (f) *box*
grille (f) *grid*
phrase (f) *sentence*
réponse (f) *answer*
Qui...? *Who...?*
bonne personne (f) *correct person*
Quelle personne? *Which person?*
en français *in French*
choisissez *choose*
complétez *complete*
décidez *decide*
écoutez *listen to*
écrivez *write*
identifiez *identify*
lisez *read*
mentionnez *mention*
remplissez *fill*
répondez *reply*

> The verbs on this page ending in – **ez** (**choisissez, écoutez, décidez**, etc.) are in the **imperative** form.

⑩ Practice

👓 What do each of the following rubrics mean in English?

❶ Écrivez **P+N** pour une opinion positive et négative.

❷ Attention! Vous pouvez utiliser la même lettre plus d'une fois.

❸ Choisissez **deux** phrases qui sont vraies.

❹ Remplissez les blancs.

❺ Identifiez la bonne personne.

❻ Quelle est la réponse correcte?

❼ Écrivez la bonne lettre dans la case.

Numbers

You will need a good understanding of numbers as they appear in a variety of contexts.

⑩ Cardinal numbers 1–100 [A–Z]

1	un	11	onze	21	vingt et un	40	quarante
2	deux	12	douze	22	vingt-deux	50	cinquante
3	trois	13	treize	23	vingt-trois	60	soixante
4	quatre	14	quatorze	24	vingt-quatre	70	soixante-dix
5	cinq	15	quinze	25	vingt-cinq	71	soixante et onze
6	six	16	seize	26	vingt-six	72	soixante-douze
7	sept	17	dix-sept	27	vingt-sept	80	quatre-vingts
8	huit	18	dix-huit	28	vingt-huit	81	quatre-vingt-un
9	neuf	19	dix-neuf	29	vingt-neuf	90	quatre-vingt-dix
10	dix	20	vingt	30	trente	100	cent

30–39, 40–49 and 50–59 follow the same pattern as 20–29.

71–79 are like saying *sixty eleven*, *sixty twelve*, etc. You need a hyphen for numbers 72–79.

80 is literally *four twenties*. For 81–99, add 1–19 to quatre-vingt.

There is an **s** on **quatre-vingts** for 80, but not for 81–99. !

⑤ More numbers [A–Z]

101	cent un	750	sept cent cinquante
200	deux cents	1.000	mille
205	deux cent cinq	1.000.000	un million

Percentages are expressed as pour cent:
dix pour cent 10%

Adding -aine to a number means *about*.

Je voudrais une dizaine de poires. *I'd like about 10 pears.*

une douzaine *a dozen*

un nombre de *a number of*

In French you use a full stop or a space to indicate thousands. A comma is used to represent a decimal point. For example **10,5%** (*10.5*%).

⑤ Ordinal numbers [A–Z]

1st	premier / première	1er (m) / 1re (f)
2nd	deuxième / second(e)	2e
3rd	troisième	3e
4th	quatrième	4e
5th	cinquième	5e
6th	sixième	6e
7th	septième	7e
8th	huitième	8e
9th	neuvième	9e
10th	dixième	10e

Ordinal numbers agree with the noun, but only premier and second have a feminine form, for example la Première Guerre mondiale. Second(e) is used when talking about the second item of two things only, whereas deuxième is used when talking about the second item in a longer list.

⑩ Practice — Grades 1–5

🎧 Listen to the results of a survey about leisure habits. Write the letter of the activity next to the correct number.

37%	
63%	
75%	
84%	

Going to the cinema	A
Going on social networks	B
Listening to the radio	C
Shopping	D
Surfing the net	E
Watching TV	F

[4 marks]

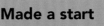 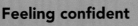

The French alphabet

You will need to be able to understand and say the letters of the alphabet in order to spell things out loud.

② About the French alphabet

French uses the same letters of the alphabet as English, but they are pronounced differently. Make sure you are able to recognise them when spoken, and that you know how to say them. You may need to be able to spell out any of the following:

- your name or a place name
- your address or email address
- a web address
- a common French acronym.

② How to say the French alphabet

A – ah	H – ash	O – oh	V – vay
B – bay	I – ee	P – pay	W – doobleh vay
C – say	J – jhee	Q – kuh	X – eeks
D – day	K – kah	R – air	Y – ee-grek
E – euh	L – ell	S – ess	Z – zed
F – eff	M – emm	T – tay	
G – jhay	N – enn	U – oo	

⑤ Common abbreviations

CDI: centre de documentation et d'information (m) *resource centre*

CES: collège d'enseignement secondaire (m) *secondary school*

EPS: éducation physique et sportive (f) *PE (physical education)*

HLM: habitation à loyer modéré (f) *council / social housing*

SDF: sans domicile fixe (m) *homeless person*

SNCF: société nationale des chemins de fer français (f) *national rail service*

TGV: train à grande vitesse (m) *high speed train*

TVA: taxe sur la valeur ajoutée (f) *VAT (value added tax)*

VTT: vélo tout terrain (m) *mountain bike*

SAMU: service d'aide médicale d'urgence (f) *emergency medical services*

le SAMU is actually pronounced as a word, not as individual letters

② Punctuation and symbols

You may need to know the following punctuation marks:

´ accent aigu (m)	' apostrophe (f)
` accent grave (m)	. point (f)
^ accent circonflexe (m)	@ arrobase (f)
¨ tréma (m)	_ tiret bas (m)
ç c cédille (f)	ABC majuscule
- trait d'union (m)	abc minuscule

⑤ Worked example Grades 1–5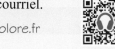

① Donne-moi ton adresse courriel.

💬 Adélaïde_Roussel@tricolore.fr

② Comment ça s'écrit?

💬 ah majuscule day euh accent aigu ell ah ee tréma day euh tiret bas air majuscule oh minuscule oo deux ess euh ell arrobase tricolore (comme le drapeau) point eff air

You can also use the link word **comme** when spelling something out, e.g. **A, comme Afrique.**

⑮ Practice Grades 1–5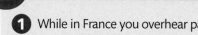

① While in France you overhear parts of conversations.

A	A bicycle	**1**	
B	Council / social housing	**2**	
C	French railway system	**3**	
D	High speed train	**4**	
E	Homeless people	**5**	
F	Resource centre		
G	A school subject		

For each extract, choose the topic from the list and write the correct letter in the box. **[5 marks]**

② Answer the following questions.

- Comment t'appelles-tu?
- Comment ça s'écrit?
- Quelle est ton adresse?
- Et ton adresse e-mail? **[4 marks]**

 Made a start   Feeling confident   Exam ready

Dates

You need to know how to say the date, and talk about months and days to describe events or important occasions.

⑤ How to say the date

In French, the days of the week and the months of the year are all masculine, and are written with a lowercase letter. You use cardinal numbers (deux, trois, quatre, cinq...) when talking about dates, except for the first of the month, which uses the ordinal number, premier.

Quelle est la date d'aujourd'hui / de ton anniversaire?
What is the date today / of your birthday?

(Aujourd'hui) c'est le douze janvier.
*(Today) it's **12 January**.*

C'est le lundi premier juin.
*It's **Monday**, **1 June**.*

en juillet *in July*

Le Salon du Chocolat à Paris a lieu au mois d'octobre.
The Salon du Chocolat takes place in Paris during the month of October.

> When you say the day of the week in the date, **le** comes before the day, instead of the number.

⑤ Days and months

Les jours de la semaine – the days of the week

lundi	Monday	vendredi	Friday
mardi	Tuesday	samedi	Saturday
mercredi	Wednesday	dimanche	Sunday
jeudi	Thursday		

Les mois de l'année – the months of the year

janvier	January	juillet	July
février	February	août	August
mars	March	septembre	September
avril	April	octobre	October
mai	May	novembre	November
juin	June	décembre	December

février prochain / dernier *next / last February*

au début / fin d'avril *at the beginning / end of April*

de mai à septembre *from May to September*

VOCABULARY LINK
PAGE
97

⑤ Worked example — Grades 1–5

Answer the following questions:

❶ Quand est-ce que tu travailles au supermarché?

💬 *Je travaille le vendredi soir.*

❷ Quand vas-tu voir tes grands-parents?

💬 *Je vais voir mes grands-parents dimanche prochain.*

❸ Qu'est-ce que tu as le mardi matin au collège?

💬 *Le mardi matin, j'ai maths et géo.*

> For something that happens regularly on the same day of the week, you use **le**, e.g. **le vendredi** means *on Fridays*.

> **prochain** means *next*; **dimanche dernier** *last Sunday*.

> To talk about a particular time of day, use **le** + day of the week + time of day, e.g. **le mardi matin / après-midi / soir** *Tuesday morning / afternoon / evening*

⑤ How to say the year

There are several ways to say the year in French:

La Révolution française a eu lieu en mille sept cent quatre-vingt-neuf / dix-sept cent quatre-vingt-neuf.
The French revolution took place in 1789.

Mon grand-père est mort en mille neuf cent quatre-vingt-dix-neuf / dix-neuf cent quatre-vingt-dix-neuf.
My grandfather died in 1999.

Ma petite sœur est née en deux mille treize. *My sister was born in 2013.*

Pendant les années soixante, les femmes portaient des jupes courtes.
In the sixties women wore short skirts.

⑤ Practice — Grades 1–5

🎧 Listen to the information about the dates of various French festivals.

1st March	A	28th May	D
21st April	B	21st June	E
17th May	C	8th December	F

Write the correct letter for each definition.

1	Start of the *Fête des lumières*	
2	Last day of Cannes Film Festival	
3	Last day of the *Fête du Citron*	
4	Date of the *Fête de la musique*	

[4 marks]

 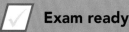

Telling the time

You should be familiar with both the 12-hour and 24-hour clock.

 About telling the time

You will need to be able to tell the time in order to understand and talk about:

- arrivals and departures

  Le train part à neuf heures. *The train leaves at nine o'clock.*

  Ma grand-mère arrive à trois heures et demie.

  My grandmother arrives / is arriving at half past three.

- the start and finish of an event

  Les cours commencent à neuf heures moins le quart.

  Lessons begin at a quarter to nine.

  Le concert a fini à neuf heures vingt. *The concert finished at twenty past nine.*

- opening and closing times

  Le musée ouvre à dix heures. *The museum opens at ten o'clock.*

  Les magasins ferment à six heures du soir. *The shops close at six o'clock.*

- a period of time

  J'ai travaillé de huit heures à quatre heures. *I worked from 8 a.m. to 4 p.m.*

The question for all these situations would begin with **À quelle heure...?** *At what time...?*

 Worked example **Grades 1–9**

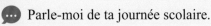 **Parle-moi de ta journée scolaire.**

Ma journée scolaire commence le matin à huit heures et demie quand j'arrive au collège. Normalement, j'ai du temps pour bavarder un peu avec mes copains pendant un quart d'heure parce que le premier cours ne commence qu'à neuf heures moins le quart, mais aujourd'hui, le bus était en retard et je n'ai pas eu le temps. J'ai cours toute la matinée, mais il y a une récréation qui dure vingt minutes, de dix heures cinquante jusqu'à onze heures dix. Après le déjeuner, j'ai encore deux cours avant la fin de la journée.

Try to use a variety of negative expressions, not just **ne … pas. Ne...que** means *only*.

Relative pronouns like **qui, que** and **dont** are another useful way to show that you can use a variety of structures.

GRAMMAR LINK PAGE 78

Quelle heure est-il?

In French you say the hour first and then the minutes.

7.00 **Il est sept heures.**

7.05 **Il est sept heures cinq.**

7.10 **Il est sept heures dix.**

7.15 **Il est sept heures quinze or et quart.**

7.20 **Il est sept heures vingt.**

7.25 **Il est sept heures vingt-cinq.**

7.30 **Il est sept heures trente or et demie.**

7.35 **Il est sept heures trente-cinq or il est huit heures moins vingt-cinq.**

7.45 **Il est sept heures quarante-cinq or il est huit heures moins le quart.**

VOCABULARY LINK PAGE 97

These are statements about what the time is in answer to the question: **Quelle heure est-il?** *What time is it?*

There is no s on **heures** for the time with **une: à une heure cinq**.

There is no e on **demi** with midday (**midi**) and midnight (**minuit**): **il est midi / minuit et demi.**

The 24-hour clock is often used in France. Make sure you know the equivalent 12-hour clock time.

1	2	3	4	5	6	7	8	9	10	11	12
13	14	15	16	17	18	19	20	21	22	23	24

You can add **du matin, de l'après-midi** or **du soir** (*in the morning, afternoon, evening*) to the end of a 12-hour clock phrase to make it clear what time of day you are describing.

Je fais de la natation à six heures du soir (or **à dix-huit heures**). *I go swimming at six in the evening.*

The best answers will use conjunctions like **quand** to join sentences and make them more complex.

You must say **pendant** (*during*) in time expressions like this, not **pour** (*for*) which should only be used when talking about the future.

 Practice **Grades 1–5**

 Listen to the extracts and write the times below.

1	The train arrival time	
2	Exhibition closing time	
3	Start of concert	
4	Bedtime	

You can use the 12-hour or 24-hour clock. **[4 marks]**

 Made a start   **Feeling confident** 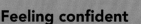 **Exam ready**

Seasons and weather

There are many contexts in which you may need to be able to talk about the weather and seasons.

 Seasons and weather

You can talk about seasons or the weather to add detail to an answer, or to show that you can use a range of tenses in the following contexts:

- discussing future plans:

Demain, il y aura du vent, alors nous pourrons faire de la voile.

Tomorrow **it will be windy** so we can (will be able to) go sailing.

- talking about a holiday:

Quand il pleuvait, nous sommes restés à l'hôtel.
When **it rained**, we stayed in the hotel.

- describing a photo:

Ils sont à la plage et il y a du soleil.
They are at the beach and it is sunny.

- giving reasons for doing or liking a particular activity:

J'adore l'hiver parce que j'aime la neige et le froid. Je peux aussi faire du ski.
I love winter because I like snow and the cold. I can also go skiing.

> Remember correct expressions for talking about the seasons:
>
> **En été / automne / hiver** In summer / autumn / winter
> But: **Au printemps** In spring

 Worked example **Grades 4–5**

👓 The weather app on your mobile phone gives you the following information.

	région	vendredi	samedi
A	Pays de la Loire	Généralement ensoleillé, mais froid	Le ciel sera très nuageux
B	Provence	Vent faible, ciel un peu nuageux	Le ciel deviendra clair
C	Normandie	Temps pluvieux et froid	Vent fort et le ciel sera couvert
D	Alsace	Risque de neige le soir	Temps glacial
E	Corse	Temps orageux	Risque de précipitations

Write the letter of the region that corresponds to the following weather conditions.

1	Snow and ice	D
2	Saturday, cloudy and windy	C
3	Friday, sunny	A
4	Possibility of rain	E

[4 marks]

 Quel temps fait-il?

météo (f) weather forecast

Several weather expressions use the verb **il y a** (in different tenses) + **du / de la / des**:

Il y a du vent / soleil / brouillard / tonnerre *It's windy / sunny / foggy / thundery.*

Il y a de la neige / brume. *It's snowing / misty.*

Il y aura de l'orage. *It will be stormy.*

Il y avait des averses / éclaircies. *There were showers / bright spells.*

You can also use **faire** and **être**:

Il fait / fera / faisait doux / beau / mauvais / frais.
The weather is / will be / was mild / fine / bad / fresh.

Le temps est / sera / était nuageux / pluvieux / variable.
The weather is / will be / was cloudy / rainy / variable.

VOCABULARY LINK
PAGE
97

 Aiming higher ⬆

Use more advanced weather phrases and idioms in your Writing and Speaking exams:

Hier, il pleuvait si fort quand nous sommes sortis que nous avons été immédiatement trempés jusqu'aux os et nous avons dû enlever nos vêtements mouillés.

| *wet* | *soaked to the skin – literally to the bone* |

You only need to look at the **samedi** column. Don't immediately go for the answer with **nuageux** as there is no mention of wind. Remember that **couvert** means *overcast* and is a synonym of *cloudy*.

 Practice **Grades 1–5**

🎧 Listen to the people talking about the weather and what they like to do. Complete the grids.
Example: **[4 marks]**

Weather	Activity
snow	skiing

 ❶

Weather	Activity

❷

Weather	Activity

 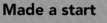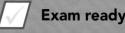

Greetings

There are many ways of greeting people in French, depending on the time of day or year, the occasion and the person to whom you are speaking.

 10 Forms of address

There are formal and informal ways of greeting and addressing people. You should use the informal form **tu** when talking to someone your own age, a friend, a child or a family member. Use the formal **vous** when talking to an adult or someone you do not know very well. You should also use **vous** when talking to more than one person. You can add **monsieur** or **madame** to your greeting to make it even more polite.

You must also use the appropriate possessive adjective and emphatic pronoun:

Comment s'appelle votre mari / ton frère / ta sœur?

What is your husband / brother / sister called?

Ça va? *How are you?*

→ **Oui, et toi / vous?** *Fine, and you?*

Je te / vous présente mon père / ma mère / mes parents.

I'd like to introduce you to my father / mother / parents.

> ### Exam focus
> You will need to read the instructions carefully in your role play exam and use the correct form of address for the situation.

> This question uses the emphatic pronoun of the informal **tu** and formal **vous.** See page 77.

 5 Worked example | **Grades 1–5**

 Listen to the following extracts from conversations. Write **F** for the use of a formal form of address, and **I** for an informal use.

1	F
2	I
3	I
4	F
5	I

1. Madame, je vous présente ma femme.
   Enchantée, madame.
2. Salut, Gaëlle! Quoi de neuf?
3. Allô, c'est toi, Marc?
4. Bonjour madame, comment allez-vous?
5. Coucou Lyse, ça va?

> This is what you say when actually answering the phone. You don't use **Allô** as a general greeting though, or when you are with someone in person, in which case you would say **Salut** or **Bonjour**.

 10 Vocabulary | A–Z

Greetings for certain occasions
bon appétit *enjoy your meal*
bon voyage *have a safe journey*
bon anniversaire *happy birthday*
bonne année *happy new year*
bonne chance *good luck*
bonnes vacances *have a good holiday*
Joyeux Noël *Happy Christmas*
Joyeuses Pâques *Happy Easter*

VOCABULARY LINK PAGE 97

Saying goodbye
For goodbyes in person or on the phone you can use:
- **Au revoir** *Goodbye*
- **À bientôt** *See you soon*
- **À demain** *See you tomorrow!*
- **À tout à l'heure** *See you later*

Writing a letter or email
For informal letters and emails, you can start with:
- **Cher Paul / Chère Christine** *Dear Paul / Christine*
- **Salut à tous!** *Hi everyone*

For formal letters and emails you should start with:
- **Monsieur / Madame** *Dear Sir / Madam*
- **Messieurs / Mesdames** *Dear Sirs / Madams*

For informal letters and emails, you can end with
- **Amicalement** *best wishes* (used between friends)

For formal letters and emails, you should use
- **Cordialement** *regards*
- **Veuillez agréer, Monsieur / Madame, l'expression de mes sentiments distingués.**
  Yours sincerely / faithfully

 5 Practice | **Grades 1–5**

 While in France you overhear snippets of conversations.

Write the letter of the occasion for each one.

A In a restaurant
B At an airport
C At Christmas
D On January 1st
E At the end of the day
F At a birthday party

1	
2	
3	
4	

[4 marks]

Opinions

You will need to be able to recognise points of view, express your own opinions and give reasons for them.

② Expressing likes and dislikes

Give an opinion by using these expressions which are followed by a noun or verb in the infinitive.

j'aime *I like* je déteste *I hate*
je n'aime pas *I don't like* je préfère *I prefer*

J'aime jouer au football. Je déteste aller chez le dentiste.

⑤ Vocabulary

Introducing opinions
je crois que *I believe that*
je pense que *I think that*
je trouve que *I think / find that*
à mon avis *in my opinion*
selon moi / lui / elle *in my / his / her opinion*
d'après moi / lui *in my / his opinion*
pour moi *for me*
personnellement *personally*

Adverbs like **totalement** (*totally*) or **tout à fait** (*completely*) can add weight to an opinion.

GRAMMAR LINK PAGE 77

Expressing agreement and disagreement
Je suis d'accord *I agree*
Je ne suis pas d'accord *I don't agree*
Moi aussi / Moi non plus *Me too / Me neither*

When expressing your opinion, you should aim to back it up with a reason using *because* (**parce que** or **car**).

Expressing emotions
ça m'énerve *that gets on my nerves*
ça me fait rire *that makes me laugh*
ça me rend triste *that makes me sad*
ça me plaît *I like it*
ça m'est égal *that's all the same to me*
ça ne me dit rien *that doesn't interest / appeal to me*
ça suffit *that's enough*
ce n'est pas la peine *it's not worth it*

VOCABULARY LINK PAGE 98

Expressing the opposite point of view
par contre / en revanche / d'un autre côté *on the other hand*
au contraire *on the contrary*
pourtant *however*

On dit qu'il y a trop de déchets, pourtant on ne recycle pas assez. *They / People say there is too much rubbish, however we don't recycle enough.*

⑩ Worked example — Grades 1–9

🖉 You see this bullet point on a writing task.
• Films - opinions

À mon avis, les films de science-fiction ne sont pas du tout réalistes. Cependant, ils sont souvent très passionnants et divertissants et je peux admirer les effets spéciaux. Par contre, je déteste absolument les films d'horreur parce qu'ils me font peur.

Learn plenty of useful adjectives like **passionnant** (*exciting*) and **divertissant** (*amusing*) to express positive opinions. Remember to make adjectives agree.

Use **À mon avis** to introduce your opinion.

When giving opinions you can expand on your answer using expressions like **cependant** (*however*) and **par contre** (*on the other hand*).

⑩ Practice — Grades 4–5

👓 Your French friend has shown you the following tweets about sport.

@noah_K On dit que le tir à l'arc est un sport très ennuyeux mais je ne suis pas d'accord. Je trouve ça absolument fascinant.

@karim J'adore la boxe parce que les boxeurs sont très forts, mais c'est un sport tout de même dangereux.

@selim_O Je ne suis pas d'accord avec les gens qui disent que le cricket est nul. À mon avis, c'est un sport totalement passionnant.

@Loulou Nager dans les couloirs de nage ne me dit rien. C'est tout à fait monotone!

What are their views on sport? Complete the table with **P** (for positive), **N** (for negative) or **P/N** (for positive and negative). **[4 marks]**

@noah_K		@selim_O	
@karim		@Loulou	

Asking questions

You will have to ask questions during the role-play and the general conversation in your speaking exam.

⑤ How to ask a question ✓

You will have to be able to ask questions about many topics and understand any questions you are asked.

There are several ways of asking a question:

❶ Using **Est-ce que...?**

This turns a statement into a question.
Il est travailleur. *He is hard-working.*
Est-ce qu'il est travailleur? *Is he hard-working?*

❷ You can combine **est-ce que** with a question word.

Pourquoi est-ce que tu ne t'entends pas avec ton frère? *Why don't you get on with your brother?*

❸ You can invert the subject and the verb and use a hyphen between them.

Peux-tu m'aider? *Can you help me?*

Comment vas-tu au collège? *How do you get to school?*

> ❗ To avoid two vowel sounds appearing next to each other, add a **t** with hyphens to the verb and subject inversion to make pronunciation easier.
> **Pourquoi a-t-elle...?** *Why has she...?*

❹ You can use intonation to make a statement sound like a question; just make your voice go up at the end of the sentence.

Il est travailleur? *Is he hard-working?*

⑩ Worked example — Grades 1–9 ✓

💬 Look at the following question prompts from a role-play. What question(s) could you ask?

❶ **?** Aller en ville – transport *(arranging to meet a friend)*

Comment est-ce qu'on va en ville (ce soir)? / On se retrouve à l'arrêt de bus?

❷ **?** Aller en ville – transport *(staying at a hotel on the outskirts of a town)*

Comment est-ce qu'on peut aller en ville? / Est-ce qu'il y a un bus pour aller en ville?

② Exam focus ✓

Your question must have a verb in it to score full marks. Don't forget that you will need to ask your teacher a question in the general conversation too. Remember to use **vous** when addressing them. In the role-play you may need to use **tu**, depending on the context.

② Question words 〔A–Z〕 ✓

qui *who*
qu'est-ce que *what*
qu'est-ce qui *what*
quand *when*
où *where*
pourquoi *why*
comment *how*
combien *how much / how many*
quel(s), quelle(s) *which*
est-ce que *do / does*

> In **qu'est-ce que**, que is used for the **object** in a question:
> **Qu'est-ce que tu fais?** *What are you doing?*
> In **qu'est-ce qui**, qui is used for the **subject** in a question:
> **Qu'est-ce qui manque?** *What is missing?*

VOCABULARY LINK PAGE 99

⑤ Using prepositions and nouns ✓

You may need to combine a question word with a preposition or a noun. Prepositions must always come before the question word and not at the end of a sentence, which is often the case in English, especially when spoken.

Avec qui vas-tu en vacances? *With whom are you going on holiday? / Who are you going on holiday with?*

Dans quelle région est-ce que tu vas rester? *In which region are you staying? / Which region are you staying in?*

À quelle heure est-ce qu'on va se rencontrer? *At what time are we going to meet? / What time are we going to meet at?*

> This task requires you to ask *how* you get into town, but your answer must fit the context.

> Here, **on** has the sense of *we – How shall we get into town?*

> Here, **on** has a broader meaning – *How can one / you get into town?*

> Asking whether there is a bus is an alternative way of completing the task.

⑩ Practice — Grades 1–9 ✓

💬 What questions could you ask for the following scenarios?

- **?** Heure du concert (at a box office)
- **?** Végétarien (in a restaurant with the waiter)
- **?** Projets pour les vacances (talking to a friend)
- **?** Tarifs pour les étudiants (museum entry)

Describing people

You need to be able to give personal information and describe your and others' appearance and personality.

⑤ Describing appearance

You will need use the verbs avoir, être and porter (*to wear*) to describe your own or someone else's appearance and personality. This is also an opportunity to show that you know a range of adjectives and how to use them.

VOCABULARY LINK PAGE 102

Je suis assez mince et de taille moyenne. J'ai les cheveux roux, longs et ondulés, et les yeux bleus. J'ai des taches de rousseur sur le visage. Je ne porte pas de lunettes. Je ressemble un peu à ma mère mais elle est plus petite et a les cheveux très bouclés. Ma meilleure amie est jolie et grande. Elle porte des vêtements cool et est très aimable.

I am quite slim and medium height. I have long red wavy hair and blue eyes. I've got freckles on my face. I don't wear glasses. I look a bit like my mother but she is smaller and has very curly hair. My best friend is pretty and tall. She wears cool clothes and is very kind.

⑤ Giving personal information

In a role-play task you may be asked for some other personal details:

Quel âge as-tu / avez-vous? *How old are you?*

J'ai quinze ans, mais dans un mois, j'aurai seize ans. *I am fifteen, but in a month's time I will be sixteen.*

Quelle est ta / votre date de naissance? *What is your date of birth?*

Je suis né(e) le 22 avril 2001 (deux mille un). *I was born on April 22nd 2001.*

Tu es / Vous êtes de quelle nationalité? *What is your nationality?*

Je suis anglais(e). *I am English.*

VOCABULARY LINK PAGE 105

⑤ Talking about personality

Quelles sont tes / leurs qualités personnelles? *What are your / their personal qualities?*

Je suis gentil(le) et très patient(e). *I am **kind** and very **patient**.*

J'ai un bon sens de l'humour. *I have **a good sense of humour**.*

Il / Elle est égoïste et jaloux / jalouse. *He / she is **selfish** and **jealous**.*

GRAMMAR LINK PAGE 70

Malgré means *in spite of*. Jacob says that his character is different from what people might expect from his appearance.

Remember to use **connaître** when talking about knowing a person or place and **savoir** when talking about knowing how to do something: **Je sais jouer du piano** (*I know how to play the piano*).

Jacob says he doesn't like talking to people he doesn't know. **Je n'aime pas parler avec les gens que je ne connais pas.**

⑩ Worked example — Grades 4–5

 Jacob is writing to his new French pen pal.

> Salut, je m'appelle Jacob. J'ai les cheveux blonds et les yeux bleus. Je suis grand et très musclé et j'adore jouer au foot et aller à la salle de gym. Malgré mon apparence, je suis parfois un peu timide et je n'aime pas parler avec les gens que je ne connais pas. Cependant, avec mes amis, je suis très bavard.

What do you learn about Jacob in the extract?

Which **two** statements are true?

A Jacob thinks that people might get the wrong impression about his character from his appearance. ✓

B Jacob says he feels comfortable talking to people he hasn't met before. ☐

C Jacob has green eyes. ☐

D Jacob enjoys being active. ✓

⑩ Practice — Grades 4–5

🎧 Listen to some extracts of people talking about what they look for in their ideal friend. Write the correct letter in the box.

A generosity
B good physique
C kindness
D patience
E sense of humour
F shyness
G talkative

1	
2	
3	
4	

[4 marks]

 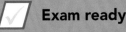

Family

You will need to be able to talk about your family, and any activities you do together, as well as family life in general.

 Introducing your family

To talk about your family, you will need to use possessive adjectives and the verbs **avoir** and **être**.

GRAMMAR LINK PAGE **72**

Voici ma famille. Mes parents sont divorcés alors on me voit avec ma mère devant mon beau-père. Il a un fils avec ma mère, mon demi-frère, et j'ai aussi une sœur cadette.

*This is my **family**. My **parents** are divorced so you can see me with my **mother** in front of my **step father**. He has a **son** with my mother, my **half-brother**, and I also have a **younger sister**.*

 Worked example   Grades 4–9

💬 Answer the following question:

Qu'est-ce que tu as fait avec ta famille le week-end dernier?

Le week-end dernier, nous sommes allés voir mes grands-parents parce que c'était l'anniversaire de ma grand-mère. Elle a maintenant soixante-dix ans. On étaient douze personnes à la fête car nos cousins étaient venus aussi. Nous avons mangé un déjeuner excellent et après, nous avons chanté «Joyeux anniversaire!» Nous nous sommes tous bien amusés. J'adore passer du temps en famille.

 Aiming higher

Look for opportunities to extend your sentences by using a relative clause or the pluperfect tense.

Nous avons mangé un déjeuner excellent que ma grand-mère avait préparé. *We ate an excellent lunch that my grandmother had prepared.*

You could also use **après avoir** + past participle

Après avoir mangé un déjeuner excellent, nous avons chanté... *After eating an excellent lunch, we sang...*

 Family life

famille monoparentale (f) *single-parent family*
belle-mère (f) *step mother*
beau-père (m) *step father*
adopté(e) *adopted*
aîné(e) *elder / older*; **ma sœur aînée** *my older sister*
cadet(te) *younger*; **mon frère cadet** *my younger brother*
célibataire *single*
séparé(e) *separated*
divorcé(e) *divorced*
jumeau (m) / jumelle (f) *twin*
garder les enfants *to look after the children*
Je suis fils / fille unique. *I'm an only child.*
famille nombreuse (f) *large family*

VOCABULARY LINK PAGE **102**

Exam focus 📌

Use a variety of verbs. In the Worked example answer there are four examples of verbs in the perfect tense; each is different and they include verbs conjugated with **avoir** and **être** as well as a reflexive verb: **Nous nous sommes tous bien amusés.** The imperfect and present tenses are also used.

Listen out for a time marker in a question; you can use it to start your answer, giving you a bit of thinking time.

This answer uses both **on** and **nous** to convey the idea of 'we'. It shows that you are able to manipulate verbs correctly.

You could extend this sentence to give a reason, e.g. **parce qu'on s'entend tous très bien** (*because we all get on well*). See page 12 for more descriptions on relationships with others.

 Practice   Grades 4–9

✏️ Vous écrivez une réponse aux questions de votre école partenaire. Décrivez:

* Activités en famille – normalement et récentes
* Avantages et désavantages d'une famille nombreuse.

Écrivez environ 150 mots en **français**.   **[32 marks]**

  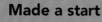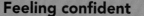

Friends and relationships

Talk about relationships between you, your friends and family, and say how you feel about different people.

⑤ What you need to know:

To talk about relationships you should know how to:

- Use reflexive verbs:

  Je m'entends bien avec mes parents.

  I get on well with my parents.

  GRAMMAR LINK PAGE **90**

- Give a reason for a good / bad relationship:

  Ils me permettent de sortir.

  They let me go out.

  Je dois faire trop de ménage.

  I have to do too much housework.

- Use adjectives to describe personality types:

  Il / elle est paresseux(euse) / égoïste / têtu(e) / généreux(euse) / travailleur(euse).

  He / she is lazy / selfish / stubborn / generous / hard-working.

- Express your opinions and feelings:

  Ce n'est pas juste! It's not fair!

  See page 7 for more on opinions.

② Vocabulary A–Z

s'amuser *to have fun*

s'entendre avec *to get on with*

s'énerver *to get annoyed*

se disputer avec *to argue with*

se fâcher contre *to get angry with*

se fâcher avec *to fall out with*

se fier à *to trust*

s'inquiéter (au sujet de) *to worry (about)*

se mettre en colère *to get angry*

se moquer de *to make fun of*

conflit (m) *conflict, argument*

dispute (f) *argument*

de mauvaise humeur *in a bad mood*

gâter *to spoil*

critiquer *to criticise*

faire des remarques sur *to comment on*

déranger *to disturb*

VOCABULARY LINK PAGE **102**

⑩ Worked example Grades 4–9

 Décrivez votre vie de famille.

> The verbs and adjectives all agree with their subjects.

Ma vie de famille est extrêmement difficile parce que je ne m'entends pas bien avec mes parents. Ils sont trop sévères car je ne peux pas sortir le soir avec mes copains. Par conséquent, je me dispute souvent avec eux. Hier, je me suis aussi fâché(e) avec mon petit frère parce qu'il a refusé de promener le chien. Je pense qu'il est vraiment paresseux. À mon avis, mes parents le gâtent trop.

> Show you know how to use direct object pronouns. Similarly, you could say of your parents: **je les trouve agaçants / gentils** *I find <u>them</u> annoying / kind.*

> This extract from a longer answer contains a good variety of vocabulary and shows that you can express an opinion and give reasons for it. It uses both present and perfect tenses with time phrases and conjunctions.

⑩ Practice Grades 4–9

 Read what these people say about their friends in an online forum. Identify the people. Write **D** (Dominique), **M** (Marc) or **D+M** (Dominique and Marc) in the box.

> **Marc:** On se dispute de temps en temps, car mes copains pensent que je passe trop de temps à la maison – ce qui n'est pas du tout vrai. Je me dispute quelquefois avec mon meilleur ami à l'école parce qu'il est très bavard et il me dérange quand je veux travailler.

> **Dominique:** Je m'entends bien avec mes amies et elles ont confiance en moi. Elles savent que je suis travailleuse et que je ne veux pas sortir avec elles tous les soirs, alors elles me laissent faire mes devoirs tranquillement. Cependant elles m'énervent parfois quand elles font des remarques sur ce que je porte.

❶ Who has friends who know that they need time to themselves? ☐

❷ Who does not agree on all matters with their friends? ☐

❸ Who likes complete peace and quiet at times? ☐

[3 marks]

 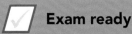

Marriage and partnership

You will need to be able to express your attitude towards marriage and partnership and whether it is something for you.

⑤ Talking about future plans

GRAMMAR LINK PAGE 87

This topic gives you the opportunity to use the future tense and the conditional:

- Je voudrais me marier un jour. I **would like** to get married one day.
- Mes noces idéales auraient lieu dans un château. My ideal wedding **would take place** in a country house.
- Je ne me marierai pas avant l'âge de trente ans. I **won't get married** before the age of thirty.
- Le mariage aura lieu en été. The wedding **will take place** in summer.
- Je ne veux pas me marier mais j'habiterais avec mon/ma partenaire. I don't want to get married but **I would live** with my partner.
- J'aime être indépendant(e), alors je resterai célibataire. I like to be independent so **I will stay** single.

② Vocabulary

VOCABULARY LINK PAGE 102

se marier *to get married*
épouser *to marry*
fiançailles (f) *engagement*
les noces (f) *wedding*
mari (m) *husband*
femme (f) *wife / woman*
partenaire (m/f) *partner*
conjoint (m) / conjointe (f) *partner*
mariage (m) civil *civil wedding / partnership*
divorce (m) *divorce*
célibataire *single*
bague (f) *ring*

⑩ Worked example   Grades 1–5

Forum about marriage

👓 You are looking at an online forum.

> Gaëlle_L is saying that she wouldn't like to be like her aunt who is single (**célibataire**).

Gaëlle_L: Ma tante est restée célibataire toute sa vie, et vit toute seule. Je ne voudrais pas être comme elle.	

Tigre_tom: À mon avis, le mariage est surestimé. Mes parents ont beaucoup d'amis qui sont divorcés.	

Susie_XX: On pourrait tout simplement vivre ensemble car les noces peuvent être très chères. C'est quand même génial de pouvoir célébrer un jour si spécial!	

What views are expressed on marriage?
For a **positive** view, write **P**.
For a **negative** view, write **N**.
For a **positive** and a **negative** view, write **P/N**.

Gaëlle_L	P
Susie_XX	P/N
Tigre_tom	N

> **Surestimé** means *overrated* in this context. Tigre_tom also mentions that many of his parents' friends are divorced.

> Susie_XX mentions the expense of weddings, but also that it is nice (**génial**) to celebrate (**célébrer**) a special day.

[3 marks]

⑤ Aiming higher ⬆

Make sure you use a range of tenses. The top answers will refer to three different time frames.

Le week-end dernier, on a fêté les fiançailles de ma sœur. Elle connaît son fiancé depuis trois ans et les noces auront lieu l'année prochaine.

Last weekend, we celebrated my sister's engagement. She has known her fiancé for three years, and the wedding will take place next year.

⑩ Practice   Grades 4–9

💬 Answer the following questions.

- Tu rêves de te marier?
- Est-ce que tu es allé(e) à un mariage récemment?
- Est-ce que le mariage est nécessaire, à ton avis?
- Est-ce que tu utiliserais Internet pour trouver un ou une partenaire?

Food

When you talk about food, you need to be able to say what you like and dislike, and to talk about healthy eating habits.

5 Talking about food

When you talk about food you will need to be able to use the following :

- the partitive article:

GRAMMAR LINK
PAGE
68

Je mange **des** céréales le matin, et **du** pain le soir.

> These words aren't used in English here, but they must be used in French.

- the correct gender of food-related nouns:
le fromage, la viande, une banane
- adverbs of frequency and negative expressions:
Je mange **très rarement** de la viande. *I rarely eat meat.*
Je **ne** mange **jamais** de biscuits. *I never eat biscuits.*
- expressions of liking and disliking, including reasons:
Je n'aime pas manger de frites parce qu'elles contiennent trop de matières grasses. *I don't like eating chips because they contain too much fat.*

2 Vocabulary A–Z

alimentation (f) **équilibrée / saine** *balanced / healthy diet*
cochonneries (f pl) *junk food*
féculent (m) *carbohydrate / starchy food*
matières grasses (f pl) *fat*
minéral (m; pl minéraux) *mineral*
plat à emporter (m) *ready meal*
protéine (f) *protein*
produit laitier (m) *dairy product*
restauration rapide (f) *fast food*
sucreries (f pl) *sweet things*
vitamine (f) *vitamin*
ça contient beaucoup de vitamines *that contains a lot of vitamins*
consommer *to eat*
contenir *to contain*
éviter *to avoid*

VOCABULARY LINK
PAGE
104

Talking about quantities
verre (m) **de / (d'eau)** *a glass of (water)*
portion (f) **de** *a portion of*
10 grammes (m) **de** *10 grams of*
tranche (f) **de** *a slice of*
cuillerée (f) **de** *a spoonful*

10 Worked example Grades 4–9

1 Qu'est-ce que tu aimes manger? C'est bon ou mauvais pour la santé?

J'aime manger des cochonneries, mais je sais qu'elles sont mauvaises pour la santé parce qu'elles contiennent trop de sucre et de matières grasses.

2 Est-ce que tu manges équilibré?

Normalement, j'ai une alimentation très équilibrée, c'est-à-dire que chaque jour, je mange au moins cinq portions de fruits et de légumes, deux portions de produits laitiers et je ne mange pas trop de viande. Cependant, je suis sorti(e) hier avec des copains et on a mangé des hamburgers et des frites.

Using **cependant** (*however*) enables you to introduce a different tense into your answer.

> **Mais je sais** means *but I know* and is a useful way of extending your answer and adding more detail.

> **C'est-à-dire** means *that is to say* and is another way of explaining and developing your answer.

10 Practice Grades 1–5

 A dietician is giving advice.

Listen to the advice. Write the correct number in the box. Choose from the numbers shown below.

10	50	75	100	125	150	200

1 Bread at breakfast: ☐ grams.

2 Fish at lunch: ☐ grams.

3 Vegetables apart from potatoes at lunch: ☐ grams.

4 Meat at evening meal: ☐ grams. **[4 marks]**

Meals

You need to be able to talk about meals and to say what your favourite meal is and why.

 5 · Talking about meals

Talking about meals gives you the opportunity to use different tenses, as well as likes and dislikes.

Normalement, au petit-déjeuner, je mange du pain.
*I normally **eat** bread for breakfast.*

Pour le goûter, j'ai mangé une pomme.
*For a snack, **I ate** an apple.*

Dimanche prochain, on mangera chez mes grands-parents.
***We'll be eating** at my grandparents' house next Sunday.*

Je préfère le goûter parce que j'aime les aliments sucrés.
I prefer snacks because I like sweet food.

10 · Worked example **Grades 1–5**

✎ Vous envoyez une photo à votre ami(e) français(e).

Qu'est-ce qu'il y a sur la photo? Écrivez **quatre** phrases en **français**.

Voici les autres membres de ma famille — nous sommes ensemble dans la cuisine et nous prenons le petit-déjeuner. Nous mangeons du pain et des croissants, et nous buvons du jus d'orange et du thé. Je pense que c'est un repas assez sain car on mange aussi des fruits comme le melon. Quelquefois, on a des pains au chocolat, c'est comme les Français!

Exam focus
The verbs in the answer above are all different and are a mix of the **nous**, **je** and **on** forms, showing that you know how to conjugate verbs in different forms. The vocabulary relates to the picture and the use of **nous** and **je** relates to the task of you sending a photo to your French friend. It has an opinion (**je pense que**) and a reason (**car**) and shows that you know how to use the partitive (**du, de la, des**).

2 · Vocabulary **A–Z**

aliment (m) *food*
petit-déjeuner (m) *breakfast*
déjeuner (m) *lunch*
goûter (m) *snack*
casse-croûte (m) *snack*
dîner (m) *dinner*
Au dîner, on mange... *For dinner, we eat...*
goût (m) *taste*
boire *to drink*
manger *to eat*
déguster *to savour*
faire la cuisine *to cook*
préparer *to prepare*
épicé *spicy*
piquant *spicy*
sucré *sweet*
salé *salty*
savoureux *savoury*

VOCABULARY LINK PAGE **104**

5 · Aiming higher

- Include more complex structures such as **après avoir / être** + past participle.
  Après avoir mangé ce repas énorme, je voulais m'endormir.
  After eating that enormous meal, I wanted to fall asleep.

- Use expressions such as **être en train de** *to be (in the process of) doing something:*
  Nous sommes en train de prendre le petit-déjeuner. *We are eating / we are in the process of eating breakfast.*

- Show you know about past participle agreements with a preceding direct object:
  On a mangé les pommes que j'avais achetées au marché. *We ate the apples that I had bought at the market.*

10 · Practice **Grades 1–9**

💬 Answer the following questions.
- Quel est ton repas préféré? Pourquoi?
- Est-ce qu'il est important de bien manger au petit-déjeuner?
- Quel repas est le plus important, à ton avis? Pourquoi?

Feeling unwell

You should be able to say the names of parts of the body and that something is wrong or hurting.

 5 Saying what is wrong

 2 Vocabulary

To talk about feeling unwell, you will need to use the following:

- avoir mal + au, à la, à l', aux:
  J'ai mal au dos / à la tête. **I've got** backache / a headache.
- part of the body + faire mal:
  Mon bras / ma jambe me fait mal. My arm / leg **hurts**.
- reflexive verbs:
  Je me suis blessé la main / le pied. I **hurt / injured** my hand / foot.
  Je me suis cassé le pouce. I **broke** my thumb.
  Il s'est tordu la cheville. He **twisted** his ankle.
- Elle s'est brûlé le doigt. She **burnt** her finger.
  Je me suis fait un bleu à la cuisse. I **bruised** my thigh.

You can use depuis + present tense to say how long you have experienced a particular symptom.

J'ai de la fièvre depuis trois jours. I have had a fever for three days.

blessure (f) *injury*

être couvert de bleus (un bleu) *to be covered in bruises*

cancer (m) du poumon *lung cancer*

fièvre (f) *fever*

grippe (f) *flu*

maladies (f pl) cardio-vasculaires *cardio vascular diseases*

obésité (f) *obesity*

être enrhumé *to have a cold*

être stressé *to be stressed*

être obèse *to be obese*

respirer *to breathe*

souffrir de *to suffer from*

tousser *to cough*

---

 10 Worked example `Grades 1–5`

 While you are in France, you overhear your exchange partner telling the class teacher what is wrong with a number of students who are absent from school.

For each person write down what the problem is and the consequence. Answer in **English**.

	Problem	Consequence
Example: Michelle	toothache	has to go to the dentist
Daniel	flu	has to stay in bed
Carole	broken arm	can't write
Henri	injured knee	has difficulty walking
Fatima	stomach ache	must stay at home

Listen once for the problem, and then a second time for the consequence. Don't try to catch everything on the first listening.

You can write short answers in response to this task.

Try to predict what you might hear. Listen out for the details as well as the overall sense. If a part of the body is mentioned, what is the specific problem?

[4 marks]

---

 10 Practice `Grades 4–9`

Read this short online article about stress.

Which **three** statements are true, according to the article? Write the correct letters in the boxes.

- **A** Stress mainly affects people who are working.
- **B** Stress can affect anyone.
- **C** The only symptoms are headaches and sleeping disorders.
- **D** Most people suffer from general exhaustion.
- **E** Physical activity is good for overcoming stress.
- **F** Having a drink can provide some relief from stress.

☐ ☐ ☐ **[3 marks]**

Le stress, c'est la maladie de la vie moderne qui touche beaucoup de gens de n'importe quel âge et de n'importe quelle occupation. À cause du stress, on peut souffrir de maux de tête, de troubles du sommeil et d'épuisement ainsi que de beaucoup d'autres symptômes.

Pour combattre les effets du stress, on devrait être actif et participer à des activités où on peut se détendre un peu. L'alcool n'est en aucun cas une solution aux problèmes de stress.

 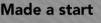

Healthy and unhealthy living

You will need to be able to talk about good and bad health habits and what you do to maintain a healthy lifestyle.

⑤ Talking about a healthy lifestyle

When you talk about healthy lifestyles, you will need to use:

- frequency adverbs:
  Je ne fume **jamais**.
  I **never** smoke.
   GRAMMAR LINK PAGE **74**
  Je dors **toujours** huit heures par nuit. I **always** sleep eight hours at night. Je fais de l'exercice **trois fois par semaine**. I exercise **three times a week**.

- sports vocabulary and verbs:
  Je fais de la musculation pour rester en forme. I do weight training to keep fit.

  For more on sport, see page 23.

- expressions like **il faut** and the verbs **devoir** and **pouvoir** to say what you could and should do:
  Il faut boire au moins six verres d'eau par jour. **You should** drink at least six glasses of water a day.

⑤ Pour rester en forme A–Z

se détendre to relax

faire de l'exercice to exercise

être en bonne santé to be in good health

grossir to put on weight

maigrir to lose weight

en surpoids overweight

fumer to smoke

essoufflé out of breath

éviter to avoid

peser to weigh

tabagisme (m) smoking

VOCABULARY LINK PAGE **102**

⑩ Worked example — Grades 4–9

🖉 Votre ami(e) français(e) vous a demandé d'écrire un article sur la vie saine pour son journal scolaire. Décrivez:

- l'importance d'une vie saine
- activités faites et à faire pour mener une vie saine.

À mon avis, il est très important de mener une vie saine pour éviter les maladies graves. De nos jours, beaucoup de gens ont une mauvaise alimentation et donc ils grossissent et deviennent même obèses. En plus, les gens qui ne font pas d'exercice, qui boivent trop d'alcool et qui fument risquent de souffrir de maladies cardio-vasculaires.

Personnellement, j'ai dû faire des efforts pour mener une vie plus saine car il y a un an, j'étais en surpoids. On m'a conseillé de manger moins d'aliments riches en calories. Par conséquent, j'ai maigri et mes copains disent que j'ai maintenant l'air vraiment bien. J'ai aussi décidé de faire de l'exercice plus régulièrement en pratiquant la natation et le jogging. Je trouve que l'activité physique m'aide à me détendre. Je ferais aussi du vélo si j'avais le temps. Malheureusement, mes études scolaires m'occupent beaucoup, ce qui est assez stressant!

② Aiming higher ⬆

Try to include a range of examples of the perfect tense, for example verbs which take **être**, reflexive verbs and irregular verbs.

Try to include some of the less common negative expressions, e.g. **Je ne consomme ni trop de viande ni trop de sucre.**

> Make sure you express your opinion. You could also use **je pense que** or **je trouve que** here.

> You could give examples of illnesses, e.g. **comme le cancer / le diabète**.

> Relative pronouns like **qui**, **que** and **dont** are useful for developing your sentences.

> Top grade answers will refer to past, present and future events. In this paragraph, there are four examples of the perfect tense, one imperfect and one conditional.

> The best answers vary the person of the verb. Most of this text uses **je**, but using **on** or **mes copains** as well shows that you know how to conjugate different verbs.

> The present participle (**en pratiquant**) is an example of an advanced structure you can use.

> Vary the start of your sentences as much as possible: avoid starting every sentence with **je**.

⑩ Practice — Grades 1–9

💬 Answer the following questions.
- Qu'est-ce qui est mauvais pour la santé?
- Qu'est-ce que tu feras ce week-end pour rester en forme?

Social issues

You need to know how to talk about social issues, such as the causes and effects of poverty and homelessness.

 5 **Causes of poverty and homelessness**

When you discuss social issues you should be able to:

- say what causes problems:
  À mon avis, la pauvreté **est due au** coût élevé de la vie.
  In my opinion, poverty **is due to** the high cost of living.

- introduce an explanation with parce que:
  Je pense que beaucoup de sans-abri boivent de l'alcool parce qu'ils veulent oublier leurs problèmes.
  *I think a lot of homeless people drink alcohol **because** they want to forget their problems.*

- use depuis + present tense

Il **est** au chômage **depuis** un mois.

2 **Vocabulary**

alcoolique *alcoholic*
améliorer *to improve*
arrêter *to stop*
centre d'accueil (m) *refuge centre*
chômage (m) *unemployment*
être au chômage *to be unemployed*
chômeur (m) *unemployed person*
logement (m) à prix raisonnable *affordable housing*
loyer (m) *rent*
mendier *to beg*
perdre son emploi (m) *to lose one's job*
sans-abri (m pl) *homeless*
SDF (m: sans domicile fixe) *homeless person*

VOCABULARY LINK
PAGE 103

15 **Worked example** | **Grades 4–9**

👓 Lisez la description de Saïd et de sa vie de sans-abri.

> Je suis un immigré d'Afrique et je suis venu en France sans ma famille pour améliorer ma qualité de vie. J'avais espéré trouver un emploi bien payé mais je n'ai pas eu de chance, bien que j'aie un diplôme d'ingénieur. J'ai gagné un peu d'argent en lavant les voitures mais ce n'était pas suffisant pour payer le loyer.
>
> On penserait que le froid serait le pire aspect de ma situation mais le soir, je peux aller au centre d'accueil où l'on nous donne un repas chaud et où on peut se doucher. Non, le pire, c'est que la vie dans les rues est dangereuse car on risque d'être attaqué par des drogués ou d'être victime d'un accident de circulation. *Saïd*

Répondez aux questions. Écrivez la bonne lettre dans la case.

1 Pourquoi Saïd est-il venu en France?

A	pour rejoindre sa famille
B	pour chercher du travail
C	pour obtenir un diplôme

B

2 Quel est le plus grand problème pour les sans-abri, selon Saïd?

A	On a froid dans les rues.
B	On n'a rien à manger.
C	On pourrait être blessé ou tué.

C

Rejoindre means *to rejoin*. Saïd says he came to France (**sans** *without*) his family.

Saïd says **On penserait que le froid serait le pire aspect de ma situation** (*one would think that the cold is the worst thing about my situation*). He then goes on to say that something else is the worst thing.

On n'a rien à manger means *You have nothing to eat.* Saïd says he can have a hot meal (**un repas chaud**) at the refuge centre (**au centre d'accueil**).

Être blessé ou tué means *to be injured or killed*. Saïd says you can be attacked (**attaqué**) or be victim of a traffic accident (**accident de circulation**).

10 **Practice** | **Grades 4–5**

🎧 While in France, you hear some extracts of interviews with four homeless people.

A	Cost of housing	D	Mental illness
B	Drug problems	E	Physical illness
C	Family problems	F	Unemployment

What is the reason for each person being homeless? Write the correct letter in the box.

1		3	
2		4	

[4 marks]

Charity and voluntary work

You need to know how to talk about different types of charities and voluntary work, including fundraising.

 On fait du bénévolat

On fait du bénévolat pour différentes raisons, par exemple: pour aider les autres; pour se donner le sentiment d'être utile et de ne pas se concentrer sur soi-même. D'autres s'engagent pour obtenir de nouvelles compétences ou pour gagner plus de confiance en soi.

There are different reasons for doing voluntary work, for example: to help others; to make oneself feel useful; and not to focus on oneself. Others get involved to gain new skills or confidence in themselves.

Soi is the emphatic pronoun used with **on**. **Soi-même** means *oneself, ourselves*.

 Fundraising activities A–Z

aider les autres *to help others*
amasser des fonds *to fundraise*
association (f) caritative *charity*
expérience (f) enrichissante *enriching experience*
faire du bénévolat *to do voluntary work*
manifestation (f) *demonstration*

mondial *worldwide*
participer à la vie de société *to take part in society*
reconnaissant *grateful*
soutenir quelqu'un *to support someone*
solidaire *supportive*
solidarité (f) *solidarity*

VOCABULARY LINK PAGE **103**

 Worked example Grades 1–9

1 Fais-tu du bénévolat?

💬 En ce moment, je ne fais pas de bénévolat, mais ◄ à l'avenir, je voudrais en faire avec une association ◄ caritative qui aide les réfugiés. Je crois que c'est important de penser aux autres.

2 Est-ce que tu as participé à un événement pour 💬 collecter des fonds?

L'année dernière, notre collège a organisé une journée au profit des victimes de catastrophes naturelles. On a payé une livre sterling pour ne pas porter notre uniforme scolaire, et j'ai participé à un concert ◄ pendant la pause déjeuner.

Use conjunctions like **mais** to introduce a different tense into your answer.

Using the pronoun **en** is a feature of a top answer. The same would apply to **y**.

Don't worry if your answer isn't strictly true. Focus on giving an answer that is varied and accurate.

 Practice Grades 1–5

🎧 Listen to this extract from a podcast in which people talk about how they raise money for charity.

What does each one do to raise money? Write the correct letter in the box.

A	Baking for a cake sale
B	Selling things online
C	Taking part in a charity run
D	Taking part in a sponsored concert
E	Using social media to raise awareness
F	Washing cars

1	
2	
3	

[3 marks]

18 | **Made a start** | **Feeling confident** | **Exam ready**

Music

You should know how to talk about your musical tastes.

⏱ (10) Discussing music

When you talk about music, you should be able to:

- say what type of music you like:
  J'adore **le rock** mais j'aime aussi **la musique classique**.
  *I love **rock** but I like **classical music** too.*

- compare musical styles:
  Le rap est **plus** monotone **que** la pop.
  *Rap is **more** monotonous **than** pop music.*

- talk about your favourite singer or musician and musical experiences:
  Hier, je suis allé à un concert de Grégoire.
  I went to a Grégoire concert yesterday.

- say how you listen to music:
  J'écoute la musique sur mon portable.
  I listen to music on my mobile phone.

- Use jouer + du / de la / de l' to say you play an instrument:
  Je joue **du** violon / **de la** clarinette / **de l'**accordéon.
  I play the violin / clarinet / accordion.

- Use the present tense + depuis to say how long you have been playing an instrument:
  Ma sœur **joue** de la batterie **depuis** deux ans / septembre.
  *My sister **has been playing** the drums **for** two years / since September.*

- Use pronouns, for example use **me** when talking about the effect that music has on you

La musique classique? J'adore ça parce que ça **me** détend.

⏱ (5) Worked example — Grades 1–9

💬 Parle-moi de ton chanteur préféré.

Mon chanteur préféré est un chanteur belge qui s'appelle Stromae. En fait, ce n'est pas son vrai nom, mais il l'a choisi pour lancer sa carrière de chanteur de rap et de hip-hop. Je trouve sa musique très accrocheuse, surtout son premier tube, Alors on danse. Je ne l'ai pas vu en concert, mais j'ai vu des vidéos de lui sur YouTube.

En fait (in fact) is a good phrase to use when you want to clarify something.

The best answers will include a range of tenses and features such as direct object pronouns.

Try to avoid repeating the same verbs. Here you could say Je ne suis pas allé à un de ses concerts, mais... You are then using a verb that takes être.

⏱ (2) Vocabulary — A–Z

chanson (f) *song*
chanter *to sing*
chanteur (m) / chanteuse (f) *singer*
groupe (m) *group*
mélodie (f) *tune*
paroles (f pl) *words / lyrics*
tube (m) *hit*
lent *slow*
vif / vive *lively*

VOCABULARY LINK
PAGE **104**

You must use the perfect and / or imperfect tense when responding to this bullet point.

You must refer to the future here. You could use the conditional to say what you would do if you don't have any future plans.

⏱ (2) Expressing opinions about music

Ça me rend heureux / triste. *It makes me happy / sad.*
La chanson a une mélodie vive / inoubliable. *The song has a lively / unforgettable tune.*
Les paroles sont faciles à comprendre. *The words are easy to understand.*

⏱ (20) Practice — Grades 1–9

✏️ Écrivez un e-mail à votre ami(e) français(e) sur vos goûts musicaux. Décrivez:

- le genre de musique que vous aimez
- votre groupe ou artiste favori
- une expérience musicale récente
- une activité musicale que vous ferez à l'avenir.

Écrivez environ **90** mots en **français**. Répondez à chaque aspect de la question. **[16 marks]**

Cinema

You need to know how to say what kinds of films you like and why.

⑤ About cinema

When you talk about films and TV programmes you can use:

- adjectives to express your opinion and give reasons for it:
  J'adore les films de science-fiction parce que les effets spéciaux sont impressionnants. *I like science fiction films because the special effects are **impressive**.*

- the comparative and superlative:
  À mon avis, Audrey Tautou est plus célèbre que d'autres actrices françaises. *In my opinion Audrey Tautou is **more famous than** other French actresses.*
  C'est le meilleur film de cette année. *It's **the best film** this year.*

- relative pronouns:
  C'est un film que j'ai vu trois fois. *It's a film **that** I've seen three times.*
  C'est un film qui parle des problèmes sociaux. *It's a film **that** talks about social problems.*

② Vocabulary

écran (m) *screen*
avoir horreur de *to hate / can't stand*
j'ai horreur des films d'arts martiaux *I can't stand martial arts films*
comédie (f) *comedy*
effrayant *scary*
faire peur / rire *to scare / to make laugh*
ce film m'a fait rire *the film made me laugh*
être fan de *to be a fan of*
film policier (m) *detective film*
film de guerre (m) *war film*
genre (m) *type (of film)*
réaliste *realistic*
passionnant *exciting*
publicités (f pl) *adverts*
vedette (f) *film star*

⑤ Worked example — Grades 1–5

❶ Quel genre de film est-ce que tu préfères?

💬 J'aime surtout les films d'action parce qu'ils sont vraiment passionnants. Pourtant, ils sont aussi parfois violents, et je déteste la violence.

❷ Quel est le dernier film que tu as vu?

💬 Le dernier film que j'ai vu était *La La Land*, une comédie musicale. Je l'ai vu avec ma famille le week-end dernier. J'ai trouvé ça absolument génial car il s'agit de deux personnes qui veulent réaliser leurs rêves.

The same question might be phrased slightly differently: **Quelle sorte de films aimes-tu? Pourquoi?**

The best answers go beyond a simple response: they give a specific example of the kind of film and might mention the last time you saw that kind of film.

Using the object pronoun in **je l'ai vu** is a feature of the best answers. However, try to avoid repeating the same verb. For example, you could say **Je suis allé(e) le voir.**

⑤ Talking about a film

Le thème du film est la guerre et la paix. *The theme of the film is war and peace.*
Il s'agit d'un vieil homme et sa petite fille. *It's about an old man and his granddaughter.*
L'action se déroule dans la banlieue de Paris. *The action takes place in the suburbs of Paris.*
La musique est / était... *The music is / was...*
Les effets (m) spéciaux sont / étaient... *The special effects are / were...*
C'est un film réalisé par... *It's a film directed by...*
Les acteurs principaux sont... *The main actors are...*
Je recommanderais ce film parce que... *I would recommend this film because...*

⑩ Practice — Grades 4–9

🎧 Listen to this podcast about a recent film.
Answer the questions in English.

❶ How did the speaker first hear about the film? **[1 mark]**

❷ In what way are the opening shots of the film memorable? **[1 mark]**

❸ How did the speaker feel when he saw the scene between the young man and his mother? **[1 mark]**

Television

You will need to know how to talk about the kind of television programmes you like and why.

(5) Your television viewing habits

Use frequency adverbs here:

Normalement, je regarde la télé le matin quand je prends mon petit-déjeuner.
Normally, I watch TV in the morning when I am having breakfast.

J'allume la télé tous les jours pour regarder les infos.
I switch on the television **every day** to watch the news.

Je ne regarde que deux heures de télé par jour.
I only watch **two hours** of television **each day**.

Give reasons:

J'aime regarder des émissions de téléréalité parce qu'elles me font rire.
I like to watch reality TV programmes because they make me laugh.

Je trouve les documentaires très utiles car il est important de s'informer de ce qui se passe dans le monde.
I find documentaries very useful as it's important to find out what's happening in the world.

(5) Worked example — Grades 1–5

💬 Qu'est-ce qu'il y a sur la photo?

Sur la photo, il y a une famille qui regarde la télé. Ils sont assis ensemble sur le canapé et regardent la même émission. Je pense que c'est une émission divertissante, comme un jeu télévisé.

(2) Vocabulary — A–Z

s'abonner à *to subscribe to*
actualités (f pl) *news*
animateur (m) *host*
chaîne (f) *television channel*
dessin animé (m) *cartoon*
divertissant *entertaining*
documentaire (m) *documentary*
émission (f) *TV programme*
émission de téléréalité *reality TV programme*
fan (m) de *fan of*
feuilleton (m) *soap (opera) or drama*
infos (f pl) *news*
s'intéresser à *to be interested in*
jeu (m) télévisé *game show*
météo (f) *weather forecast*
programme (m) *channel*
série (f) *series*
télécommande (f) *remote control*
télé (f) de rattrapage *catch-up TV*
télévision (f) sur demande *on-demand TV*

VOCABULARY LINK
PAGE **104**

(5) Comparing TV programmes

À mon avis, les documentaires sont plus éducatifs que les jeux télévisés. *In my opinion, documentary programmes are more educational than game shows.*

Remember to use the definite article for things that you are comparing.

Add detail by explaining further: **parce que les membres de la famille sont heureux et ils sourient.** *because the family members are happy and are smiling.*

(5) Aiming higher ⬆

Use the imperfect tense to talk about what you used to watch, and use pronouns to refer to things you have already mentioned:

Avant, **je regardais** beaucoup de dessins animés. Cependant, maintenant, **je les trouve** bêtes. *Before, I used to watch a lot of cartoons, however I find them stupid now.*

(10) Practice — Grades 1–9

💬 Answer the following questions.

- Quelles émissions est-ce que tu regardes régulièrement?
- Quels sont les avantages de regarder un film à la télé?
- Voudrais-tu participer à une émission de télé-réalité?
- Qu'est-ce que tu as regardé à la télé hier?

Eating out

You should know the language you need for ordering and talking about a meal out. See Food (page 13) and Meals (page 14) also.

---

② In a restaurant

You need to know how to ask for things in a restaurant:

Je voudrais la carte / l'addition, s'il vous plaît.
***I'd like** the menu / bill, please.*

J'ai besoin d'un couteau / une cuillère / une fourchette / un verre. I need *a knife / spoon / fork / glass.*

Qu'est-ce que vous avez comme plat végétarien?
What kind of** vegetarian dishes **do you have?

La bouillabaisse, qu'est-ce que c'est? What is *'bouillabaisse'?*

Est-ce que le service est compris? Is *service included?*

---

② Talking about your food

appétissant *appetising*
acide *acidic*
amer *bitter*
dégoûtant *disgusting*
délicieux / délicieuse *delicious*
frais / fraîche *fresh*

La soupe n'était pas appétissante car elle était froide et manquait de sel. *The soup wasn't appetising because it was cold and lacked salt.*

---

⑩ Worked example   Grades 4–9

💬 Vous parlez avec un serveur / une serveuse dans un restaurant.

- Réservation hier + heure et nom.
- Location de table.
- Quoi manger (2 détails).
- !
- ? Wi-Fi

– Bonsoir, je peux vous aider?
– **J'ai fait une réservation hier pour une table à sept heures au nom de Miles.**
– Bon. Où est-ce que vous voulez vous asseoir?
– **Je voudrais une table près de la fenêtre.**
– D'accord. Qu'est-ce que vous voulez comme entrée et plat principal?
– **Je prends l'assiette de crudités et le poulet rôti.**
– Pourquoi est-ce que vous avez choisi notre restaurant pour votre repas ce soir?
– **Le menu n'est pas trop cher!**
– Ah bon!
– **Est-ce qu'il y a du Wi-Fi ici?**

This means *yesterday*, so you will need to use the perfect tense: **J'ai réservé une table hier...** *I reserved a table…*

Alternatives are: **dans le coin** *in the corner;* **sur la terrasse** *on the terrace.*

Make sure that your answer is appropriate. You would need to say something different if you were asked: **Qu'est-ce que vous voulez comme dessert?**

Other possible answers include:
Votre restaurant est près de mon hôtel. *Your restaurant is near to my hotel.*
Un ami l'a recommandé. *A friend recommended it.*
J'ai vu des recommandations sur Internet. *I saw some recommendations on the internet.*

---

⑤ Practice   Grades 4–5

👓 Read the following report about restaurant habits.

Selon un sondage sur les habitudes des Français au restaurant, 21% des hommes mangent au restaurant chaque semaine contre 12% des femmes. Pour 45% des gens sondés, un bon restaurant est un endroit où on peut passer un moment convivial. Pour 19%, il faut que le service soit accueillant et amical, et pour 11% un repas copieux est le plus important. Quant à un mauvais restaurant: pour 20%, c'est un établissement trop bruyant, pour 22%, c'est un temps d'attente trop long et pour 29%, c'est un mauvais rapport qualité / prix.

What percentage of the people surveyed would say the following? Write the figures in the boxes.   **[4 marks]**

| 1 | Friendly staff are the mark of a good restaurant | ___ % | 3 | A generous amount of food is important | ___ % |
| 2 | A bad restaurant is where it is too noisy | ___ % | 4 | If I have to wait too long it is not good | ___ % |

    Made a start **Feeling confident** **Exam ready**

Sport

You will be expected to know how to talk about sports you like and why you like them.

⑤ Talking about sport

You should be able to talk about:

- what sports you like doing and why: **J'adore le tennis parce qu'il demande de bons réflexes.** *I love tennis because it requires good reflexes.*
- how often you do a sport: **Je fais du roller deux fois par semaine.** *I go roller skating twice a week.*
- how long you have been doing a sport: **Je fais de la voile depuis deux ans.** *I have been going sailing for two years.*
- benefits of your favourite sport: **Le footing est bon pour le cœur.** *Jogging is good for your heart.*

For team sports use **jouer + à: je joue au foot / basket** *I play football / basketball.*

For individual sports use **faire + de** or **pratiquer + le / la: je fais du patinage** *I go skating;* **je pratique l'escrime** *I do fencing.*

② Vocabulary A–Z

championnat (m) *championship*
se détendre *to relax*
équipe (f) *team*
s'entraîner *to train*
faire partie de *to be a member of*
oublier ses soucis *to forget one's worries*

participer à *to take part in*
respirer *to breathe*
c'est un sport rapide / ludique *it's a fast / fun sport*
sport individuel / d'équipe / nautique (m) *individual / team / water sport*
sportif / sportive *sporty*

VOCABULARY LINK
PAGE **105**

⑩ Worked example Grades 4–9

✎ Translate the following passage into French.

> Use the imperfect tense to translate 'we were'.

My favourite sport is tennis and I play twice a week at the sports club with my brother. He prefers football because he likes team sports. Last year we saw lots of cyclists on the road when we were on holiday in west of France. I think that cycling can be dangerous when there is too much traffic.

Mon sport préféré c'est le tennis et j'y joue deux fois par semaine au centre sportif avec mon frère. Il préfère le foot parce qu'il aime les sports d'équipe. L'année dernière, on a vu beaucoup de cyclistes sur la route quand on était en vacances dans l'est de la France. Je pense que le cyclisme peut être dangereux quand il y a trop de circulation.

The past participle of the verb **voir** is **vu**.

If you don't know the word for traffic, you could rephrase this using words you do know, such as 'a lot of cars'.

Many of these nouns need a definite article (**le/la**) where they don't in English. Go to page 65 to check the rules.

⑩ Practice Grades 1–9

💬 Answer the following questions.
- Qu'est-ce qu'il y a sur la photo?
- Qu'est-ce que tu fais normalement pour rester en forme?
- Parle-moi d'un événement sportif que tu as vu récemment.

You will be asked **two further questions** you have not prepared.

 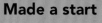

Travel and transport

Look at language for describing journeys you've been on, how you travel regularly, and arranging to use public transport.

⑤ Talking about travel

You will need to be able to:

- say how you travelled to a place and what the journey was like: **On est allés en Écosse en voiture. Ce n'était pas très confortable car le voyage a duré six heures.** *We went to Scotland by car. It wasn't very comfortable because the journey lasted six hours.*

- use the pronoun y to mean *there*: **Nous y allons en train / avion / bateau / car.** *We go **there** by train / plane / boat / coach.*

- Compare means of transport

L'avion est **plus** rapide **que** le train.

⑩ Worked example — Grades 4–9

💬 Vous parlez avec un employé dans une gare à Paris.

- Billets de train – où et type.
- !
- ? Tarif – étudiants.
- Projets pour visite en France (2 détails).
- Opinion sur la cuisine française + raison.

- Je peux vous aider?
- Je voudrais un aller simple pour Marseille, s'il vous plaît.
- Quand est-ce que vous voulez voyager?
- Je veux voyager cet après-midi.
- Très bien.
- Est-ce qu'il y a un tarif réduit pour les étudiants?
- Oui, il y a une réduction de vingt pour cent. Qu'est-ce que vous avez l'intention de faire en France?
- Je vais passer un mois avec une famille pour améliorer mon français et je visiterai quelques régions de France.
- C'est bien, ça. Et qu'est-ce que vous pensez de la cuisine française?
- Je l'adore, surtout les gâteaux parce que j'aime les aliments sucrés.

Any time phrase, such as **à midi** or **demain** in response to **quand** would work here.

② Vocabulary A–Z

aéroport (m) *airport*
agence (f) de voyages *travel agency*
attacher sa ceinture *to put on one's seat belt*
autoroute (f) *motorway*
durer *to last*
guichet (m) *ticket office*
horaire (f) *timetable*; **Quelles sont les horaires du train?** *What are the train times?*
passer par le péage *to go through the toll gate*
quai (m) *platform*
salle d'attente (f) *waiting room*

VOCABULARY LINK PAGE 105

Exam focus

With this scenario you may also be required to do the following tasks:

- Ask whether you have to change train / bus: **Est-ce qu'il faut changer de train / bus?**

- Ask for the arrival or departure time of a train / bus: **Le train / bus arrive / part à quelle heure?**

Note where this role-play is set. Don't ask for a ticket to Paris. You could mention any other French town.

Projets means *plans* so you must refer to the future.

⑩ Practice — Grades 4–5

1 🎧 You overhear some French people talking about journeys they have made. How did they travel and what problems did they have? Answer in **English**.

	Transport	Problem
Example	taxi	expensive
1		
2		
3		
4		

[4 marks]

2 💬 Answer the following questions.

- Comment vas-tu au collège?
- Quel est ton moyen de transport préféré? Pourquoi?
- Est-ce que tu es allé(e) en France? Décris ton voyage.
- Comment voyagerais-tu si tu avais le choix?

Planning a holiday

Being able to talk about your holiday plans and the things you like doing on holiday is important.

(5) Talking about holiday plans

To talk about your holiday plans use:

- the future tense:

Cette année, j'irai en Espagne avec mes copains pour deux semaines. *This year, I **will go** to Spain with my friends for two weeks.*

Nous ferons du camping à la montagne parce que nous voulons faire de l'escalade. *We **will camp** in the mountains because we want to go climbing.*

- the conditional:

Si j'avais beaucoup d'argent, je logerais dans un hôtel quatre étoiles au lieu d'une auberge de jeunesse. *If I had a lot of money, I **would stay** in a 4-star hotel instead of a youth hostel.*

 GRAMMAR LINK PAGE **88**

(10) Worked example — Grades 4–5

👓 Lisez les commentaires sur un forum au sujet des vacances.

A	Je m'intéresse plutôt aux activités culturelles. Je préfère les grandes villes plutôt que la campagne.
B	Le camping n'est pas mon truc, surtout quand il pleut!
C	En vacances, mon frère adore faire du canoë-kayak ou de l'escalade, mais moi, je déteste ça. Je préfère me détendre et me faire bronzer sur la plage.
D	Mes vacances idéales seraient sur les pistes couvertes de neige dans les Alpes.
E	Mes vacances idéales seraient sur une île tropicale où je pourrais faire du ski nautique et de la plongée sous-marine.
F	Normalement, je passe mes vacances dans un gîte rural en Bretagne, mais cette année, j'irai en Grèce pour faire de la voile.

Identifiez la bonne personne. Écrivez la bonne lettre dans la case.

1	En vacances, j'adore faire des sports d'hiver.	D
2	J'ai l'intention de visiter des musées quand je serai en vacances.	A
3	Cette année, je ferai quelque chose de différent.	F
4	En vacances, je ne suis pas très actif.	C

[4 marks]

(2) Vocabulary A–Z

avoir l'intention de *to intend to*
croisière (f) *cruise*
à l'étranger *abroad*
en plein air *in the open air / outdoor*
faire une excursion *to go on an outing*
location (f) de voitures *car hire*
monument (m) *monument*
passer *to spend (time)*
repos (m) *rest*
au bord de la mer / d'un lac *by the sea / a lake*
à la campagne *in the countryside*
à la montagne *in the mountains*
près d'une plage *near a beach*
vacances (f pl) *holidays*

 VOCABULARY LINK PAGE **106**

The last sentence means *I prefer to relax and sunbathe* and is similar in meaning to *I am not very active.*

Les pistes couvertes de neige means *slopes covered with snow.*

(5) Aiming higher ↑

Use conjunctions such as **pourtant**, **cependant** and **d'un autre côté** to introduce different tenses:

J'aime les vacances en famille sur un terrain de camping. Pourtant, si j'avais le choix, je passerais une quinzaine sur une île tropicale.

Use expressions such as **avant de** and **afin de**:

J'irai en Espagne afin de perfectionner mes compétences linguistiques.

Visiting museums is a cultural activity (**activités culturelles**).

This means *I'll do something different.* Key words to look out for are **normalement** and **mais**.

(5) Practice — Grades 1–9

💬 Answer the following questions.

- Est-ce que tu préfères les vacances d'été ou les vacances d'hiver?
- Comment seraient tes vacances idéales?
- Selon toi, est-ce que les vacances sont importantes? Pourquoi / pourquoi pas?
- Quel type de vacances préfères-tu et pourquoi?

Reservations

You need to know how to talk about and book hotel accommodation.

⑤ Accommodation

When you talk about accommodation you can mention:

- the location: **L'hôtel est situé non loin de la gare.** *The hotel is located not far from the station.*
- what the hotel is / was like:
  C'est / c'était un hôtel charmant, mais aussi un peu démodé. *It is / was a charming hotel but also a bit old-fashioned.*
- what your room is / was like: **Ma chambre est / était confortable / petite / sale.** *My room is / was comfortable / small / dirty.*

⑩ Worked example — Grades 1–9

💬 Vous êtes à la réception d'un hôtel.

> - Réservation hier – chambre (2 détails).
> - !
> - Nombre de nuits.
> - ? Repas – heure.
> - Choix de l'hôtel – raison.

- Bonjour, je peux vous aider?
- **Bonjour, j'ai fait une réservation hier pour une chambre à deux lits avec balcon.**
- Bon, c'était sous quel nom?
- **Mon nom est Atkins.**
- Merci, et, pour confirmer, vous allez rester pour combien de temps?
- **Je resterai une semaine.**
- Alors, vous avez la chambre 313 au troisième étage.
- **Merci. Le petit-déjeuner est à quelle heure?**
- De sept à neuf heures du matin. Pourquoi avez-vous choisi notre hôtel?
- **J'ai choisi votre hôtel parce que je voulais loger dans un hôtel au centre-ville.**

⑤ Accommodation problems

L'ascenseur était en panne. *The lift was out of order.*

Il y avait un chantier de construction en face. *There was a building site opposite.*

La connexion Wi-Fi / la télévision ne fonctionnait pas. *The wifi connection / television wasn't working.*

Il n'y avait pas d'eau chaude. *There was no hot water.*

Ma chambre donnait sur le parking. *My room overlooked the car park.*

② Vocabulary — A-Z

balcon (m) *balcony*
chambre familiale (f) *family room*
clé (f) *key*
climatisation (f) *air conditioning*
coffre-fort (m) *safe*
douche (f) *shower*
étage (m) *floor*; **au deuxième étage** *on the 2nd floor*
au rez-de-chaussée *on the ground floor*
logement (m) *accommodation*
robinet (m) *tap*
vue (f) **sur la mer** *view of the sea*

VOCABULARY LINK PAGE **106**

⑤ Asking about hotel facilities

Est-ce qu'il y a une piscine / un ascenseur? *Is there a swimming pool / lift?*

Est-ce que vous offrez la pension complète ou la demi-pension? *Do you offer full board or half board?*

> Use the perfect tense to complete this part of the task. You could say: **J'ai téléphoné hier pour réserver.**

> Alternative types of room could include different facilities (**avec Wi-Fi / douche / salle de bains / vue sur la plage**) or location (**au rez-de-chaussée / premier étage**).

> The unpredictable question here could be: **Vous êtes de quelle nationalité?** *What is your nationality?*

> Alternative answers to this could include **j'ai lu beaucoup de bonnes recommandations en ligne** *(I read a lot of good reviews online)*, or **le tarif n'est pas trop cher** *(the room rate is not too expensive)*.

⑤ Practice — Grades 4–5

🎧 Listen to these comments made about a hotel during a radio consumer programme.

For a **positive** view, write **P**.
For a **negative** view, write **N**.
For a **positive and a negative** view, write **P/N**.

1	
2	
3	
4	

[4 marks]

Describing your holiday

You should be able to describe your holiday, what you did and what it was like.

⑤ Talking about past events

Use both the imperfect and perfect tenses to describe what you did on your holiday:

Quand il y avait du soleil, nous sommes allés à la plage où nous nous sommes bronzés. *When it* **was** *sunny, we* **went** *to the beach where we* **sunbathed**.

Use a variety of time phrases:

L'année dernière *Last year*; en août *in August*; pendant les vacances *during the holidays*; il y a six mois *six months ago*.

② Vocabulary

se bronzer *to sunbathe*
décoller *to take off*
découvrir *to discover*
donner sur *to overlook*
foule (f) *crowd*
faire du tourisme *to go sightseeing*
lunettes (f pl) de soleil *sunglasses*
paysage (m) *landscape*
sable (m) *sand*
séjour (m) *stay*
trajet (m) *journey*
visite guidée (f) *guided visit*

VOCABULARY LINK
PAGE
105

⑤ Worked example **Grades 1–5**

🖉 Vous êtes en vacances et vous écrivez à votre ami(e) français(e). Mentionnez:

- l'endroit où vous êtes
- le logement
- vos activités en vacances
- la météo.

Écrivez environ **40** mots en **français**.

Make sure that you cover all the bullet points from the question and structure your different sentences around them.

Salut, ca va? Me voici dans le sud de la France. Je passe une semaine dans un petit hôtel au bord de la mer. C'est super parce que je peux faire de la natation et me bronzer tous les jours. En ce moment, il fait très chaud et il y a du soleil.

Ben

Check that you have the correct verb endings and spellings, and that adjectives agree. Also check your word count, to make sure you have written enough, as required by the question.

⑩ Practice **Grades 4–9**

① Read the following account of a holiday.

> Normalement, j'aime les vacances actives et je vais souvent à la montagne où je peux faire des randonnées et de l'escalade. Quand il ne pleut pas, c'est formidable d'être en plein air! Cependant, cette année, j'ai décidé de faire une croisière en Méditerranée. Chaque jour, on a découvert un nouvel endroit, ce qui a été une expérience très enrichissante. Bien sûr, tout était inclus, y compris les repas, et on pouvait faire de l'exercice dans la piscine ou dans la salle de sport à bord. Le seul problème, c'est que j'avais parfois le mal de mer. **Guy**

What is one advantage and one disadvantage of the type of holiday Guy went on **this year**? **[2 marks]**

② Listen to these extracts of conversations about holiday experiences.

What is each person talking about? Write the correct letter in the box. **[4 marks]**

A	An accident	
B	A theft	
C	Beach activities	
D	Buying a souvenir	
E	Sightseeing	
F	Travel documents	
G	The weather	

1	
2	
3	
4	

Before you listen, try to predict which words you need to listen out for and jot them down.

Social media

You should be confident in talking about using social media and the advantages and disadvantages of using it.

Using social media

Use the verb **pouvoir** to say what you can do with social media.

GRAMMAR LINK
PAGE 82

- **Je peux rester en contact avec ma famille en utilisant les réseaux sociaux.** *I can stay in contact with my family by using social networks.*
- **On peut tchatter et discuter de n'importe quoi.** *You can chat and discuss anything.*
- **C'est un outil utile pour les entreprises qui peuvent informer leurs clients sur leurs produits.** *It's a useful tool for businesses who can inform their customers about their products.*

Worked example — Grades 1–5

💬 Answer the following questions.

1 Quand vas-tu sur des réseaux sociaux?

Je vais sur les réseaux sociaux tous les jours du matin au soir, tout le temps, même en cours. J'y suis tout à fait accro!

2 Quels réseaux sociaux est-ce que tu préfères? Pourquoi?

Je préfère les réseaux sociaux où l'on peut mettre des photos en ligne, car je pense que c'est génial de voir ce que font mes amis.

Aiming higher

Use the following expressions to present an argument:

d'une part ... d'autre part *on the one hand, on the other hand*

en revanche *on the other hand*

cependant; pourtant *however*

D'une part, c'est génial de partager des photos avec ses copains, mais d'autre part, on ne devrait pas les partager avec des gens qu'on ne connaît pas.

On the one hand, it is great to share photos with friends, but on the other hand, you shouldn't share them with people you don't know.

C'est facile de s'exprimer sur n'importe quoi, pourtant, il faut réfléchir avant de poster un commentaire.

It's easy to express yourself about anything, however you must think before posting a comment.

Vocabulary

avantage (m) *advantage*
dangereux *dangerous*
face à face *face to face*
forum (m) *chat room*
inconvénient (m) *disadvantage, drawback*
mettre en ligne *to upload*
outil (m) *tool*
partager des photos *to share photos*
passer du temps *to spend time*
portable (m) *mobile phone*
réseau social (m) (pl réseaux sociaux) *social network*
rester en contact *to stay in contact*
site Internet / web (m) *website*
tchatter *to chat*
télécharger *to download*
utiliser *to use*

VOCABULARY LINK
PAGE 106

You could avoid repeating **sur les réseaux sociaux** by using **y** here – **J'y vais tous les jours.**

Use the pronoun **y** to say *I am addicted to them.*

Say what you like doing with social media to answer this question rather than just naming the social media you use.

You could also introduce a perfect tense here: **ce que mes amis ont fait.**

Practice — Grades 4–5

🎧 Listen to these extracts from a street survey about social media. Do they express positive or negative opinions?

For a **positive** view, write **P**.

For a **negative** view, write **N**.

For a **positive and a negative** view, write **P/N**.

1	
2	
3	
4	
5	

[5 marks]

 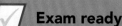

Mobile technology

You will need to be able to talk about how you use the internet and your mobile device.

5 Online activities

Avec mon portable ou ma tablette, je peux envoyer des textos ou des e-mails, surfer sur Internet pour obtenir des renseignements, faire des achats en ligne, télécharger et écouter de la musique, regarder des vidéos, tchatter avec mes copains, mettre des photos en ligne et passer des coups de fil.

With my mobile phone or tablet, I can send texts or emails, surf the web to find information, shop online, download and listen to music, watch videos, chat with my friends, upload photos and make phone calls.

Exam focus

This answer covers size, colour and what you do with your phone. The vocabulary in this answer could be adapted to answer a similar question about a tablet or computer.

Une marque très connue means a *well-known brand.*

10 Worked example | Grades 1–9

1 Décris ton portable. / Fais-moi une description de ton portable.

Mon portable est un téléphone intelligent avec un écran tactile. Il est assez grand et argenté. C'est une marque très connue. Il y a une quarantaine d'applis dessus que j'utilise régulièrement, comme la caméra et une appli pour retoucher les photos.

2 Est-ce que les portables sont nécessaires, à ton avis?

À mon avis, les portables sont une partie indispensable de notre vie quotidienne. Ils fonctionnent comme réveil matin, horloge, carnet d'adresses, agenda, torche, calculatrice ainsi qu' ordinateur et outil pour faire des recherches sur Internet. Quand je sors le soir, mes parents ne s'inquiètent pas parce qu'ils savent que je peux les appeler.

3 Comment as-tu utilisé ton ordinateur le week-end dernier?

Le week-end dernier, j'ai utilisé mon ordinateur pour faire mes devoirs et pour faire des recherches en ligne.

Develop your answer by using **quand** and **parce que**.

This response shows that you can use verbs in the singular and plural, and in the 1st and 3rd persons, as well as reflexive verbs and pronouns correctly.

2 Vocabulary

accès Wi-Fi (m) *wi-fi access*
appeler quelqu'un *to phone someone*
avoir besoin de *to need*
e-mail (m) *email*
lecteur (m) MP3 *MP3 player*
obtenir des renseignements *to find information*
ordinateur portable (m) *laptop*
sauvegarder *to save*
tablette (f) *tablet*
transporter *to transport*
Wi-Fi (m) *wi-fi*
vérifier *to check*

VOCABULARY LINK PAGE **106**

10 Practice | Grades 4–5

👓 Your French friend shows you some comments about technology on a forum.

Fatima	Un avantage de la technologie est que je peux rester en contact avec ma famille en Espagne.
Léon	Pour moi, un grand avantage est que je ne suis plus obligé de regarder les émissions de télé au moment où elles sont diffusées.
Nora	Ce que je trouve vraiment bien, c'est que je ne dois plus apporter des tas de livres avec moi quand je vais en vacances.
Guy	Le problème du harcèlement en ligne devient de plus en plus sérieux.

What is each person talking about?

Write the correct letter for each person.

A	Cost of technology
B	Cyberbullying
C	Gaming
D	Reading books
E	Technology and entertainment
F	Technology and family life
G	Technology and school life

Fatima	
Léon	
Nora	
Guy	

[4 marks]

My home

You should be able to describe your home and say what you like and dislike about it.

 Talking about your home

To talk about your home you can use:

- prepositions:

  Ma maison est située dans une rue tranquille **à côté d**'un parc. *My house is located in a quiet street **next to** a park.*

- adjectives and qualifiers:

  Mon appartement est **très petit** et **assez démodé**. *My flat is **very small** and **quite old fashioned**.*

- demonstrative pronouns:

  Ma maison est plus petite que **celle** de mes cousins. *My house is smaller than my cousins' house. (i.e. **that** of my cousins.)*

 GRAMMAR LINK PAGE **78**

 Vocabulary A–Z

arbre (m) *tree*
fenêtre (f) *window*
fleur (f) *flower*
HLM (habitation à loyer modéré) *low cost home*
immeuble (m) *block of flats / building*
jardin (m) *garden*
maison (f) individuelle / jumelée / mitoyenne *detached / semi-detached / terraced house*
grenier (m) *attic*
pièce (f) *room*
sous-sol (m) *basement*

VOCABULARY LINK PAGE **107**

 Describing your house

Voici ma maison. Directement en face de la porte d'entrée se trouve la cuisine. Au rez-de chaussée, nous avons aussi un salon ouvert avec salle à manger. L'escalier mène au vestibule du sous-sol où on trouve la machine à laver. Au premier étage, il y a deux chambres: celle de mes parents et ma chambre, ainsi que la salle de bains avec douche et toilette. Le grenier a été converti en deux chambres. À l'extérieur, nous avons un joli jardin avec beaucoup d'arbres et de plantes.

This is my house. Directly opposite the front door is the kitchen. There is also an open plan sitting room and dining room on the ground floor. Stairs lead from the hall to the basement where the washing machine is. On the first floor there are two bedrooms – my parents' and mine, as well as a bathroom with a shower and toilet. The attic has been converted into two bedrooms. Outside we have a pretty garden with lots of trees and plants.

 Worked example Grades 1–9

Answer the following question:

💬 Depuis combien de temps habites-tu dans ta maison?

Model answer 1

J'habite dans ma maison depuis six ans. Auparavant, nous habitions dans une maison mitoyenne à la périphérie de la ville.

Model answer 2

J'habite dans ma maison depuis mon enfance, c'est tout ce que je connais et je l'aime bien, mais si j'avais le choix, j'aurais un bel appartement au centre-ville.

You must answer this question, using the present tense and a period of time.

Use **auparavant** *previously* to extend your answer to where you lived before.

The best answers extend a simple response. Here, the imperfect and the conditional add more detail.

 Practice Grades 1–9

💬 Answer the following questions.

- Que penses-tu de ta maison?
- Comment serait ta maison idéale?

  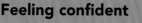

The neighbourhood

You should know how to describe your neighbourhood and express opinions about it.

(5) Describing your neighbourhood

To describe your neighbourhood you can use:

- the verb pouvoir to say what you can or can't do there:
  On peut y faire des achats / visiter le musée / aller au théâtre. **You can** go shopping / visit the museum / go to the theatre there.
  On ne peut pas aller au cinéma. **You can't go** to the cinema.
- adjectives to describe and compare places in town:
  Il y a une église ancienne qui est plus grande que la cathédrale. There is an old church that is bigger than the cathedral.
- opinions: J'aime habiter à Manchester parce que c'est une grande ville agréable. I like living in Manchester because it is a pleasant city.
- negatives: Il n'y a ni cinéma ni théâtre. There is **neither** a cinema **nor** a theatre.
- qualifiers: Il n'y a absolument rien pour les jeunes. There is **absolutely** nothing for young people.

(10) Worked example — Grades 4–9

👓 Read these comments posted on an online forum reviewing a town.

> Dans cet espace énorme, on trouve une centaine de boutiques sous le même toit où on vend des choses à des prix incroyables. On n'a jamais besoin de sortir avec son parapluie!

> Pendant la saison touristique, on peut bien s'y amuser, mais on s'ennuie tellement le reste de l'année.

> Trouver un espace de stationnement au centre-ville est presque impossible. Cependant, au parc relais à la périphérie, un espace de stationnement est garanti.

> Pour les tout-petits, il y a plein de choses à faire, avec des aires de jeux et une ferme urbaine mais pour les ados, il n'y a même pas de club de jeunes.

What do the writers think about the following? :

Write **P** for a **positive** opinion.

Write **N** for a **negative** opinion.

Write **P/N** for both **a positive and a negative** opinion.

1	Activities for young children and teenagers	P/N
2	Life outside the tourist season	N
3	Shopping facilities	P
4	Using the park and ride	P

(2) Vocabulary

aire (f) de jeux *play area*
banlieue (f) *suburb*
bruit (m) *noise*
circulation (f) *traffic*
embouteillage (m) *traffic jam*
heure (f) de pointe *rush hour*
quartier (m) *district*
piste (f) cyclable *cycle lane*
transports (m pl) en commun *public transport*
zone piétonne (f) *pedestrian zone*
animé *lively*
bruyant *noisy*
calme *calm*
pollué *polluted*
tranquille *quiet*

PAGE 107

This comment refers to the shopping facilities, and in particular the great prices and the fact that everything is under one roof (**sous le même toit**).

This contrasts the out of town parking (park and ride) with that in the centre of town.

This comment contrasts the facilities for young children with those for teenagers (**les ados**).

(2) Aiming higher

Use the imperfect tense to compare where you live now and have lived previously, or what your town is like now and was like in the past.

Avant, j'habitais au centre de cette ville industrielle mais il y a deux ans, on a déménagé en banlieue. *Before, I lived in the centre of an industrial town, but two years ago we moved to the suburbs.*

Avant, il y avait un grand château mais il est maintenant en ruines. *Before, there used to be a big castle, but now it is in ruins.*

(15) Practice — Grades 4–9

✏ Vous écrivez un article sur votre ville pour un magazine français.

Décrivez:

- votre ville maintenant et dans le passé
- les avantages et les inconvénients de vivre en ville.

Écrivez environ **150** mots en **français**. Répondez aux deux aspects de la question. **[32 marks]**

Shopping

To talk about shopping, you should be able to describe the product, as well as the facilities where you live and whether or not you shop online.

 Buying things

Use adjectives, including demonstrative adjectives, when talking about things you want to buy:

Je voudrais acheter / échanger **ce** pull vert, **cette** chemise blanche et **ces** chaussettes noires.
I would like to buy / exchange this green jumper, this white shirt and these black socks.

Use intensifiers when giving your opinion:

Il / elle est **trop** / **assez** grand(e) / petit(e) / cher / chère. It's **too** / **quite** big / small / expensive.

GRAMMAR LINK
PAGE
72

Il est **trop** grand!

 Vocabulary

A–Z

cadeau (m) *present*
caisse (f) *till*
carte (f) bancaire *bank card*
chercher *to look for*
compte (m) *account*
dépenser *to spend money*
échanger *to exchange*
économiser *to save*
fermer *to close*
livraison (f) gratuite *free delivery*

mode (f) *fashion*
moyen (m) de paiement *means of payment*
offrir *to offer*
ouvrir *to open*
panier (m) *basket*
prix (m) *price*
portefeuille (m) *wallet*
porte-monnaie (m) *purse*
réduire *to reduce*
réduit *reduced*

retourner *to return*
soldes (m pl) *sale;* en soldes *in the sales*
vendeur (m) / vendeuse (f) *shop assistant*
vitrine (f) *shop window*
vos commandes (f) *your orders*
bon marché *cheap*
cher / chère *expensive*
démodé *old fashioned*

VOCABULARY LINK
PAGE
107

 Worked example   Grades 4–9

💬 Vous parlez avec un(e) vendeur(euse) dans une boutique de mode.

- Vêtement acheté – couleur et taille.
- !
- Problème (2 détails).
- ? Autre.
- Ville – opinion – raison.

- J'ai acheté ce pantalon bleu grande taille.
- Je l'ai acheté hier.
- Il manque un bouton et il y a un trou.
- Est-ce que je peux échanger le pantalon?
- J'aime cette ville parce qu'il y a beaucoup de choses à faire.

Answer the following question.

Est-ce que tu aimes faire du lèche-vitrine?

J'adore la mode mais je n'ai pas beaucoup d'argent, alors j'aime faire du lèche-vitrine avec mes copains / copines. Normalement, nous allons en ville le week-end. Samedi dernier, nous avons vu de très beaux vêtements dans les grands magasins et les boutiques indépendantes.

Use the perfect tense.

Try to predict what the unprepared question might be.

You could mention a different item of clothing and a different size: **une chemise petite taille.**

Quand est-ce que vous l'avez acheté(e)? Alternatives would be **la semaine dernière** or **lundi.** An alternative unpredictable question might be: **C'était combien?**

An alternative would be not liking the colour (**Je n'aime pas la couleur**) or it being the wrong size.

This responds to **Alors, vous êtes touriste ici? Que pensez-vous de la ville?**

 Practice   Grades 4–9

🎧 You hear a discussion about online shopping.

Answer the following questions in **English**.

❶ What is the main advantage of shopping online? **[1 mark]**

❷ What does the speaker see as a disadvantage? **[2 marks]**

 Made a start   **Feeling confident**   ✓ **Exam ready**

Town and region

It's important to know how to describe where you live and how to give some of its advantages and disadvantages.

 Describing your region

To talk about your region you can:

- describe where it is and the type of area it is:

  C'est une région rurale dans le sud-ouest de l'Angleterre. *It is a rural area in the south-west of England.*

- use adjectives and make comparisons:

  C'est une région très pittoresque, mais elle est moins touristique que d'autres régions. *It is a picturesque region, but it is less touristy than other regions.*

- use the pronoun y to say what you can do there:

  On peut y faire du tourisme. *You can go sightseeing there.*

GRAMMAR LINK PAGE 79

 Worked example | **Grades 4–9**

🎧 **La vie à la campagne et en ville**

Écoutez ces extraits d'un podcast. Des gens parlent de leur région.

Notez l'avantage et l'inconvénient de l'endroit où ils habitent **maintenant**. Complétez la grille en **français.**

	L'avantage	L'inconvénient
1	La vie est plus tranquille.	Il y a peu de magasins.
2	La vie culturelle est riche et variée.	trop bruyant le samedi soir
3	transports en commun sont meilleurs	beaucoup de circulation aux heures de pointe
4	absence / moins de pollution	trajet / voyage plus long

Use **depuis** + present tense here.

Remember to make adjectives agree.

 Aiming higher

Use superlatives to add weight to your opinions and descriptions.

Le pire, c'est qu'on ne peut pas respirer d'air frais. *The worst thing is that you can't breathe fresh air.*

La meilleure chose de la vie ici, c'est... *The best thing about life here is...*

  Vocabulary

champ (m) *field*
se déplacer *to get around / move*
colline (f) *hill*
ferme (f) *farm*
fleuve (m) *river*
à la montagne *in the mountains*
paysage (m) *landscape*
randonnée (f) *walk / hike*
région (f) *region*
rivière (f) *river*
rural *rural*
usine (f) *factory*
village (m) *village*
vivre *to live*

VOCABULARY LINK PAGE 107

This tells you the context for the texts you will hear. Try to predict what advantages and disadvantages might be mentioned.

Note maintenant is stressed. This implies that the texts may refer to places where the people talking have lived in the past. Listen carefully for the relevant information.

If the question is in French you should answer in **French**. Section B on both the reading and listening papers has questions and answers in French.

 Practice | **Grades 1–9**

1 Translate the following passage into French.

✏️ I have been living on a farm in the country for three years. I like living here because I can go for walks in the fields with my dog. However, my brother hates the village because it is too small. He would like to live in a big city. Last year he spent six months with a family in the USA.

[12 marks]

2 Answer the following questions.

💬
- Qu'est-ce qu'on peut faire dans ta région?
- Où voudrais-tu habiter dans l'avenir?
- Tu aimes habiter dans ta région?
- Tu voudrais vivre à l'étranger? Pourquoi / pourquoi pas? **[4 marks]**

 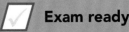

The environment

Talking about environmental issues needs specific vocabulary like 'recycling' and modal verbs like 'we should' and 'we could'.

5 Being environmentally friendly

To say what you should, could, or must do, use the verbs **devoir** and **pouvoir** and the following expressions. They are all followed by another verb in the infinitive.

- **Il faut** éteindre les appareils électroniques et la lumière en quittant une pièce.
  It is necessary to / One must switch off appliances and lights when leaving a room.
- **Il est important d'**acheter des produits verts.
  It is important to buy green products.
- **On doit / Nous devons** protéger l'environnement.
  One / We must protect the environment
- **On devrait / Nous devrions** utiliser du papier recyclé.
  One / we should use recycled paper.
- **On a besoin de** recycler autant que possible.
  We need to recycle as much as possible.

> This includes relevant 'environmental' vocabulary, an opinion with a reason, and a perfect tense.

2 Vocabulary

arrêter *to stop*
baisser *to lower*
chauffage (m) central *central heating*
centre (m) de recyclage *recycling centre*
déchets (m pl) *rubbish*
détruire *to destroy*
économiser *to save*
emballage (m) *package*
éviter *to avoid*
gaspillage (m) *waste*
ordures (f pl) *rubbish*
poubelle (f) *dustbin*
réduire la consommation de *to reduce the consumption of*
sac (m) (en) plastique *plastic bag*
séparer *to separate*
trier *to sort (out) waste*

VOCABULARY LINK PAGE 108

5 Worked example — Grades 1–9

1 Tu aimes recycler? Pourquoi / pourquoi pas?

💬 J'aime bien recycler et je pense que c'est important parce qu'on doit éviter le gaspillage et réduire les déchets. La semaine dernière, on a apporté des boîtes en carton au centre de recyclage. Chez moi, nous compostons toujours les déchets de cuisine.

2 Qu'est-ce que tu as fait récemment pour protéger l'environnement?

Récemment, nous avons baissé le chauffage chez nous et on a tous mis un pull! De cette façon, nous pouvons utiliser moins d'énergie. Cela est important pour protéger notre planète contre les effets du réchauffement de la Terre.

2 Aiming higher 🔼

Expand on main points expressed in a variety of ways:

Avant, chez nous, on ne faisait rien afin de protéger l'environnement, mais mon oncle nous a dit de faire un effort, alors mon père a décidé d'installer des panneaux solaires et de baisser le chauffage central pour ne pas gaspiller d'énergie. Actuellement, on consomme moins d'électricité, mais il faut qu'on en fasse encore plus.

> This answer uses conjunctions (**mais, alors, pour**) and a variety of tenses to produce a complex sentence.

You don't need to use the subjunctive at GCSE, but if you feel confident about how to use it you could include an example. Useful ones are: **qu'on fasse / qu'on puisse / qu'on aille** (from **faire / pouvoir / aller**).

GRAMMAR LINK PAGE 96

10 Practice — Grades 4–9

🎧 You are listening to a discussion programme about environmental issues.

Which issue does each person mention as being of greatest concern to them? Write the correct letter in the box.

1		3	
2		4	

A	Packaging	D	Recycling
B	Renewable energy sources	E	Saving water
C	Food waste	F	Energy use

[4 marks]

✓ **Made a start** ✓ **Feeling confident** ✓ **Exam ready**

Global issues

To talk about global issues, you will need to know vocabulary for natural and man-made disasters.

 Talking about causes and effects

Causes and effects can be expressed by using words such as mener à (*to lead to*), contribuer à (*to contribute to*), à cause de and à la suite de (*because of*).

Dans les pays pauvres le déboisement tropical par les habitants pour la production des récoltes alimentaires ou l'élevage d'animaux contribue à l'effet de serre et mène au rechauffement de la terre et à la disparition de plusieurs espèces de plantes et d'animaux.

In poor countries the deforestation of the tropical rain forests by the inhabitants to produce crops or to raise animals contributes to the greenhouse effect and leads to global warming and to the extinction of several animal and plant species.

L'élévation du niveau de la mer est provoquée par le rechauffement de la terre.

Rising sea levels are caused by global warming.

Beaucoup de gens ont perdu leur maison et toutes leurs affaires à la suite de l'ouragan qui a ravagé leur pays.

A lot of people have lost their homes and all of their possessions following the hurricane that ravaged their country.

 Worked example | **Grades 4–9**

👓 Lisez ce témoinage de Hassan qui parle des problèmes de son pays.

> Les problèmes dans la République du Tchad duraient depuis des années. Au début, il y avait la sécheresse et la terre ne pouvait rien produire à manger. Tout le monde avait faim et je perdais du poids. Heureusement, on a reçu de l'aide de la France, ce qui nous a permis de vivre plus facilement. *Hassan*

Écrivez les bonnes lettres dans les cases.

Les problèmes dans le pays d'Hassan étaient principalement suite…

A	au climat.
B	à un désastre créé par l'homme.
C	à la situation politique du pays.

A

La conséquence de ces problèmes était……

A	la guerre.
B	la mort.
C	la famine.

C

 Vocabulary A–Z

combustion (f) de combustibles fossiles – *the burning of fossil fuels*

déboisement (m) tropical – *deforestation of tropical rain forests*

défavorisé – *disadvantaged*

desertification (f) – *desertification*

disparition (f) des espèces – *extinction of species*

effet(m) de serre – *greenhouse effect*

éruption (f) volcanique – *volcano eruption*

famine (f) – *famine*

glissement (m) de terrain – *land slip*

guerre (f) – *war*

incendie (m) – *fire*

inondation (f) – *flood*

ouragan (m) – *hurricane*

pauvreté (f) – *poverty*

rechauffement (m) de la Terre – *global warming*

sécheresse (f) – *drought*

séisme (m) – *earthquake*

service (m) d'urgence – *emergency service*

tremblement (m) de terre – *earthquake*

VOCABULARY LINK
PAGE
108

Try to predict what words you might hear for each problem and jot them down before you listen. For example, natural disaster could be **séisme, ouragans, éruption volcanique.**

 Practice | **Grades 4–9**

🎧 You are listening to a discussion programme about environmental and global issues.

A	Energy sources	E	Pollution
B	Extinction of species	F	Population growth
C	Global warming	G	War
D	Natural disasters		

What does each person mention as the most serious problem? Write the correct letter in the box.

1	
2	
3	
4	

My studies

You will need to be able to give your opinions about school subjects and give reasons for them.

⑤ School subjects

To talk about school subjects you should:

- express likes and dislikes with reasons:

  Ma passion, c'est l'histoire parce que je trouve l'étude des événements du passé fascinante.
  My passion is history because I find the study of events in the past fascinating.

- make comparisons:

  Je pense que l'allemand est plus utile que le dessin.
  I think that German is more useful than art.

- use the conditional to express wishes:

  Si j'avais le choix, je n'étudierais pas les maths.
  If I had the choice, I wouldn't study maths.

⑤ Aiming higher ⬆

Phrases like **d'ailleurs** (*moreover / besides*) and **néanmoins** (*nevertheless*) are useful when you want to give a more extended answer to a question or point.

> You can extend your answer by saying what someone else's preferences are.

⑤ Worked example — Grades 1–9

❶ Tu préfères les sciences ou les langues?

💬 J'aime les deux, car je les trouve faciles. En plus, les profs enseignent ces matières d'une manière stimulante. Cependant, ma copine n'aime pas les langues, parce qu'elle les trouve trop difficiles.

❷ Quelles matières est-ce que tu as trouvées difficiles cette année? Pourquoi?

💬 Cette année, j'ai trouvé la technologie difficile parce que je ne suis pas tellement créatif et il faut avoir de bonnes idées. D'ailleurs, je ne suis pas fort en dessin et on doit faire un dessin de nos idées.

❸ Pourquoi as-tu choisi d'étudier le français?

💬 En fait, je ne l'ai pas choisi car nous devons tous étudier le français. Cependant, je pense que c'est une matière très utile car on apprend à communiquer avec des gens qui parlent une autre langue.

> This answer uses two tenses, adjectives, an impersonal verb and a modal verb.

> This is a detailed response that includes **je**, **nous** and **on** forms of verbs as well as a relative clause (**qui**).

② Vocabulary A–Z

apprendre *to learn*
bulletin (m) scolaire *school report*
comprendre *to understand*
cours (m) *lesson*
demander *to ask*
devoirs (m pl) *homework*
échouer *to fail*
emploi du temps (m) *timetable*
études (f pl) *studies*
examen (m) *exam*
matière (f) obligatoire / facultative *compulsory / optional subject*

VOCABULARY LINK PAGE **109**

⑤ Talking about subjects and teachers

J'aime mon prof de maths parce qu'il me fait rire.
I like my maths teacher because he makes me laugh.

Je trouve le prof de chimie trop impatient. Il n'enseigne pas bien et on n'apprend rien dans son cours.
I find the chemistry teacher too impatient. He doesn't teach well and we don't learn anything in his lessons.

⑤ Talking about your ability

Je suis très fort en biologie mais assez faible en espagnol. Par contre, mon copain est doué en langues.
I am very good at biology but quite weak in Spanish. On the other hand, my friend is gifted in languages.

> **Exam focus** 📌
> With longer listening passages, listen for the main points on the first listen, and then for the details on the second listen.

⑤ Practice — Grades 4–9

🎧 Listen to this extract from a radio discussion about school subjects.
Answer the questions in **English**.

❶ What specific subject does the speaker like?

❷ What reason is given for this?

❸ What is their least favourite subject?

❹ What reasons are given for this? (2 details)

[5 marks]

Your school

Knowing how to describe your school and give your opinion on aspects of school life, such as school rules, is important.

(5) About your school

- The school day:

  La journée scolaire commence à huit heures et demie et finit à quatre heures. *The school day starts at 8.30 a.m. and finishes at 4.00 p.m.*

- What your school is like (size, age, equipment):

  Mon collège est un collège mixte pour environ mille élèves. Il est très bien équipé car il y a des tableaux interactifs dans toutes les salles de classe, un réseau Wi-Fi partout dans les bâtiments et on utilise des tablettes en cours. *My school is a mixed school for about a thousand pupils. It is very well equipped as there are interactive boards in all the classrooms, a wi-fi network throughout the buildings and we use tablets in lessons.*

- Your opinion about school matters, such as rules:

  À mon avis, le directeur est trop strict et les règles sont injustes. *In my opinion, the head teacher is too strict and the rules are unfair.*

(10) Worked example — Grades 4–9

🖉 Translate the following into French.

My school is quite big but the buildings are old. I have to get up early because lessons start at quarter to eight. Normally I go home by bus, but yesterday I had a detention and the bus left without me. In the evening we have to do so much homework! It's not fair!

Mon école est assez grande mais les bâtiments sont vieux. Je dois me lever tôt parce que les cours commencent à huit heures moins le quart. Normalement, je rentre à la maison en bus, mais hier j'ai eu une retenue et le bus est parti sans moi. Le soir, nous devons faire tellement de devoirs! Ce n'est pas juste!

(2) Vocabulary A–Z

activités (f pl) périscolaires *extra-curricular activities*
bien équipé *well-equipped*
cantine (f) *canteen*
installations scolaires (f pl) *school facilities*
directeur / directrice (m/f) *headteacher*
harceler *to bully*
redoubler *to repeat the year*
retenue (f) *detention*

VOCABULARY LINK
PAGE 109

(5) Talking about rules

To say what you are or are not allowed to do, use:

- devoir: Nous **devons** porter un uniforme scolaire.
  We have to wear a school uniform.

- permettre + de: Il nous est **permis d'**utiliser nos portables pendant la récré.
  We are allowed to use our mobile phones during break.

  On ne nous **permet** pas **de** porter du maquillage.
  We are not allowed to wear make-up.

- the phrase il est interdit + de: **Il est interdit de** courir dans les couloirs. *You are not allowed to run in the corridors.*

(2) Comparing French and English schools

En France:

On ne porte pas d'uniforme. *You don't wear a uniform.*

La journée commence vers huit heures. *The day begins at about eight o'clock.*

On n'étudie pas la religion. *You don't study RE.*

On doit redoubler si on ne fait pas assez de progrès. *You have to repeat the year if you don't make enough progress.*

Les grandes vacances durent deux mois. *The summer holidays last for two months.*

(10) Practice — Grades 1–9

1 Écoutez ces extraits d'un micro-trottoir sur le collège.

🎧 Écrivez **N** pour une opinion **négative**.
Écrivez **P** pour une opinion **positive**.
Écrivez **P+N** pour une opinion **positive et négative**.

1		3	
2		4	

[4 marks]

2 Answer the following questions.
💬
- Que penses-tu de la journée scolaire?
- Que penses-tu du règlement scolaire?
- Comment était ton école primaire?
- Qu'est-ce que tu as fait au collège hier?

Jobs and careers

You will need to know how to talk about different types of jobs and describe your own skills and qualities.

Talking about jobs

When saying what job someone has in French, you do not use an article (even though English uses *a*):

Je voudrais être avocat. *I would like to be a lawyer.*

Mon père est médecin. *My father is a doctor.*

To talk about where someone works, you can use **chez** or **à** with the name of a company.

Ma mère travaille chez / à Boots. *My mother works at Boots.*

Talking about your skills and qualities

Quelles sont vos compétences et vos qualités personnelles?

What are your skills and personal qualities?

Je suis bien organisé(e) / plein(e) d'énergie / enthousiaste / fidèle / travailleur(euse) / honnête.

I am well organised / full of energy / enthusiastic / loyal / hard-working / honest.

J'aime faire partie d'une équipe. *I like to be part of a team.*

Je parle deux langues étrangères. *I speak two foreign languages.*

Worked example — Grades 4–9

💬 **As-tu un emploi à temps partiel?**

Depuis six mois, j'ai un emploi à temps partiel dans un supermarché près de chez moi. Je dois travailler à la caisse et aider les clients à trouver des produits dans les rayons. Je travaille le vendredi soir et le samedi. J'aime bien mon petit boulot parce que le travail est varié.

Use the present tense with **depuis** to say how long you have been doing something.

This detailed answer says what you do, where and when. It also gives and opinion and a reason.

Aiming higher

The top answers may include sentences that use the subjunctive:

Il faut que je finisse / fasse / aie / aille / trouve.
It is necessary that I finish / do / have / go / find.

Il faut que je fasse un travail intéressant.
It is necessary for me to do interesting work.

GRAMMAR LINK PAGE **96**

Vocabulary A–Z

boulot (m) *job*
faire quelque chose d'enrichissant *to do something enriching*
entretien (m) *interview*
entreprise (f) *firm / business / enterprise*
espérer *to hope*
gagner *to earn*
métier (m) *job*
recevoir *to receive*
varié *varied*

VOCABULARY LINK PAGE **110**

Practice — Grades 4–9

👓 Votre ami français vous a écrit un e-mail sur le genre d'emploi qu'il voudrait faire.

Sujet: Mon travail

Mes copains aiment bien les emplois où on arrive à neuf heures et on repart à cinq heures, mais ça ne me conviendrait pas du tout. En fait, si je devais faire le même travail tous les jours, je m'ennuierais. Quant au salaire, cela n'a aucune importance pour moi car mes besoins ne sont pas grands. Avant tout, je voudrais m'entendre avec mes collègues et éviter un long trajet dans les transports en commun!

A	Je cherche un emploi avec des horaires réguliers.
B	Il n'est pas essentiel de gagner beaucoup d'argent.
C	Je veux avoir des collègues sympa.
D	Je voudrais des horaires flexibles.
E	Je voudrais gagner beaucoup d'argent.
F	Je voudrais travailler près de chez moi.
G	Je voudrais voyager pour le travail.
H	Les collègues sont moins importants que le salaire.

Choisissez **quatre** phrases qui sont vraies. Écrivez les bonnes lettres dans les cases.

[4 marks]

Made a start ☑ Feeling confident ☑ Exam ready

Ambitions

You should know how to talk about your future plans and ambitions.

(5) Stating your ambitions

You can use the present tense and the conditional to talk about your hopes and ambitions:

J'ai envie d'aller à l'université. ***I want to*** *go to university.*

J'ai l'intention de faire du bénévolat auprès des personnes âgées. ***I intend to*** *do volunteering with the elderly.*

GRAMMAR LINK PAGE 88

Mon but est de gagner beaucoup d'argent. ***My aim is to*** *earn a lot of money.*

J'espère faire de bonnes actions. ***I hope*** *to do some good.*

Je n'ai aucune intention de vivre à l'étranger. ***I have no intention of*** *living abroad.*

Je rêve d'avoir ma propre entreprise. ***I dream of*** *having my own business.*

J'aimerais prendre une année sabbatique. ***I would like*** *to take a gap year.*

Je ne voudrais pas travailler dans un bureau. ***I wouldn't like*** *to work in an office.*

(10) Worked example — Grades 4–9

 Listen to this extract from a street survey in which a young person talks about his plans and ambitions.

1 What is the first reason the speaker gives for changing his mind about what he wanted to do in life?

He wasn't good enough at science.

2 What kind of languages is he particularly interested in?

Languages that use a different alphabet

3 What has he still got to make up his mind about?

Whether or not to take a gap year

4 In what way could he use his language skills if he went travelling?

He could get to know other people and cultures.

Think about what possibilities there are for different **kinds** of languages.

Listen carefully and focus on the **first** reason mentioned.

Note down some ideas for this and then listen to see if your ideas are correct.

Think about what this might be, given the context of plans and ambitions.

(2) Talking about the future

Use the future tense to talk about your definite plans:

Je serai interprète. *I will be an interpreter.*

J'aurai mon propre appartement. *I will have my own flat.*

Je gagnerai un bon salaire. *I will earn a good salary.*

(2) Vocabulary

débouché (m) *job prospect / opportunity*

se détendre *to relax*

espoir (m) *hope*

fonder une famille *to start a family*

mettre de l'argent de côté *to save money*

utiliser les langues *to use languages*

VOCABULARY LINK PAGE 110

Read the questions carefully and think about the context. Try to predict what the answer might be in each case.

(5) Aiming higher

avant de + infinitive (*before doing something*)
après avoir / être + past participle (*after doing* or *after having done* something)

Avant d'aller à l'université, je prendrai une année sabbatique. *Before going to university, I will take a gap year.*

Après avoir fait du bénévolat, j'aurai de nouvelles compétences. *After having done some voluntary work, I will have some new skills.*

Après être allé(e) à l'université, je chercherai un emploi intéressant. *After going to university, I will look for an interesting job.*

(10) Practice — Grades 1–9

... Answer the following questions.

- Tu veux aller à l'université ou trouver un emploi? Pourquoi?
- Est-ce que tu voudrais étudier à l'université à l'étranger dans l'avenir? Pourquoi / pourquoi pas?
- Tu voudrais prendre une année sabbatique dans l'avenir? Pourquoi / pourquoi pas?
- Quel emploi est-ce que tu voulais faire quand tu étais plus jeune? **[4 marks]**

Education post-16

You will need to know the language relating to your plans for further education, at school and beyond.

 Talking about your plans

Use the future tense to talk about your future studies:

J'étudierai les sciences. *I will study sciences.*

J'irai au lycée pour étudier pour mon bac. *I will go to sixth form college to study for my A levels.*

Je deviendrai apprenti. *I will become an apprentice.*

Je laisserai tomber les maths. *I will drop maths.*

Je ne porterai plus d'uniforme scolaire. *I will no longer wear school uniform.*

En septembre, **j'entrerai** en première. *In September, I will go into Year 12 / Lower Sixth.*

J'aurai plus de liberté. *I will have more freedom.*

J'apprendrai une nouvelle langue. *I will learn a new language.*

 Vocabulary

diplôme (m) *degree / qualification*
année (f) sabbatique *gap year*
apprenti(e) (m/f) *apprentice*
avoir l'intention (de) *to intend (to)*
bac(calauréat) (m) *A level(s)*
en seconde *in Year 11*
en première *in Year 12 / Lower Sixth*
en terminale *in Year 13 / Upper Sixth*
étudier *to study*
laisser tomber *to drop*
liberté (f) *freedom*
lycée (m) *sixth form college*

VOCABULARY LINK
PAGE
110

 Worked example **Grades 4–9**

👓 Lisez les commentaires d'un forum sur les études scolaires et l'avenir.

Aimée	Je passerai le bac parce que je suis forte en langues, surtout en anglais et en espagnol. Cependant, j'ai parfois des difficultés en langues anciennes. Si j'avais le choix, je ne ferais plus de maths car c'est une matière qui ne m'intéresse pas, malheureusement, ce n'est pas une matière facultative. En ce moment, je pense à faire carrière comme interprète.
Marc	En fin de troisième, j'ai décidé de faire un bac pro cuisine parce que les études universitaires ne m'attirent pas. Je m'intéresse au secteur restauration et ce bac me prépare pour une carrière soit de chef de cuisine soit de directeur de restaurant. Je continue à étudier les maths car on doit savoir calculer dans le métier que j'ai choisi. Heureusement, c'est une matière que j'aime.

Identifiez la bonne personne.

Écrivez **A** pour Aimée. Écrivez **M** pour Marc.

Écrivez **A+M** pour Aimée et Marc.

1	Je dois continuer à étudier une matière que je n'aime pas.	A
2	J'ai une idée assez claire de ce que je voudrais faire dans l'avenir.	A+M
3	J'aurai probablement de bonnes notes.	A
4	Mon bac mettra à l'épreuve mes compétences pratiques.	M

Une matière facultative means *an optional subject.* Don't overlook the first part of the sentence where Aimée says she doesn't like maths.

Aimée says she is good (**forte**) at languages, from which you can infer that she also gets good marks.

Marc says he is going to do the **bac pro cuisine** and mentions that it can prepare him for a career as a chef.

 Practice **Grades 1–9**

✏️ Translate the following sentences into French.

• In September I will study the subjects that interest me the most. **[2 marks]**

• I am happy to drop geography because it's boring. **[2 marks]**

• Most of my friends intend to go to university. **[2 marks]**

• I think you can get a better job if you have been to university. **[2 marks]**

• I would like to find a job or an apprenticeship. **[2 marks]**

 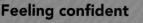

Francophone countries

You may need to be familiar with where French is spoken around the world for a range of topics, such as education, music, food, religious customs, festivals (**le Carnaval de Québec**, **la Fête des Masques** in Mali, for example) and holidays.

 Where is French spoken?

On parle français dans plusieurs pays de l'Afrique de l'ouest, par exemple au Sénégal, au Mali, au Burkina Faso, au Niger, au Togo, au Cameroun et en Côte d'Ivoire ainsi que dans les pays nord-africains comme le Maroc, l'Algérie et la Tunisie. En Asie du Sud-Est, on parlait français au Vietnam, au Laos et en Cambodge. Le Canada est aussi un pays francophone.

French is spoken in several West African countries, for example Senegal, Mali, Burkina Faso, Nigeria, Togo, Cameroon and Ivory Coast as well as North African countries such as Morocco, Algeria and Tunisia. In South East Asia, they used to speak French in Vietnam, Laos and Cambodia. Canada is also a francophone country.

 Worked example   Grades 4–9

👓 Lisez ces conseils pour les visiteurs en Guadeloupe.

Essayez d'éviter la saison des pluies entre juillet et novembre car il y a aussi un risque d'ouragans. Par contre, le temps sec et chaud de décembre à mai est très agréable.

N'oubliez pas que cet archipel des Caraïbes est un département d'outre-mer de la France alors vous pouvez utiliser les euros pour vos achats.

Prévoyez suffisamment de temps quand vous vous déplacez car le service de bus et de bateau entre les îles n'est pas très fréquent. Si vous louez une voiture sachez conscient que la condition des routes est moins bonne qu'en Europe.

1 Pourquoi est-ce qu'une visite en Guadeloupe n'est pas conseillée au mois d'août?

parce qu'il fait mauvais temps

2 Qu'est-ce que les touristes venant d'Europe n'ont pas besoin de faire s'ils veulent visiter la Guadeloupe?

changer de l'argent

3 Comment est-ce que l'état des routes pourrait affecter les déplacements en voiture? ←

Ils seraient assez lents.

Moins vites or moins confortables would also be possible here.

 Practice   Grades 4–9

🎧 Listen to this report about school life in Cameroon.
Complete the sentences in English.

1 In 91% of primary schools in Cameroon it is sometimes too _____ for classes to be held.
This is because _____ **[2 marks]**

2 69% primary school children in Cameroon would have problems if they are _____ at school because **[2 marks]**
_____

3 59% of primary schools don't have _____ This results in _____ **[2 marks]**

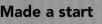 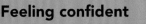

French customs

Knowing about French customs and traditions can help you understand the context of some reading and listening texts.

VOCABULARY LINK PAGE 111

⑤ Christmas traditions in France

Au réveillon, on mange un grand repas en famille. On mange des fruits de mer comme les huîtres, et comme dessert, il y a la bûche de Noël.

On Christmas Eve, families eat a big meal. They eat seafood, like oysters, and there is chocolate log for dessert.

Comme en Grande Bretagne, on met des cadeaux sous le sapin de Noël. *Like in Great Britain, people put presents under the Christmas tree.*

② Vocabulary

anniversaire (m) *birthday / anniversary*

cadeau (m) *present*

célébrer *to celebrate*

église (f) *church*

fêter *to celebrate*

messe (f) *mass*

mosquée (f) *mosque*

musulman *Muslim*

Noël (m) *Christmas*

veille de Noël (f) *Christmas Eve*

Réveillon (m) *Christmas Eve dinner*

Pâques (f pl) *Easter*

poisson d'avril (m) *April Fools' Day*

Toussaint (f) *All Saints' Day*

⑩ Worked example   Grades 4–9

 Read this short article about religion in France.

> Le catholicisme est la religion la plus importante en France, malgré le fait que de plus en plus de gens déclarent qu'ils n'ont aucune religion. Beaucoup de français ne vont à l'église qu'à l'occasion des grandes fêtes religieuses de l'année, c'est-à-dire à Pâques et à Noël. Quant aux autres religions, le nombre de musulmans et de mosquées en France augmente, tandis que les chiffres concernant les juifs et les synagogues diminuent.

Answer the questions in **English**.

❶ What does this article say about trends in church attendance?

It's decreasing, as many French people only go to church at Christmas and Easter.

❷ What does it say about Islam and Judaism?

The numbers of Muslims and mosques are increasing and numbers of Jews and synagogues are decreasing.

⑮ Practice   Grades 1–9

❶ Listen to these extracts from a podcast about customs and traditions in France.

Which four things are discussed? For each speaker, write the correct letter in the box.

A	Christmas festivities
B	Easter traditions
C	Family celebrations
D	French tradition of food
E	Mother's Day
F	Playing a joke
G	Remembering the dead

1		3	
2		4	

 [4 marks]

Try to predict what these might be. They will be related to the theme. Perhaps: **Comment est-ce que tu fêtes le Nouvel An? Est-ce que les fêtes en famille sont importantes?**

Use your knowledge of French life and culture to predict what vocabulary you need to listen out for.

❷ Answer the following questions.
- Qu'est-ce qu'il y a sur la photo?
- Quel est ton cadeau d'anniversaire idéal?
- Qu'est-ce que tu as fait pour fêter ton anniversaire l'année dernière?

  You will be asked **two** further questions you have not prepared.

You can repeat part of the question in your answer to give yourself thinking time: **Mon cadeau d'anniversaire idéal, c'est...**

French festivals

You should be aware of events and festivals in France as they may be referred to in spoken and written texts.

 La fête des Rois

La fête des Rois est le six janvier. On mange un gâteau spécial qui s'appelle la galette des Rois. On cache une fève dans la galette et la personne qui la trouve est le «Roi» ou la «Reine» et porte une couronne.

Twelfth Night / Epiphany is 6 January. They eat a special cake called 'la galette des Rois'. A bean is hidden in the cake and the person who finds it becomes the 'king' or 'queen' and wears a crown.

② **Vocabulary**

s'amuser *to have fun*
cacher *to hide*
carnaval (m) *carnival*
défilé (m) *parade / procession*
se déguiser *to disguise oneself / dress up (in a costume)*
fête (f) des Mères *Mother's Day*
feu (m) d'artifice *firework*
jour (m) de l'an *New Year's Day*
jour (m) férié *bank holiday*
mondial *worldwide*
(le) Nouvel An *New Year*
réunion (f) *meeting*
Saint-Sylvestre (f) *New Year's Eve*
veille (f) de Noël *Christmas Eve*

⑩ **Worked example** Grades 4–5

 Lisez cet extrait d'un site Internet.

> La période de carnaval commence le 6 janvier (la fête des Rois) et se termine le Mardi Gras. Les carnavals de Rio et de Venise ont une renommée mondiale, mais il y a aussi des carnavals partout en France; les plus célèbres sont ceux de Nice et Dunkerque. Ces fêtes vous donnent l'occasion de vous déguiser, de chanter, de danser et surtout de vous amuser. Souvent, les enfants se déguisent en adultes, les adultes en enfants, les femmes en hommes, les hommes en femmes, etc.

Choisissez **deux** phrases qui sont vraies. Écrivez les bonnes lettres dans les cases.

Ne … que means *only*. The text mentions the carnivals in Rio (Brazil) and Venice (Italy).

A	Le carnaval n'existe qu'en France.
B	Le début du carnaval est douze jours après Noël.
C	Le carnaval est le temps d'être heureux.
D	On porte ses vêtements de tous les jours quand on fête le carnaval.

 B   C

Début means *start*.

⑤ **La fête nationale française**

La fête nationale française est le quatorze juillet. C'est l'anniversaire de la prise de la Bastille pendant la Révolution française en 1789. Il y a des défilés dans les rues des grandes villes et le soir, on peut voir un grand feu d'artifice.

Bastille Day is 14 July. It's the anniversary of the taking of the Bastille during the French revolution in 1789. There are parades in the streets of big towns and in the evening you can see a big firework display.

L'occasion de s'amuser has the same meaning as this.

This means *everyday clothes*. The text says that carnival is the time to **se déguiser** (*disguise oneself*).

⑤ **Practice** Grades 1–9

💬 Answer the following questions.
- Que penses-tu des fêtes françaises?
- Tu es déjà allé(e) à une fête en France? C'était comment?

Pronunciation strategies

Understanding the link between the sound and spelling of a word will help you understand and say French words more accurately. You will gain marks for correct pronunciation in your speaking exam.

② General rules

- ☑ The same sound in French may have several different spellings.
- ☑ Many final consonants are silent.
- ☑ There is a liaison (the final consonant is pronounced) when a silent consonant is followed by a vowel.
- ☑ Cognates are invariably pronounced differently from their English equivalent.

⑤ Same sound / different spelling

Some vowel sounds in French can be spelled in different ways, but all are pronounced the same:

- aller / allez / allé / nez
- des / j'ai / lait / forêt / dès / craie / palais
- dans / dent / étudiant / vend / grand.

> Remember vowels before **n** and **m** are nasal sounds in French, unless the n or m are followed by another vowel or are doubled, as in **une, vinaigre** and **pomme**.

⑤ Final consonants

As a general rule, the following consonants are **not** pronounced when they are at the end of a word:

- **d**: chaud, froid, nord
- **g**: long, sang
- **m**: parfum, nom
- **n**: vin, fin, juin, selon
- **p**: trop, drap
- **s**: souris, chats, puis, alors, anglais
- **t**: mot, vert
- **x**: heureux, noix, faux, choux
- **z**: chez

> Some common exceptions to this rule are: **sud, mars, huit, oust, strict** and **gaz**. ❗

⑤ Cognates

Most cognates are nearly always pronounced differently. In particular, you should know how to recognise and say words ending in –ion (nation, éducation) and words that begin with im- (impossible, important, impoli) and in- (incapable, incident, inconnu).

⑩ Making the liaison

You need to pronounce the final consonant when it is followed by a vowel or silent h:

- when there is an adjective in front of a masculine singular noun: un grand‿hôtel / un petit‿ami / un mauvais‿exemple
- after determiners: son‿ami / mon‿espagnol / les‿examens / ces‿assiettes
- after monosyllabic prepositions: chez‿eux / aux‿États-unis / en‿Afrique / dans‿un‿instant
- after on, nous, vous, ils and elles: on‿a mangé / nous nous‿amusons / vous‿avez faim / ils‿écrivent des lettres / elles‿arrivent
- after est and ont: le train est‿arrivé / ils‿ont‿une petite maison
- after numbers: trois‿oignons / deux‿oranges.

> Although pronounced when followed by a vowel and also when at the end of a sentence, the letter **x** in **dix** and **six** is not pronounced when followed by a noun beginning with a consonant: **Je voudrais six bananes. / Je serai là dans dix minutes**. ❗

The following consonants **are** usually pronounced when they are at the end of a word:

- **b**: club, flashmob, snob
- **c**: choc, parc
- **f**: neuf, vif, bœuf, chef
- **k**: anorak, folk, rock
- **l**: mal, calcul
- **q**: cinq, coq
- **r**: four, hiver, par

Words that come from other languages invariably have the final consonant pronounced: **stop, clown, Islam, autobus, grog, forum**.

This also includes words that come from Latin, for example: **maximum, minimum, amen, aluminium, aquarium**.

> Some common exceptions are: **plomb, estomac, blanc, clef, gentil, sommeil, fusil**. ❗

⑩ Practice

Practise saying the following phrases and then listen to the audio clips to check your pronunciation.

- Ils espèrent trouver la station de métro.
- Nous achetons du riz, du miel, des noix et six bouteilles de vin fin.
- Elles écoutent leur musique sur Internet.

☑ **Made a start**   ☑ **Feeling confident**   ☑ **Exam ready**

Speaking strategies

In your speaking exam you can use non-verbal strategies, such as facial expressions and gestures, and verbal strategies to keep talking and complete the tasks.

Saying what you want to say

If you don't know or have forgotten the French word for something, here are three strategies that can help:

1 paraphrase: paresseux – *lazy*
C'est quelqu'un qui ne fait pas beaucoup de travail.

2 describe the item: its size, colour, material, shape or position – *a sprout*
C'est un légume vert un peu comme un chou, mais plus petit.

3 refer to the function of an item using words like un objet, un truc or un machin.
C'est un objet qu'on peut utiliser pour couper du bois. This could be accompanied by a non-verbal gesture (couper comme ça) to show whether you mean an axe or a saw.

Filler phrases

Sometimes you may need to give yourself a little time to think as you answer. Filler phrases can be useful as you can be thinking while you say the phrase:

alors *so*

eh bien *well*

c'est-à-dire *that is to say / what I mean*

tu sais / vous savez *you know*

tu vois / vous voyez *you see*

bon *okay*

bon ben *anyway*

euh *uh / um*

bref *in short*

tout simplement *in short*

bien sûr *of course*

Aiming higher

To gain top marks remember to:

- expand on your answer by using adjectives and adverbs to add details
- use a range of tenses. This can be done by making comparisons between different time frames.

Qu'est-ce que tu veux faire après avoir terminé tes études?

Le plus important, selon moi, est de faire quelque chose de gratifiant. Après avoir terminé mes études, j'aimerais faire du bénévolat, peut-être en Chine, puisque c'est un pays qui m'intéresse et me fascine beaucoup. Plus tard, mon rêve serait de travailler dans l'informatique vu que c'est le secteur qui m'attire le plus.

Changing the subject

If you don't automatically have an answer to a question, you should try to say something, even if it isn't strictly true. For example:

Qu'est-ce que tu as fait récemment pour réduire des déchets chez toi?

Don't say Rien.

You could say:

En fait, je n'ai pas fait grand-chose pour réduire les déchets, mais mes parents ont trié les déchets pour les recycler.

> Words like **mais**, **cependant** and **pourtant** are useful if you want to steer the conversation in a different direction.

> Although these can be helpful phrases, don't overuse them and don't string them together!

Answering questions

You can repeat words and phrases from a question in your answer to give yourself some time to think.

Où es-tu allé(e) pendant les grandes vacances l'année dernière?

L'année dernière, pendant les grandes vacances, je suis allé(e) au pays de Galles...

If you understand the question but are not sure what to say initially, you could use phrases like:

Ça, c'est une question intéressante... *That is an interesting question...*

Laissez-moi réfléchir un moment. *Let me think for a moment.*

Ça dépend... *That depends ...*

Je dirais (que)... *I would say (that) ...*

Laissez-moi réfléchir un moment.

Exam-style practice

Répondez aux questions suivantes.

- Quels sont les effets du réchauffement de la Terre?
- Qu'est-ce qu'on doit faire pour protéger l'environnement?

 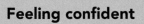

 BBC

Asking for clarification strategies

It is useful to know what you can say if you are not sure how to answer a question.

 Exam focus

You may find that you are not sure how to answer a question in your speaking exam. You may not have fully understood the question or you may not have heard what was asked. You will get some credit in the exam if you are able to keep the conversation going by using phrases to ask for clarification or repetition.

 Asking for repetition

There are several ways to ask your teacher to repeat the question:

- Pouvez-vous répéter la question, s'il vous plaît?
- Pourriez-vous répéter la question?
- Tu peux répéter la question, s'il te plaît?
- Vous pouvez parler plus lentement, s'il vous plaît?
- Tu peux parler plus lentement, s'il te plaît?

The conditional **pourriez** is an even more polite way of asking the question.

In the role-play scenario, use the **tu** form if your teacher is playing the part of a friend.

Exam focus

Remember to make your voice go up at the end of these sentences to make them into questions.

 Worked example

Look at these three different ways to check the meaning of something.

Qu'est-ce que tu fais comme activités périscolaires?

Activités périscolaires? Qu'est-ce que ça veut dire?

Pardon, je ne comprends pas le mot « périscolaire ». Qu'est-ce que ça veut dire?

Activités périscolaires? Ce sont les activités après la fin de la journée scolaire?

Activités périscolaires? What does that mean?
Repeating the word and making it sound like a question is a simple way to communicate that you have not understood it.

I'm sorry, I don't understand the word 'périscolaire'. What does it mean?
This makes it clear you don't understand the word and want to know what it means.

Activités périscolaires? Are these after school activities?
Here, you have an idea of what the phrase means, but are just checking.

 Useful phrases A–Z

Qu'est-ce que ça veut dire? *What does that mean?*
Je ne comprends pas *I don't understand*
Qu'est-ce que vous voulez dire? *What do you mean?*
Comment dit-on « dégustration » en anglais? *How do you say 'dégustation' in English?*
Je ne sais pas *I don't know*
Comment ça s'écrit? *How do you write that?*
Peux-tu / Pouvez-vous expliquer le mot...?
Can you explain the word...?

 Aiming higher

If you do need to use one of these strategies, try to use a phrase that demonstrates that you can use a range of tenses.

Je suis désolé(e), je n'ai pas bien compris le mot « dégustation ». Pourrais-tu / Pourriez vous l'expliquer s'il te / vous plaît?

I am sorry, I haven't understood the word 'dégustation'. Could you explain it please?

This is a good phrase because it also uses an object pronoun.

  Made a start **Feeling confident** **Exam ready**

General conversation

In the speaking exam, you choose the first overall theme for the general conversation. You will be allocated a photo card on one of the other two broad themes and you will also be asked questions relating to the third theme in the general conversation.

⑩ Worked example

In this example the student has chosen 'Local, National, International and Global Issues' as the theme and the second part is based on 'Current and Future Study and Employment'.

> If you don't understand the question, ask your teacher: **Les SDF qu'est-ce que ça veut dire?**

❶ Comment est-ce que tu trouves ta ville?

J'aime bien ma ville, car elle n'est ni trop grande ni trop petite, et il n'y a pas trop de circulation comme dans les grandes villes. On peut se déplacer facilement parce que les transports en commun sont excellents. Pour ceux qui aiment la culture, il y a plusieurs musées et un théâtre, mais il n'y a pas de cinéma, ce qui est dommage!

❷ Dans beaucoup de grandes villes, on voit souvent des SDF. Qu'est-ce qu'on pourrait faire pour les aider?

À mon avis, la meilleure façon d'aider les SDF est de soutenir les associations caritatives qui travaillent avec eux. On pourrait par exemple aider à préparer des repas pour les SDF ou donner des vêtements chauds.

❸ Quels sont les avantages de vivre à la campagne?

> You can develop your answer by talking about the disadvantages as well as the advantages of living in the countryside.

Je pense que le plus grand avantage de vivre à la campagne est que l'air est plus frais et il y a moins de pollution. Cependant, les moyens de transports en commun sont souvent moins fréquents et on doit aller en ville pour faire des achats.

> Use the same tense as the question in your answer. Here it is the conditional.

❹ Comment seraient tes vacances idéales?

Mes vacances idéales seraient au bord de la mer parce que j'aime me détendre et me bronzer. Pourtant, s'il fait mauvais, je trouve intéressant de faire des activités culturelles comme visiter un musée.

❺ Qu'est-ce que tu as fait pendant tes vacances l'année dernière?

> You must ask a question during the conversation. Remember to use **vous**.

L'année dernière, je suis allé(e) au pays de Galles où on a fait du camping. Il faisait beau et nous pouvions faire des randonnées presque tous les jours. Un jour, nous sommes montés en haut du Snowdon et nous avons eu une vue magnifique, c'était formidable! Est-ce que vous êtes allé(e) au pays de Galles?

❻ Quelles sont tes matières préférées à l'école et pourquoi?

Je trouve les sciences fascinantes, mais ma matière préférée est l'histoire parce que je m'intéresse beaucoup à ce qui s'est passé dans le passé.

> Vary the way you introduce your opinions and use vocabulary. **Établissement** is an alternative for **école** or **collège**.

❼ Que penses-tu de l'uniforme scolaire?

Je pense que l'uniforme scolaire est une bonne idée parce qu'on n'a pas besoin de passer du temps le matin à décider de ce qu'il faut porter. En plus, ça donne une identité visible à ton établissement. Pourtant, j'ai parfois envie de porter mes propres vêtements comme on le fait en France!

❽ Qu'est-ce que tu as fait comme travail scolaire hier?

> This answer is developed by making reference to differences from France.

Hier, j'ai révisé pour mes examens. Je devais lire les notes dans mes cahiers et j'ai fait des exercices de maths. Pour préparer mon examen de français, j'ai enregistré mes réponses à des questions sur mon portable.

❾ Quels sont tes projets pour l'année prochaine?

> **Projets** is a clue that you need to use the future tense.

L'année prochaine, je serai en première et j'étudierai les sciences et les maths, parce que je veux être ingénieur et ces matières sont nécessaires pour obtenir une place à l'université.

⑩ In the exam

- use a range of vocabulary and grammatical structures that refer to past, present and future time frames
- express opinions and give a reason for them.
- You must also ask a question.

⑤ Exam-style practice

Listen to the questions recorded on the audio clip and answer them. The first theme is Current and Future Study and Employment and the second is Identity and Culture.

Pages
9–12
LINKS

Using the photo card or picture stimulus

There is a photo card or picture stimulus task in the speaking exam at both tiers, and on the writing paper at Foundation tier.

⑤ About the photo card task

The photo card or picture stimulus will be related to one of the three broad overall themes for which you should know the key vocabulary.

The first question in the photo card and the Foundation picture stimulus task is always:

Qu'est-ce qu'il y a sur la photo? *What is in the photo?*

The question and answer section of the task will last for 2 minutes for Foundation tier and 3 minutes for Higher tier.

② Describing the photo

To describe the photo card or picture stimulus, think about how you could answer the following questions:

- ☑ Who is in the photo?
- ☑ Where are they?
- ☑ What are they doing?
- ☑ When or what is the time of year / occasion?
- ☑ What is the mood of the photo?
- ☑ Other details, e.g. What is the weather like?

⑩ Worked example

Look at the photo and make notes. You will be asked questions about the photo and topics related to **me, my family and friends.**

You will be asked these questions and two more that you have not prepared:

- Qu'est-ce qu'il y a sur la photo?
- Que penses-tu des familles nombreuses?
- Qu'est-ce que tu as fait en famille le week-end dernier?

Model answer 1

Sur la photo, il y a huit personnes. Ce sont probablement les membres d'une famille. Ils prennent un selfie et ils sont très heureux. Ils rient. Ils sont à la campagne.

This answer provides quite a lot of information, but the language is simple and the sentences are short.

Model answer 2

Sur la photo, il y a huit personnes qui sont peut-être membres d'une famille. Ils sont en train de prendre une photo et ils ont l'air très heureux puisqu'ils rient. Je pense qu'ils font une promenade à la campagne.

Qui is a relative pronoun – use it to join sentences.

Words like **peut-être** and **probablement** can be used to make inferences about what is in the photo.

Use connectives like **puisque** or **parce que** to introduce a reason for your statement.

⑤ Aiming higher

Replace **il y a** with a phrase that shows you can manipulate a verb, such as **je vois**, **on voit** or **on peut voir**.

Use **peut-être** (*perhaps*) to speculate about the photo. It could be a way of introducing another tense:

Ils vont peut-être partager la photo sur des réseaux sociaux.

Perhaps they are going to share the photo on social networks / media.

⑤ Exam-style practice

Qu'est-ce qu'il y a sur la photo?

Role-play (Foundation)

In the role-play, at Foundation tier, you will have to complete five tasks, including responding to an unprepared question and asking a question of your own.

② About the role-play

Read the instructions on the card carefully. Make sure you understand what your role in the scenario is and the role that your teacher will play. You will be instructed to use **tu** or **vous**, depending on the context.

During your preparation time, work out what you will say for the four bullet points with information on the card.

Remember that you will have to ask a question. It will be marked **?**.

There will be an unprepared question, to which you will have to respond. It is marked **!**. Listen carefully to what you are asked.

The role-play will last for approximately 2 minutes.

⑤ Task instructions

✓ **description** – You must describe the item mentioned; this could be size, colour, shape.

✓ **une raison** – You must give a reason for your answer – **parce que c'est utile.**

✓ **projet** – You will need to refer to future plans.

✓ **combien de personnes / fois?** *How many people / times?*

✓ **où?** *where?* You need to give a place in your answer.

✓ **quand?** *when?*

✓ **sorte de** *kind of.* For example, **musique – sorte de.** Here you will need to talk about a kind of music, but listen carefully to the question you are asked. **Quelle sorte de musique est-ce que tu aimes?** OR **Quelle sorte de musique est-ce que tu n'aimes pas?**

⑤ Worked example 💬

Tu parles de la technologie avec ton ami(e) français(e).

- Internet – une activité.
- Ton opinion d'Internet (1 détail).
- !
- L'informatique à l'école – combien de fois.
- ? Portable.

1. Je fais du shopping en ligne.
2. Je pense qu'Internet est très utile.
3. J'utilise Internet le soir.
4. J'ai un cours d'informatique une fois par semaine.
5. Comment est ton portable?

This tells you whether you should use the **tu** or **vous** form in the role-play.

You only need to say one thing you do on the internet. Focus on what you know how to say.

Try to predict what you might be asked for here. If you don't understand, you can ask your teacher to repeat the question. This unprepared question is: **Quand est-ce que tu utilises Internet?**

You should be ready to ask this question without being prompted. Remember to use the correct form of address (**tu** or **vous**).

Alternative responses:
1. Je fais des recherches pour l'école.
2. À mon avis, Internet est très dangereux.
4. On a un cours par semaine (le mardi matin).
5. As-tu un portable? Qu'est-ce que tu as comme portable? Qu'est-ce que tu fais avec ton portable?

② Exam focus 📌

- Focus on saying enough to complete the task. There is no need to expand on your answers. You will be awarded ten marks (two per task) for communication and five for knowledge and use of language.
- If you don't understand the unprepared question (**!**) you can ask your teacher to repeat the question: **Pardon? Vous pouvez répétez la question, s'il vous plaît?**

⑤ Exam-style practice 💬

Vous parlez avec l'employé d'un office de tourisme.

- Votre nationalité.
- En France – combien de temps.
- Logement – description (2 détails).
- ! (Comment trouvez-vous la France? Pourquoi?)
- ? Gare.

Pages
24–27

LINKS

Role-play (Higher)

In the role-play at Higher tier you will have to complete five tasks also, like at Foundation tier.

② About the role-play ✓

The Higher role-play consists of five tasks, including responding to an unprepared question (marked **!**) and asking a question yourself (marked **?**).

One or more tasks may require you to use the perfect or future tense. Look out for the clues where this is required on the role-play card: **activité récente** – *recent activity*. Use the perfect here.

Read the instructions on the role-play card carefully. Note whether you need to use **tu** or **vous**.

② Exam focus 📌 ✓

- There are ten marks (two per task) for communication and five for knowledge and use of language.
- Focus on saying enough to complete the task. There is no need to expand on your answers.
- The role-play will last approximately 3 minutes.
- If you don't understand the unprepared question (**!**) you can ask your teacher to repeat it: **Pardon? Vous pouvez répéter la question, s'il vous plaît?**

⑤ Task instructions ✓

In addition to the instructions that appear on Foundation role-play cards (see page 49), you might see the following on a Higher role-play card:

- ☑ references to the past: **récent(e/s)**, **récemment**, **hier**, **dernier(ière)** or a past participle such as **acheté**. Use the perfect and imperfect tenses here.
- ☑ references to the future: **projets**, **en septembre**, **prochain**. Use the future tense here.
- ☑ reference to the present: **en ce moment**. Use the present tense here.
- ☑ **avantages / inconvénients**: You will have to talk about advantages and disadvantages of something. If the card has + **raison** on it, you will have to give a reason.
- ☑ **problème / activité – 2 détails**: You will have to say what the problem / activity is and give two pieces of information about it.
- ☑ **opinion + raison**: You must say what you think about the topic and give a reason.
- ☑ **utilisation**: You must say something about your use of something.

⑩ Worked example 💬 ✓

Vous parlez avec l'employé dans un bureau des objets trouvés.

> - Objet perdu – quand et où.
> - **!**
> - En France – pourquoi (2 détails).
> - **?** Activités – région.
> - Projets – week-end (1 détail + raison).

- J'ai perdu mon porte-monnaie hier dans le bus.
- Il est marron et en cuir.
- Je suis en France avec un échange scolaire pour perfectionner mon français.
- Qu'est-ce qu'on peut faire dans cette région?
- Ce week-end, je vais visiter des monuments parce que je trouve ça intéressant.

You must address your teacher as **vous** in this task.

Use the perfect tense to say what you have lost, where and when.

Try to predict what you might be asked for here, given the context and the other tasks.

You must give two pieces of information about why you are in France.

You should use the future tense or immediate future here.

Alternative responses

1. J'ai perdu mon portable / appareil photo / sac à dos + different place / time

3. Je fais du tourisme, je rends visite à des amis.

4. Qu'est-ce qu'il y a à faire dans cette région?

5. Ce week-end, on ira au restaurant pour fêter l'échange / j'irai au stade pour voir un match de foot.

⑩ Exam-style practice 💬 ✓

Tu viens d'arriver chez ton ami(e) français(e).

> - Maison – opinion.
> - **!** (Comment était le voyage?)
> - Projets pendant visite (2 activités).
> - **?** Utilisation – technologie.
> - Aliment préféré + raison (2 détails).

Listening strategies

Get to know the strategies that will help you in your listening exam.

 Preparing for your exam 2

- Learn as much vocabulary as you can for all the topics on the syllabus.
- Listen to as much French as you can. Ask your teacher for suggestions for suitable websites.
- Make sure you understand the link between sound and spelling. Following a transcript as you listen can help. (See page 44.)

 Extra strategies 2

- If you get stuck with a word, repeat it in your head and try to use your knowledge of phonics to transcribe it. Remember that cognates are nearly always pronounced differently in French.
- Listen out for words that mean the same (or opposite) as a word in the question: monotone = répétitif.
- Focus on the words you do know and try not to be put off by any unknown language. Use familiar words to eliminate options.

 Worked example 5

«J'ai toujours rêvé d'être médecin, mais on n'est jamais certain de gagner une place pour étudier la médecine, alors j'ai décidé de faire autre chose».

The speaker…

A is certain to study medicine.

B is not planning to study medicine. ✓

C might study medicine.

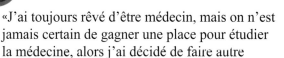
alors j'ai décidé de faire autre chose *so I decided to do something else.*

The speaker says **certain**, but uses it with **jamais** (*never*).

 Before you listen 5

- Read the questions carefully. Do you need to listen out for a specific detail? Or do you need to draw a conclusion having heard the whole extract?
- Try to predict what you may need to listen out for in order to complete a task. If you are given the following headings to match to news reports, jot down some key words.

  fire (incendie / feu / pompiers / brûler)

  flood (inondation / pluie / tempête / pleuvoir)

  murder (meurtre / tuer / mort / mourir / assassiner)

  robbery (voler / voleur / vol / vole / cambriolage + any item that could be stolen)

- Look at the title as this may help you with key words. You may not know that piste cyclable is a cycle lane, but if you see 'Cycle lanes' as the title of the exercise and you hear the word you should be able to make the connection.

While listening 5

- Try to concentrate on just listening when you hear the extract for the first time. If you start to make notes you may miss an important detail.
- Listen for the main points the first time you hear the recording and then for the details the second time.
- If you are listening out for someone's opinion or intentions, keep in mind that little words can change the meaning of a sentence:

cependant	*however*
pourtant	*however*
mais	*but*
sauf	*except*
alors	*so*
malgré	*in spite of*
de l'autre côté	*on the other hand*

- Listen to the whole extract before you draw any conclusions. An important piece of information may come at the end.

 Exam-style practice 10

Listen to this report about the Olympic Games. Answer the following questions in **English**.

(a) What advantages of being a host country are mentioned in the report (2 details)? **[2 marks]**

(b) What are the disadvantages (2 details)? **[2 marks]**

Listening 1

In the listening paper of your exam, you will need to be able to complete tasks with questions and answers in French.

 Before answering the question(s)

- Read the questions carefully before you listen.
- Try to predict what words you need to listen out for.
- Use the wording of the questions to help you understand what the extract is about.
- Listen to the whole extract before you make any notes and draw conclusions. You could miss an important detail!
- Concentrate on listening for the main details the first time and for the details the second time.

Worked example

Écoutez ce reportage sur *France Culture* au sujet des fêtes en France.

Choisissez **deux** phrases qui sont vraies et écrivez les bonnes lettres dans les cases.

1

A	La Fête des Lumières a lieu en été.
B	À l'origine, c'est une fête religieuse.
C	La première Fête des Lumières a eu lieu au seizième siècle.
D	Uniquement les édifices municipaux sont illuminés.
E	Les habitants de Lyon participent à la fête en allumant des chandelles dans leurs maisons.

[B] [E]   **[2 marks]**

> The extract says that the festival takes place in December.

> You can infer that this festival has its origins in religion from the reference to **la Vierge Marie, la mère de Jésus Christ.**

> The sixteenth century is mentioned in the extract, but this was not when the festival first started.

> **Uniquement** means *only*. The public buildings are not the only things illuminated.

> **Les habitants de Lyon** and **les Lyonnais** are synonyms. **Allumant des chandelles dans leurs maisons** means the same as **illuminent leurs fenêtres et balcons avec des bougies.**

2

A	La Fête du Citron a lieu dans une ville au centre de la France.
B	Cette fête est célébrée en automne.
C	Presqu'un quart de million de personnes visitent Menton pendant la fête.
D	La fête a lieu dans les rues et les espaces verts de la ville.
E	On peut voir de grandes structures créées avec des fruits de toutes les couleurs.

[C] [D]   **[2 marks]**

> The report says that Menton is *on the coast* (**sur la Côte d'Azur**).

> The report says the festival takes place in February.

> More than 230,000 people go to the festival.

> The report mentions **défilés** (*parades*); **espaces verts** can be inferred from the mention of **jardins publics.**

> The report only refers to lemons and oranges, not fruits of all colours.

Exam-style practice

Écoutez le reportage et choisissez la bonne lettre.

- **A** Violence au collège
- **B** Mort d'un prisonnier
- **C** Accident de la route
- **D** Noyade accidentelle dans une piscine

[ ]   **[2 marks]**

✓ **Made a start** ✓ **Feeling confident** ✓ **Exam ready**

Pages 37, 12, 24 LINKS

Listening 2

In the listening paper of your exam, you will need to be able to complete tasks with written answers in English and French.

② Before answering the questions

Read the questions carefully before you listen. Make sure you understand what kind of information you need to listen out for, and that you select the relevant bits.

You must write down all the information you are asked to give, but do not need to answer in full sentences.

⑩ Worked example 🎧

Listen to this radio programme where some pupils from a French private school are talking about school uniform.

For each speaker write down one advantage and one disadvantage:

❶ Florence

Advantage	Disadvantage
don't have to spend time deciding what to wear	jacket is quite expensive

[2 marks]

❷ Didier

Advantage	Disadvantage
Pupils are better behaved when wearing school uniform.	can't express his personality

[2 marks]

Notre comportement est meilleur means *our behaviour is better.*

⑤ Worked example 🎧

Vous écoutez des jeunes qui parlent de l'argent dans un café.

Répondez aux deux aspects de la question:

❶ Gérard paie son café avec

sa carte sans contact.

❷ Selon lui, c'est plus

pratique.

[2 marks]

② Exam focus 📌

You will hear the extract twice and then there will be a pause for you to write down your answer.

Only note down key details while you are listening to the extracts, otherwise you might miss an important piece of information.

Don't worry if there are words you don't understand. Focus on the words you do know.

Practical would also be acceptable.

jacket is not elegant would also be possible here.

Un moyen d'exprimer ma personnalité means *a way of expressing my personality.* **L'uniforme scolaire m'empêche de faire ça** means *school uniform prevents me from doing that.*

⑮ Exam-style practice 🎧

❶ Écoutez ces jeunes ados qui parlent à la radio au sujet du mariage. Complétez la grille avec **un** inconvénient et **un** désavantage.

	Avantage	Inconvénient
Claire		
Hubert		

❷ While waiting for a flight you overhear people talking about their holiday problems.

For each speaker write down one problem and one solution.

Speaker 1

Problem	Solution

[2 marks]

Speaker 2

Problem	Solution

[2 marks]

Reading strategies

Learning strategies that can help you work out the meaning of a text is extremely useful.

Decoding skills

Knowing common patterns between French and English words, as well as the meaning of French prefixes and suffixes, can help you work out the meaning of a text.

English pattern	French pattern	Examples
-c(al)	-que	musique, comique, romantique
-ary	-aire	militaire, grammaire
-y	-ie	comédie, tragédie, géographie
-ory	-oire	histoire, gloire, victoire
-ous	-eux	délicieux, nombreux, nerveux
-ty	-té	liberté, beauté, université
-ive	-if	positif, actif, négatif
-ing	-ant	dégoûtant, charmant
-ly	-ment	rapidement, complètement

Other changes between French and English:

English	French	Examples
s	é or es	espace, éponge, état
s	ô, ê	forêt, hôpital, tempête
dv	v	avantage, aventure
ni	gn	oignon, compagnon
dis	dés	désagréable, désastre

Prefixes and suffixes

Understanding French prefixes and suffixes can help you work out meanings.

re (r') or **ré** = repeated or again
refaire *to redo / do again*; **réouverture** *reopening*

in-, im-, ir-, il-, mal-: make opposite meanings, often equivalent to un-, il-, in-, dis- in English.
malhonnête (*dishonest*); **illimité** (*unlimited*)

Translation into English

- Check you use the correct tense in your translation.
- Don't forget to translate time phrases, adverbs and adjectives.
- Watch out for pronouns like **y**:
  on y voit... *you see... there.*

Strategies for working out meaning

There are bound to be a few words on the reading paper (Paper 3) which you do not know, but you can have strategies for working out the meaning. These include:

- using visual clues, such as images
- using your knowledge of word families to work out the meaning of a word: **ami, amical, amicalement** – *friend, friendly, in a friendly way*
- looking for cognates and near cognates (words that are either the same or very similar to English or another language that you know)
- using your knowledge of grammar, work out whether the unknown word is a verb, noun or adjective, etc., from its position in a sentence or the endings
- using the context and your knowledge of the French speaking world
- paying attention to high frequency words and what they mean, particularly those that can change the meaning of a sentence: **cependant** (*however*) or **mais** (*but*).

False friends

False friends are words that look like an English word but have a completely different meaning, for example:

actuellement *currently*	**en fait** *actually*
car (m) *coach*	**voiture** (f) *car*
chance (f) *luck*	**occasion** (f) *chance*
coin (m) *corner*	**pièce de monnaie** (f) *coin*
crayon (m) *pencil*	**crayon de couleur** (m) *crayon*
effectif *real*	**efficace** *effective*
éventuellement *possibly*	**finalement** *eventually*
gentil *kind*	**doux / douce** *gentle*
gros *fat*	**dégoûtant** *gross* (*disgusting*)
journée (f) *day*	**voyage** (m) *journey*
large *wide*	**grand** *large*
sensible *sensitive*	**raisonnable** *sensible*
sympathique *nice*	**compatissant** *sympathetic*

Using context

For unknown words, look at other words nearby to see if there is anything that can help you. Translate the following:

On a transporté le blessé de la scène de l'accident à l'hôpital sur un brancard.

You might not know **brancard**, but you could use other words as clues: **transporté** (*transported*), **blessé** (*injured*) and **hôpital** (*hospital*), to work out that **un brancard** is a *stretcher*.

Reading 1

In the reading paper of your exam, you will need to be able to complete different tasks with questions and answers in English.

Exam focus

Look at the number of marks allocated to each question or question part. This will indicate the amount of information and detail that is required.

Reading the introductory text will set the context for the extract and reading the question(s) may help you understand words you don't know. Read the whole text through before answering any questions.

Worked example

Read this article about healthy living.

You may not know this word, but from the context you should be able to work out that it means *hints*.

Du robinet is given as an alternative to eau minérale, so you can make an educated guess that it means *tap water*.

If you don't know what these words mean, use the context of advice about physical exercise to help you (l'escalier = stairs / l'ascenseur = lift).

Mineral water is mentioned in the text, but as an alternative to *tap water*.

Astuces pour une vie saine

N'oubliez pas que le corps est constitué à 70% d'eau. Essayez de boire au moins huit verres d'eau (soit du robinet soit de l'eau minérale) pendant la journée, de préférence le matin, l'après-midi et le soir ainsi qu'avant les repas. De cette façon, vous mangerez des portions plus petites et vous ne grossirez pas.

Une alimentation équilibrée, riche en produits frais sans trop de féculents ou de matières grasses, est indispensable pour éviter les maladies liées au mode de vie, comme le diabète de type 2 et les maladies cardiaques.

Au moins trente minutes d'exercice physique chaque jour est essentiel. Pour ceux qui passent leur journée assis devant un ordinateur, il vaut mieux monter par l'escalier que prendre l'ascenseur.

Dormez suffisamment. Le manque de sommeil empêche la consolidation de la mémoire et la récupération du cerveau.

Soit ... soit is a high frequency expression meaning *either ... or*.

Knowing conjunctions and time phrases like this is important as they can help you understand the sense of a text.

Use the cognates and the context in this paragraph to help you work out the meaning of any words you do not know.

Le manque and empêcher, meaning *lack* and *to prevent*, often appear in a range of contexts. Make sure you know them.

Answer the following question:

According to the text, what is the most important thing about drinking water?

Choose the correct answer and write the letter in the box.

A	It is mineral water.
B	You drink it regularly.
C	It forms 70% of your liquid intake during the day.

The advice in the text is to drink water in the morning, afternoon and evening.

This figure is given in the text, but it refers to the composition of the body, not the amount of water consumed in a day.

B

Exam-style practice

Now answer the following questions about the text.

1 How can a glass of water before dinner help you to avoid putting on weight?

2 What advice is given for office workers?

3 What is affected by insufficient sleep? **[3 marks]**

Pages
7, 21
LINKS

Reading 2

In the reading paper of your exam, you will need to be able to complete different tasks with questions and answers in French.

② Before answering

Reading the introductory text will set the context for the extract and reading the question(s) may help you understand words in the text that you do not know. Make sure you read the whole text through before answering any questions.

⑮ Worked example

Lisez les commentaires dans un forum sur la télévision.

La télé et les habitudes

> Chez nous, la télévision reste allumée toute la journée, même si personne ne la regarde. Pour moi, la télé, c'est un bruit de fond, mais pour ma grand-mère qui passe des heures entières toute seule, le petit écran est son compagnon constant.
>
> **Manon (17 ans)**

The television is described as a companion for Manon's grandmother.

> Au moment où je rentre chez moi, j'allume la télé et le week-end, je m'assieds devant l'écran et je regarde de nouveaux films que je ne veux pas manquer. Parfois, je suis tellement absorbée par le petit écran que je n'arrive pas à compléter mes tâches ménagères.
>
> **Agnès (24 ans)**

1 Identifiez la bonne personne. Écrivez **A** pour Agnès, **M** pour Manon, ou **A + M** pour Agnès et Manon.

A Je suis une accro de la télé.

B La télé a une grande importance pour quelqu'un que je connais.

> **accro** means *addicted to* or *hooked on*. Manon describes TV as **bruit de fond** (*background noise*), whereas Agnès watches TV all the time at home.

A

M

⑩ Exam-style practice

1 Lisez cet extrait du livre *Les Misérables* de Victor Hugo. Complétez le texte suivant avec les mots de la liste ci-dessous. Écrivez la bonne lettre dans chaque case.

Vers le ☐ de la nuit, Jean Valjean s'est réveillé. Il était d'une ☐ famille de paysans du nord de la France. Dans son enfance, il n'avait pas ☐ à lire. (…) Sa mère s'appelait Jeanne Mathieu; son père Jean Valjean ou Vlajean, (…) contraction de Voilà Jean. Jean Valjean était d'un caractère ☐ sans être triste. (…) Il avait perdu en très bas âge son père et sa mère. Sa mère était ☐ d'une fièvre de lait mal soignée.

A	anglais	E	morte
B	appris	F	née
C	fini	G	pauvre
D	milieu	H	pensif

[5 marks]

2 Lisez ce commentaire dans un forum sur les héros.

> À mon avis, les gens qu'on voit dans les médias sont souvent de mauvais modèles, surtout s'ils ont été impliqués dans scandale où ils n'ont pas dit la vérité. *Paulette*

Complétez la phrase suivante.

Pour Paulette, un modèle positif serait probablement quelqu'un qui _____ **[1 mark]**

 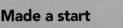

Reading 3

In the reading paper of your exam, you will need to be able to read information and find opinions or draw conclusions from it.

⑤ Exam focus

- Start by looking at the title for each extract. This gives you the context of the text and you can start to predict what words you might see.
- Read through the text carefully first, focusing on what you know. Don't worry too much about words you don't know, they may not be important. Try to understand the overall of the gist of the text and some of the main ideas.
- Read the questions carefully before you read the text for a second time. Make sure you understand what the question is asking you to do. Answer in English where it tells you to, and in French when this is required.
- Sometimes, the words in the questions may help you understand a word you didn't know in the text.
- Answer the questions you are most sure of first. You don't have to answer them in order.

⑩ Worked example

Family life

Read this extract from a news article.

Read the statements carefully, paying close attention to negatives and words like *both* and *only*.

It may help to start by eliminating the statements that you think are false.

mercredi **LA VOIX** **le 5 juin 2017**

 Selon une étude récente en France, un enfant sur dix vit dans une famille recomposée, c'est-à-dire dans une famille où les enfants ne sont pas tous ceux du couple actuel. Le plus souvent, c'est un enfant qui vit avec sa mère et un beau-père. En plus, le nombre de familles monoparentales a augmenté.

If you don't recognise **recomposée**, you will be expected to work it out from the context and apply your knowledge of how prefixes **re-** (*again*) and cognates work.

Look at the questions to help you work out the meaning of **monoparentales** if you don't know it.

Which **three** statements are true, according to the article? Write the correct letters in the boxes.

A   It is common for children in France to live with their father and his partner.

B   A child in France will often live with their mother and stepfather.

C   One in ten children in France do not live with both of their biological parents.

D   Only one in ten children in France lives with their biological parents.

E   The number of single parent families has decreased.

F   There are now more single parent families than before.   B C F

⑤ Exam-style practice

School life

Read this comment from an online forum.

> À mon avis, deux mois, c'est trop long. On oublie beaucoup de ce qu'on avait appris et on ne voit pas ses copains pendant plusieurs semaines.

What aspect of school is being discussed? ← You need to read the information and draw a conclusion.   **[1 mark]**

Reading 4

In the reading paper of your exam, you may come across longer texts or literary texts that contain unfamiliar vocabulary.

⑤ About longer texts ✓

You will not be expected to understand every word of a longer text. Read the text first to get the overall gist and then the questions to find out what information you need to extract. This may also help you to understand any language that is not clear to you on first reading. Don't waste time trying to work out the meaning of unnecessary details. You may need to infer to answer a question. You may also have to make deductions by looking at the clues and working out an answer.

⑮ Worked example 👓 ✓

Read this extract from the short story *Souvenirs* by Guy de Maupassant.

> Oh! Comme je suis surtout traversée par des souvenirs brusques de mes promenades de jeune fille. Là, sur mon fauteuil, devant mon feu, j'ai retrouvé étrangement, l'autre soir, un coucher de soleil que j'ai vu, étant bien jeune, sur une plage de Bretagne. Je l'avais oublié, certes, depuis longtemps, et il m'est revenu tout à coup, sans raison, ou peut-être parce qu'une lueur de tisons rouges aura réveillé dans ma mémoire la vision de cette lueur géante qui embrasait l'horizon ce soir-là! Je me suis tout rappelé: le paysage, ma robe, et même des détails de rien du tout, un petit bobo que j'avais au doigt depuis quelques jours, et cela si vivement, que j'ai cru en souffrir encore. J'ai senti l'odeur salée, humide et fraîche des sables mouillés (…), et je me suis mise à respirer à longs traits l'air marin qui me soufflait dans la figure. Oui, vraiment, j'ai eu seize ans pendant quelques minutes.

The title tells you the story is about memories.

The ending on the past participle (**traversée**) is a clue that the narrator is female.

Feu is a key word. If you don't know it, the options in Question 3 may help you work it out.

re (*again*) + **trouvé** = *found again* = *remembered*.

Use word patterns to work out the meaning of this word: **é** = *s* in English, **-ment** = *ly* → *strangely*.

This is a description of the fire, linking the red of the fire and the memory of a sunset (**coucher de soleil**).

The writer says **jeune fille**, but this is an older person looking back.

The writer makes no reference to sounds so you can eliminate option A. Smell (**odeur**) is mentioned but it is in the memory itself, not the trigger.

The word *sea* (**mer**) is not used, but implied through language such as **plage** (*beach*), **l'air marin** (*marine air*) and **sables** (*sand*).

Read the following statements and choose the correct option:

1 At the time of writing this extract the narrator is …

- A a young girl. ☐
- B an old woman. ✓
- C an old man. ☐

2 The narrator's memory was probably triggered by something they…

- A heard. ☐
- B smelt. ☐
- C saw. ✓

3 The memory relates to an experience…

- A to do with fire. ☐
- B by the sea. ✓
- C in the countryside. ☐

⑤ Exam-style practice 👓 ✓

Answer these questions about the text from *Souvenirs*.

1 The narrator's memory of the event uses their

- A senses of sight and smell. ☐
- B senses of touch and sound. ☐
- C senses of sound and smell. ☐

[3 marks]

2 The narrator's memory of the experience…

- A comes on suddenly and is brief. ☐
- B comes on gradually but lasts a long time. ☐
- C comes on suddenly and lasts a long time. ☐

[3 marks]

✓ **Made a start**   ✓ **Feeling confident**   ✓ **Exam ready**

Translation into English

At the end of the reading paper, you will have a short passage to translate into English.

② Translation into English

At Foundation level, the passage will consist of about 35 words, and at Higher level about 50 words.

There will be references to the past, present and future in both passages.

At Higher level you can expect a wider range of vocabulary and grammatical structures to feature in the passage.

⑤ Translating idioms

Some words and phrases are expressed differently in French and English. Watch out for the following when you have to translate them:

- expressions with **avoir**:
  J'ai quinze ans *I am 15* (**not** *I have 15 years*); **avoir froid / chaud / peur / de la chance** *to be cold / hot / afraid / lucky* (**not** *to have cold / hot / afraid / luck*); **il y a** *there is / are*

- weather expressions:
  Il y a du vent / du soleil. *It is windy / sunny.* **Il y a de l'orage.** *It is stormy.*

- **de** to show possession: **le copain de ma sœur** *my sister's friend* (**not** *the friend of my sister*)

- articles used in French, but not in English and vice versa:
  J'adore le cyclisme. *I love cycling.* **Il est professeur.** *He's a teacher.*

- **chez** *at someone's house*: **chez moi** *at my home*

- **à, de** and **en** can all have different meanings depending on the context in which they are used.

- **depuis** used in the present tense can mean *have done / been doing* something since a specific date or for a length of time. **J'apprends le français depuis cinq ans.** *I have been learning French for five years.*

- **venir de** used in the present tense means to have just done something. **Il vient de téléphoner.** *He has just rung.*

- watch out for false friends. (See Reading Strategies, page 54)

⑩ Worked example

Translate the passage into English.

Dans mon collège, il y a une bibliothèque et une salle d'informatique. Hier, en cours d'informatique, j'ai travaillé sur ordinateur. Quelquefois, j'utilise mon portable pour acheter quelque chose. Le week-end prochain, je vais acheter un nouveau pantalon.

In my school, there is a library and an IT room. I worked on the computer in IT lessons yesterday. Sometimes I use my mobile phone to buy something. Next weekend, I am going to buy a new pair of trousers.

This is *secondary school*, not college.

Salle d'informatique is literally *room of IT*, but make sure that what you write sounds natural in English.

Pour does **not** mean *for* here – it means *to* in the sense of *in order to*.

French sometimes uses an article where it is left out in English.

Trousers is a singular noun in French, unlike English.

⑩ Exam-style practice

1 Translate the following into English.

(a) Avec une télécommande, on peut changer d'émission de télévision sans quitter sa chaise ou le canapé.
[2 marks]

(b) Je suis allé à la pharmacie avec l'ordonnance que le médecin m'avait donnée pour obtenir des médicaments.
[2 marks]

2 You read the following review for a hotel on a website. Your friend asks you to translate it into English.

> Je viens de passer une semaine dans cet établissement au bord de la mer. On l'a récemment remis à neuf avec de nouveaux meubles partout. Au rez-de-chaussée, il y a une belle salle à manger où on sert le dîner chaque soir. Ce que j'ai aimé le plus, c'était la piscine chauffée. J'aimerais bien y retourner l'année prochaine.

Writing strategies

Checking your work and making sure you have completed all aspects of the task is key to success in written tasks.

 Checking for communication

Check your work for communication and make sure that you have:

- addressed all elements of the task
- used the correct number of words.

 Checking for quality of language

Aim to include a wide variety of vocabulary and structures in your written work. This includes a variety of:

- tenses – past (imperfect, perfect and pluperfect); present; future and conditional
- time phrases: **il y a un mois / à l'avenir / maintenant**
- opinions: **Je pense que / À mon avis**
- justification and reasons for opinions: **parce que / car / à cause de**
- connectives: **et, mais, pourtant**
- comparatives and superlatives: **plus / moins que**
- negatives: **ne jamais / plus / rien**

 Writing checklist

✓ **Different ways of saying things**
Be flexible in your thinking. If you are not sure whether you have expressed an idea correctly, try to go about it another way. For example, you could express *I visited my friends* as **Je suis allé(e) voir mes ami(e)s, J'ai rendu visite à mes ami(e)s** or **J'ai vu mes ami(e)s.**

✓ **Be consistent**
When writing an email or letter, stick to either **tu** or **vous** form all the way through. Check verb endings as well as the possessives **ton/ta/tes** and **votre/vos.**

✓ **Improving your work**
Look for ways to improve your work by adding some interesting adjectives and adverbs or by varying the way you express your ideas. For example, you could express disliking something as **Je n'aime pas du tout (la natation), Je déteste (la natation)** or **(La natation) ne me plaît pas.**

✓ **Know your problem areas**
You will probably be aware of the kinds of mistakes you make when you are writing in French. If you know that you often leave off accents or have difficulty with verb endings, give these extra attention in your exam.

✓ **Time management**
Manage your time so that you have a few minutes to check your work once you have finished writing it.

 Checking for accuracy

Once you have completed a written task, check it carefully for spelling and grammatical accuracy. Look out for the following:

Adjectives
- Do they agree? **Les fleurs sont jolies; des problèmes énormes**
- Are they in the correct position? **Il a les cheveux gris; une bonne raison**

Verbs
- Have you got the correct ending for the subject of the verb? **Est-ce que tu manges...? Mon ami et moi allons...**
- Is the verb reflexive or irregular, or does it have spelling changes? **Je me lève...; Les filles vont...; nous mangeons**
- Have you used the correct tense? **Le week-end prochain je ferai une randonnée.** (future); **Hier soir nous avons vu nos amis** (perfect tense for a single action in the past); **Pendant l'été je voyais mes amis tous les jours** (imperfect tense, for a repeated action over time); **Quand j'étais jeune je lisais beaucoup** (imperfect tense for description and for when something used to happen.)
- Does the past participle need to agree? **Elles sont allées; Paul et Marc sont arrivés.**

Gender
- Have you used the correct gender for nouns, pronouns and possessives? **J'ai deux frères, ils s'appellent...; Ma maison est grande et elle est entourée par des arbres.**

Spellings
- Are accents used correctly and plurals of nouns formed correctly? **Des chevaux** (sing. = **cheval**); **des gâteaux délicieux.**
- Do you need capital letters? **Le mardi; en mai.**

 Exam-style practice

Vous décrivez votre anniversaire pour votre blog.
Décrivez:
- votre anniversaire – comment fêté
- dates importantes dans votre famille
- les rapports dans la famille
- projets – weekend prochain.

Écrivez environ 90 mots en **français**. Répondez à chaque aspect de la question.

Try out the strategies on this page while you practise.

Translation into French (Foundation)

As part of the writing paper, you will have short sentences to translate into French.

About the translation task

At Foundation tier, the translation will consist of five different, short sentences. You will be expected to get the key messages across and to show that you know how to accurately apply the grammar and structures appropriate to Foundation level. In particular, you should pay attention to:

- verb forms: do you need the 'I', 'he, she, it' or some other form of the verb?
- verb tense: do you need to use the present tense or the future? The perfect or imperfect?
- adjective agreements: is the adjective describing a singular or plural noun? Is it masculine or feminine?

Exam focus

You could be asked to translate sentences that contain:

- a verb that refers to someone else, e.g. a friend
- references to simple opinions such as likes or dislikes and negatives
- different verbs in each sentence, and at least one sentence in a tense other than the present
- common idioms, time phrases and high frequency language, e.g. **il y a** *there is / are*
- references to time and place
- vocabulary covering more than one context.

Worked example

Translate the following sentences into **French**.

1. My sister is small.
2. I don't like playing football at school.
3. On Saturdays, I go shopping in town.
4. There is a park next to the cinema.
5. Yesterday, I watched television with my parents and my brother.

1. Ma sœur est petite.
2. Je n'aime pas jouer au football au collège.
3. Le samedi, je vais faire des courses / du shopping / des achats en ville.
4. Il y a un parc à côté du cinéma.
5. Hier, j'ai regardé la télévision avec mes parents et mon frère.

The possessive adjective **ma** and adjective **petite** must agree with **sœur**.

Ne ... pas must go round the verb. The verb **aimer** (to like) is followed by the infinitive. You need the correct form of **à** to go with school: **au collège / à l'école**.

Days of the week are spelled with a lowercase letter. Use the definite article + day of the week to convey the idea that something happens regularly.

Cinéma is masculine, so **de** (à côté de) changes to **du**.

Make sure you use the correct part of the verb **avoir** and that you have the correct past participle. The possessive adjective (*my*) must agree with parents (plural) and brother (singular).

Remember to use the verb **avoir** when you say how old someone is.

Use the correct word for *library* in French. **Librairie** means *bookshop* and is a 'false friend'.

Think: do you need **avoir** or **être** to make the perfect tense of the verb **aller**?

There is more than one way of saying *people*. It doesn't matter which you use.

Do you need **à** or **de** when you talk about playing a musical instrument?

 Exam-style practice

Translate the following sentences into **French**.

1. My brother is 13 years old. **[2 marks]**
2. In the morning I have breakfast in the kitchen. **[2 marks]**
3. There is a library opposite the supermarket. **[2 marks]**
4. Last week I went to the theatre with my family. **[2 marks]**
5. There are four people in my family. **[2 marks]**
6. I don't like doing homework. **[2 marks]**
7. My sister plays the piano in the evening. **[2 marks]**

 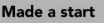 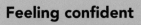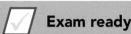

Translation into French (Higher)

As part of the writing paper, you will have a short passage to translate into French.

② About the translation task

At Higher tier the translation will consist of a passage of at least 50 words. It is likely to consist of the following features:

- a mix of subject and vocabulary areas
- higher level grammar structures and vocabulary.

You will be assessed both for your ability to convey the message and for the accuracy of the grammar and spelling.

② Exam focus

The passage that you will have to translate is likely to include:

- verbs that refer to someone other than yourself
- reference to opinions such as likes or dislikes with reasons
- a variety of verbs (regular and irregular) and tenses: present, perfect, imperfect, future and conditional
- references to time, place and comparisons.

⑩ Worked example

Translate the following passage into **French**.

Last week I went to a restaurant in town to celebrate my father's birthday. My mother had chicken and we drank mineral water. I like cooking at home and sometimes I prepare dinner on Saturdays. Next week I will go to a classical music concert with my friends. If I had the choice we would see a film in the cinema.

La semaine dernière, je suis allé(e) dans un restaurant pour fêter l'anniversaire de mon père. Ma mère a pris du poulet et nous avons bu de l'eau minérale. J'aime faire la cuisine à la maison et quelquefois, je prépare le dîner le samedi soir. La semaine prochaine, j'irai à un concert de musique classique avec mes copains. Si j'avais le choix, je verrais un film au cinéma.

> You must make the noun and adjective agree.

> Remember to use **de** (of my father) when you have to translate 'apostrophe s' showing possession.

> The verb **aimer** is followed by an infinitive.

> You need the future tense here. **Aller** is irregular in the future.

> Use **de** here – a concert of classical music.

> You need to use the imperfect and the conditional in this sentence.

> **Célébrer** could also be used, instead of **fêter**.

> You could use **mangé** instead of **pris**.

② Exam focus

Remember to check your translation carefully.

- Word order – Are the adjectives and pronouns in the correct position?
- Have all the necessary agreements been made: gender (masculine / feminine) and singular / plural?
- Verbs – Have you used the correct tense and have you conjugated the verb correctly?
- Spelling – Have you spelled words correctly?

⑮ Exam-style practice

① Translate the following passage into **French**.

In the summer, I went on holiday with my family to the south of Spain. The hotel was quite small and my room was dirty. My parents like Spanish food but I prefer spicy dishes. Next week it is my brother's birthday. I will buy him some white socks and a book. **[12 marks]**

② Translate the following passage into **French**.

In February, I went on a school trip to France. The journey was too long and I was seasick. In the future I would prefer to travel by plane. I stayed with a nice family who lived in the town centre. Next year my French friend will come to my house and we will go sightseeing. **[12 marks]**

Made a start | Feeling confident | Exam ready

Writing (Foundation)

In the writing paper of your exam at Foundation tier, you will need to complete different tasks involving writing in French.

② About Task 1

You must write four sentences about the picture, which are marked for communication only, not for accuracy. Focus on using words and language that you know. You could:

- set the scene
- say what one or more people are doing
- use an adjective to say what something is like
- add one further piece of information, e.g. weather, mood, further description.

② About Tasks 2 and 4

In both Task 2 and Task 4, you have to write about all four bullet points. If, for example, you don't cover two of the bullet points the maximum mark you can get for content is 5.

In Task 2 you will need to write approximately 40 words in French.

In Task 4 you will need to write approximately 90 words in French.

⑩ Worked example

1 Vous envoyez cette photo à votre ami(e) français(e).

Qu'est-ce qu'il y a sur la photo? Écrivez **quatre** phrases en **français**.

C'est à la plage. La famille fait un pique-nique.
La fille porte un tee-shirt blanc. Il fait chaud.

This first sentence sets the scene. You could also write: **C'est au bord de la mer.**

2 Vous écrivez un e-mail à votre ami(e) français(e) sur vos intérêts. Mentionnez:

- musique
- sport
- technologie
- films.

Écrivez environ **40** mots en **français**.

Salut! J'aime la musique rock mais je déteste le folk. En été, je joue au tennis tous les jours. Quand il fait mauvais, je vais à la piscine. J'adore la technologie. Je regarde des films sur mon portable. Je préfère les films romantiques.

Here you could also write: **Des personnes / Des gens prennent le déjeuner.**

You could describe the appearance of a different person: **La mère a les cheveux noirs.**

You could use another weather expression here: **Il y a du soleil.**

⑳ Exam-style practice

Vous avez passé des vacances en France. Écrivez une carte postale à votre ami(e) français(e). Décrivez:

- où vous êtes et activités récentes
- différences entre la France et la Grande-Bretagne
- projets pour les vacances l'année prochaine
- l'importance des vacances.

Écrivez environ **90** mots en **français**. **[16 marks]**

You will need the perfect tense here.

You must use descriptive language, with adjectives, here.

This will require the future tense.

You must give your opinion.

Writing (Higher)

In the writing paper of your exam at Higher tier, you will need to complete different tasks involving writing in French.

 ② About the longer writing task

The task will consist of two bullet points that you must cover in approximately 150 words. For top marks, try to include all of the following in your written piece:

adjectives (and intensifiers); variety of verbs and tenses; opinions (with reasons); conjunctions and connectives to link everything; adverbs; details and originality (something a bit different).

Make sure you answer in the correct tense for the bullet point – past, present or future. If you wish, you can incorporate other verb tenses where appropriate, to show off the range of language you are confident with.

 **② Checking your work**

Remember to check your work for the following:

- spellings, accents and capital letters (for proper nouns – a person's name, towns and countries) are used correctly
- gender (masculine or feminine) and adjective agreements, including position
- verbs: tenses and formation; correct auxiliary (**avoir** or **être**) in the perfect tense.

See page 60 for more on Writing strategies.

 ⑩ Worked example

Vous écrivez un article sur les échanges scolaires pour un magazine français. Écrivez environ **150** mots.

Décrivez:

- un échange scolaire auquel vous avez participé
- l'importance des échanges scolaires.

L'année dernière, j'ai passé une semaine en France en échange scolaire. Avant d'y aller, j'avais envoyé des e-mails à mon correspondant pour faire sa connaissance. Lui et sa famille étaient très gentils et on s'est bien entendus pendant mon séjour. Un jour, nous avons fait une excursion en car à un vieux château de la région. J'ai trouvé le paysage très

beau et l'histoire du château était fascinante. Les autres jours, je suis allé au collège où j'ai assisté aux cours avec mon correspondant.

À mon avis, l'échange m'a permis de me familiariser avec un nouveau pays et une nouvelle culture, c'était une expérience que je n'oublierai jamais. J'ai remarqué par exemple que les repas sont plus importants pour les Français que pour nous, puisqu'il faut beaucoup de temps pour les préparer, et ensuite on passe toute la soirée à table. Cependant, je pense que la chose la plus importante de l'échange est qu'on peut améliorer son français et communiquer avec d'autres gens.

> You have to write about your experience on an exchange and give your opinion about the importance of exchanges. Make something up if you have to!

> **On s'est bien entendus** is an example of a reflexive verb in the perfect tense.

> You can introduce the pluperfect tense (**j'avais envoyé**) with **avant de** (before + ing).

> Try to include a comparative or superlative.

> The future tense is included here (*I will never forget*).

 ⑤ Aiming higher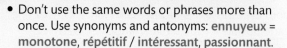

- Don't use the same words or phrases more than once. Use synonyms and antonyms: **ennuyeux = monotone, répétitif / intéressant, passionnant.**
- Justify your opinions using different phrases: **parce que / car** – *because*; **pour** + infinitive – *(in order) to*; **afin de** + infinitive – *in order to*; **alors, par contre, mais, puisque.**
- Include higher level language and structures: pluperfect tense, perfect infinitive (**après avoir / être** + past participle).
- Use the conditional to write about what you would or could do in the future.

⑳ Exam-style practice

Un magazine français en ligne tient un concours pour un article au sujet de «l'amitié» avec un prix de 100 euros.

Vous écrivez un article. Décrivez:

- comment vous avez été un bon ami / une bonne amie récemment
- ce que vous ferez avec les 100 euros.

Écrivez environ **150** mots en **français**. **[16 marks]**

  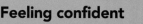

Articles

Articles are the little words that mean *the* (le, la, l', les) and *a*, *an* or *some* (un, une, des).

② About articles

In French, the article changes depending on whether the noun it goes with is masculine, feminine or plural.

	masc	fem	plural
definite article (*the*)	le / l'	la / l'	les
indefinite article (*a / an / some*)	un	une	des

L' is used in front of a vowel or a silent 'h': l'arbre, l'homme.

② Using the indefinite article

Un and une are used more or less in the same way as you would use *a* in English.

They are left out when saying someone's job or profession:
Il est professeur. *He is a teacher.*
Ma mère est médecin. *My mother is a doctor.*

⑤ Using the definite article

The definite article is used to refer to something specific.
Le château est très grand. *The castle is very big.*

In French the definite article (le, la, l', les) is used with some nouns where it is left out in English, such as:

- school subjects: On doit étudier les maths et l'anglais.
- languages: Le chinois est une langue difficile.
- parts of the body: Il a les yeux bleus et les cheveux blonds.
  Il s'est cassé la jambe.
- likes and dislikes: J'aime les pommes, mais je déteste les bananes.
- countries: La France est plus grande que la Suisse.
- abstract nouns and generalisations: La gastronomie française est très connue.
- with quantities when referring to the price: quatre euros le litre.
- time phrases: le week-end dernier; le samedi (meaning *every Saturday*).

> Exceptions are with **parler** and **en**: je parle français; Comment dit-on ... en français?.

On prend **le** petit-déjeuner à sept heures.

⑮ Practice

1 Complete the following with the correct form of the article.

(a) J'apprends _____ portugais.

(b) Qu'est-ce qu'il fait _____ soir?

(c) Je me suis blessé _____ dos.

(d) _____ Allemagne a une frontière avec _____ Pays-Bas.

(e) Les oranges sont deux euros _____ kilo.

(f) _____ année prochaine, je vais visiter _____ Italie.

(g) J'aime regarder _____ tennis à _____ télé.

(h) _____ poste se trouve entre _____ banque et _____ hôtel de ville.

(i) J'adore _____ cuisine française.

(j) _____ racisme est un problème dans quelques pays.

2 Translate the following into French.

(a) He has grey hair and green eyes.

(b) She is a nurse and she works in a hospital.

(c) There are some shops in the village.

(d) We eat dinner in the kitchen.

(e) I visited Spain last summer.

Prepositions

Prepositions are short words like *in*, *on*, *at* and *with*. They provide important information in a sentence.

 About prepositions

Prepositions usually go in front of a noun or pronoun and tell you about how, where, when or for whom something is.

dans *in*	sur *on / on top of*
devant *in front of*	sous *under*
derrière *behind*	à travers *across / through*
entre *between*	vers *towards*
contre *against*	chez *at someone's house, shop or business*

Je regarde la télé **dans** le salon. *I watch TV **in** the living room.*

chez le boucher **at** *the butcher's*

Other common prepositions:

avec *with*	sauf *except*
malgré *in spite of*	selon *according to*
parmi *among*	pour *for*
sans *without*	

 The preposition *en*

En is used without an article, directly in front of a noun and has a different meaning depending on its use.

- with feminine countries, continents and regions it means *to* or *in*:
  Je vais **en** France. *I am going to France.*
  J'habite **en** Angleterre. *I live in England.*

- with means of transport it means *by*:
  en avion (*by plane*); **en** voiture (*by car*); **en** train (*by train*); **en** vélo (*by bike*).

  > You can also say **par le train** and **à vélo**.

- with languages to say *in*:
  Comment dit-on ... **en** anglais? *How do you say... in English?*

- with months and seasons to say *in*:
  en juillet (*in July*), **en** été / automne / hiver (*in summer / autumn / winter*)

  > *In spring* is **au** printemps.

- to describe what something is made out of:
  un porte-monnaie **en** cuir *a leather purse*; une écharpe **en** soie / coton / laine *a silk / cotton / woollen scarf*; une bague **en** argent / or *a silver / gold ring*

- to form the present participle (see page 94) and a lot of common expressions:
  en bas *downstairs*; **en** haut *upstairs*; **en** bonne santé *in good health*; **en** fait *in fact*; **en** tout cas *in any case*; **en** même temps *at the same time*; **en** plein air *in the fresh air*; **en** vacances *on holiday*; **en** route pour *on the way to*.

 Expressions of time

The following prepositions tell you when something happens.

avant le dîner **before** *dinner*

après les cours **after** *lessons*

vers six heures **at about** *(towards) six o'clock*

Nous avons cours **jusqu'à** quatre heures. *We have lessons **until** four o'clock.*

Le train part **dans** dix minutes. *The train leaves **in** ten minutes.*

pendant la journée **during** *the day*

J'ai fait mes devoirs **pendant** trois heures. *I did my homework **for** three hours.*

J'irai en France **pour** une semaine. *I will go to France **for** a week.*

> **Pour** can only be used to translate *for*, when referring to a specific length of time in the future. **Pendant** can be used to translate *for* when talking about a specific length of time in the past, present or future. If an action started in the past and is still going on, then use **depuis** with the present tense (e.g. **je joue du piano depuis dix ans** *I have been playing the piano for ten years*).

Some time expressions that have a preposition in English do not need one in French:

le week-end *at the weekend*

le dimanche *on Sundays (every Sunday)*

le matin *in the morning*

 Practice

🖉 Translate the following prepositional phrases.

(a) *towards* the station
(b) *against* England
(c) *in spite of* the rain
(d) *among* my friends
(e) *for* my birthday
(f) *at* my house
(g) *without* milk
(h) *except* Tuesdays
(i) *according to* a survey

The preposition à

The preposition à often means *to* or *at*, but has other meanings too so is a very useful little word.

⑤ About the preposition à

Take care when à is followed by le or les. À combines with these articles to form au and aux.

le	la	l'	les
au	à la	à l'	aux

Some common uses of à:

- with towns to mean *to* or *in*:
  Je vais à Paris. *I am going to Paris.*
  Mon frère habite à Nice. *My brother lives in Nice.*

- with places to mean *to* or *at*:
  Je vais au parc. *I am going to the park.*

  On se rencontre au cinéma?
  Shall we meet at the cinema?

  Cet après-midi, on va aux Champs-Élysées.
  We are going to the Champs-Élysées this afternoon.

- with masculine or plural countries to mean *to* and *in*:
  Je suis allé au Japon. *I've been to Japan.*

  Ma sœur habite aux Pays-Bas. *My sister lives in the Netherlands / Holland.*

> Remember that feminine countries take **en**:
> **L'année prochaine, je vais en Allemagne.**
> *Next year, I'm going to Germany.*
> **La Grande Muraille est en Chine.** *The Great Wall is in China.*

J'ai mal **à la** tête.

⑩ More uses of à

- To give the flavour or style of something: une crêpe au chocolat *a pancake with chocolate*; une glace à la vanille *a vanilla ice cream*.

- To mean *with* when describing someone or something: le garçon aux cheveux roux *the boy with red hair*.

- To mean *on*: au rez-de-chaussée *on the ground floor*; à cheval *on horseback*; à pied *on foot*; à la télé *on television*.

- With time phrases and occasions: à dix heures *at ten o'clock*; au printemps *in spring*.

> For the other seasons use **en** to mean *in*: **en été / en automne / en hiver**.

- To indicate distance and direction: à cent cinquante mètres d'ici *150 metres from here*; Prenez la deuxième rue à droite. *Take the second road on the right.*

- With the verb jouer + sport: jouer au tennis / football; jouer aux échecs *to play tennis / football / chess*.

> Remember that **jouer** + *de* is used when talking about playing an instrument.

- With avoir mal à + part of the body, meaning *to hurt*: Elle a mal au dos. *Her back hurts / she has backache.*

- To show possession (with emphatic pronouns): C'est à qui? *Whose is this?* C'est à moi. *It's mine.*

- After some verbs, to link them to another verb: s'amuser à, apprendre à, commencer à, s'intéresser à, ressembler à.

  Il commence à pleuvoir. *It's starting to rain.*
  Je m'intéresse aux sports nautiques. *I'm interested in water sports.*

- Other common expressions: à mon avis *in my opinion*; à vélo *by bike*; peu à peu *little by little*.

⑩ Practice

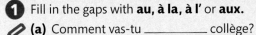

1 Fill in the gaps with **au, à la, à l'** or **aux.**

  (a) Comment vas-tu _____ collège?

  (b) J'irai _____ États-Unis pendant les vacances.

  (c) Pour aller _____ hôpital, s'il vous plaît?

  (d) Je vous attends _____ gare.

  (e) J'ai fait du ski _____ Canada.

2 Translate the following into English.

  (a) Je voudrais un sandwich au jambon.

  (b) C'est la fille aux yeux bleus.

  (c) Mon appartement est au troisième étage.

  (d) J'avais mal à l'estomac.

  (e) Ils sont en train de jouer au volley.

3 Translate the following into French.

  (a) I have earache.

  (b) How much is the coffee ice cream?

  (c) They are playing cards.

  (d) I love onion soup.

Partitives and preposition *de*

The word **de** means *some* or *any*, and it is also a preposition meaning *from* or *of*.

 Forms of the partitive

The partitive article **de** combines with definite articles (**le, la, l', les**).

	partitive
masculine singular de + le	du
feminine singular de + la	de la
before a vowel / h singular de + l'	de l'
plural de + les	des

Use it to refer to an unknown quantity of something. In English, you can sometimes leave out *some* or *any*, but you can't in French.

Je voudrais du pain et des tomates. *I'd like some bread and tomatoes.*

Avez-vous du beurre? *Have you got any butter?*

Est-ce que vous vendez de l'eau minérale? *Do you sell (any) mineral water?*

 **Using *de* or *d'* on its own**

Use **de / d'** for the following:

- after a negative:

  Il n'a pas mangé de fromage. *He didn't eat any cheese.*

  Je n'ai pas d'argent. *I haven't got any money.*

  Les végétariens ne mangent pas de viande. *Vegetarians don't eat meat.*

  Il n'y avait pas de pêches au marché. *There weren't any peaches in the market.*

- after an expression of quantity:

  Il y a beaucoup d'arbres et de fleurs. *There are a lot of trees and flowers.*

  un kilo de pommes de terre *a kilo of potatoes*

- When a plural adjective comes in front of a noun:

  Elle a de grandes oreilles. *She has big ears.*

  Il y a de jolies fleurs. *There are some pretty flowers.*

 Showing possession with *de*

The preposition **de** is also used to indicate ownership.

le copain de Paul *Paul's friend*

 Prepositions + *de*

Several preposition phrases contain **de**:

autour de *around*
au bord de *at the side / edge of*
au bout de *at the end of*
à cause de *because of*
à côté de *next to*
en dehors de *outside*
au dessous de *below*
au dessus de *above*

à droite de *to the right of*
en face de *opposite*
au fond de *at the back of*
à gauche de *to the left of*
au lieu de *instead of*
loin de *far from*
au milieu de *in the middle of*
près de *near to*

La gare est loin du centre-ville. *The station is far from the town centre.*

L'hôtel est en face de la poste et à côté du musée. *The hotel is opposite the post office and next to the museum.*

 Verbs followed by *de*

A number of common verbs are followed by **de** to link them to another verb.

avoir envie de *to feel like*
avoir besoin de *to need*
choisir de *to choose to*
décider de *to decide to*
essayer de *to try to*
finir de *to finish*
penser de *to think of / about*
refuser de *to refuse*

J'ai décidé / choisi d'étudier l'histoire. *I've decided / chosen to study history.*

This means *to think of / about* in the sense of an opinion:

Que penses-tu de ce livre? *What do you think of / about this book?*

To think of / about in the sense of 'something on your mind' is **penser à**, so be careful:

J'ai pensé à toi! *I thought of / about you!*

 Practice

Translate the following sentences into French.

(a) I have bought some milk, some meat and some eggs.

(b) He hasn't got any fish.

(c) My sister's boyfriend is quite tall.

(d) The park is next to the castle.

(e) I tried to do my homework.

Nouns

Nouns are words that name people, places, things and abstract concepts.

About nouns

Nouns are words that you can usually put *a* or *the* in front of. In French, all nouns have a gender: either masculine (m) or feminine (f). The gender of a noun is always listed in a dictionary, but when you learn nouns you should learn their gender too.

Masculine nouns

The following are always masculine:

- days, months and seasons: le lundi, le mois, le printemps
- languages: le français, le portugais
- weights and measures: un kilo, un litre, un kilomètre
- male people and members of the family: le professeur, le grand-père, le frère
- nouns formed from infinitives: le devoir.

Masculine noun endings

The following endings are generally masculine:

ending	example
-age, -ège	le fromage, le village, le collège
-eau, -ou	le bateau, le gâteau, le bijou, le genou
-ier	le quartier
-eur	un ascenseur, le moniteur
-ment	un appartement, le monument
-isme	le tourisme, le cyclisme, le rascisme
-phone, -scope	le téléphone, le microscope

Exceptions are **la peau** and **l'eau**.

Exceptions are **la page**, **la plage**, **la cage** and **l'image**.

Plurals of nouns

Most nouns form the plural by adding -s: un arbre, des arbres. Nouns that end in -s, -x, or -z do not change: une souris / des souris; la voix / des voix; le nez / les nez.

Words with the following endings make the plural as follows:

- -al changes to -aux: un animal, des animaux
- -eau changes to -eaux: un chapeau, des chapeaux
- -ou changes to -oux: un bijou, des bijoux.

A few nouns have an irregular plural form:

un œil → des yeux; monsieur → messieurs; madame → mesdames; mademoiselle → mesdemoiselles.

Feminine nouns

The following are always feminine:

- most shops: la boulangerie, la pharmacie (not le supermarché)
- continents: l'Asie, l'Europe
- most countries: la France, la Belgique, la Suisse

Exceptions include **le Canada**, **les États-Unis**.

- female people and family members: la directrice, la tante, la sœur, la mère
- most rivers: la Seine, la Loire, but not le Rhône or le Rhin.

Feminine noun endings

The following endings are generally feminine:

ending	example
-tion, -aison	la nation, la combinaison
-ette, -esse	la chaussette, la toilette
-ence, -ance, -ense, -anse	la patience, l'enfance, la défense, la danse
-ité	la cité, une université, une activité
-ure	la nature, la culture
-ode, -ade, -ude	la méthode, la limonade, l'attitude

Masculine and feminine jobs

Many jobs and occupations have different endings depending on whether they refer to a man or a woman.

change	masculine	feminine
add -e	avocat	avocate
-ier → -ière	fermier	fermière
-ien → -ienne	musicien	musicienne
-eur → -euse	vendeur	vendeuse
-er → -ère	boulanger	boulangère
-teur → -trice	acteur	actrice

VOCABULARY LINK
PAGE
110

Practice

✎ What is the gender of the following nouns?

(a) mercredi (e) rire

(b) pharmacienne (f) serveuse

(c) révolution (g) nourriture

(d) chinois (h) chou

Adjectives

You need to take care with agreement and position of adjectives in French.

Adjective agreement

In French, adjectives must agree with the gender (masculine or feminine) and number (singular or plural) of the noun that they describe. Most adjectives add an -e in the feminine form, and add an -s in the plural.

m sing	un chat noir	*a black cat*
f sing	une table noire	*a black table*
m pl	des chats noirs	*black cats*
f pl	des tables noires	*black tables*

If the adjective already ends in -e it does not add another, so the masculine and feminine forms are the same.

un problème grave *a serious problem*
une maladie grave *a serious illness*

If the adjective already ends in -s, the masculine singular and masculine plural are the same:

un lapin gris *a grey rabbit*; des lapins gris *grey rabbits*

Irregular adjectives

The following adjectives are irregular and have a different masculine singular form used in front of a vowel or silent h.

	beautiful	old	new
masc sing	beau	vieux	nouveau
masc + vowel	bel	vieil	nouvel
fem sing	belle	vieille	nouvelle
masc pl	beaux	vieux	nouveaux
fem pl	belles	vieilles	nouvelles

un vieil homme, le Nouvel An, un bel arbre

Position of adjectives

Most adjectives in French go after the noun they describe, unlike in English. This always happens with adjectives relating to colour, shape or nationality:

la maison blanche *the white house*; la langue française *the French language*; une table ronde *a round table*.

The following adjectives go in front of the noun:

beau; bon; grand; gros; haut; jeune; joli; long; mauvais; nouveau; petit; premier; vieux.

e.g. une grande maison *a big house*

Some adjectives change their meaning depending on whether they go before or after the noun.

une chambre propre *a clean room*
ma propre chambre *my own room*

Other adjectives like this are: ancien *former / ancient*, même *same / even* and seul *only / lonely*.

Spelling changes in adjectives

Some adjectives double the final consonant and add an -e for the feminine form: bon / bonne; gros / grosse.

Adjectives ending in –al change to –aux in the masculine plural: un journal national / des journaux nationaux.

Adjectives with the following endings have a different form in the feminine form:

masc ending	fem ending	example
-er / ier	-ère	cher / chère; premier / première
-x	-se	heureux / heureuse
-et	-ète or -ette	inquiet / inquiète; cadet / cadette
-aux	-ausse	faux / fausse
-ien	-ienne	ancien / ancienne
-f	-ve	actif / active; neuf / neuve
-c	-che	blanc / blanche

Other irregular feminine forms: frais → fraîche; favori → favorite; long → longue.

> Masculine adjectives that end in -x do not change in the plural: un sport dangereux / des sports dangereux. Sec changes to sèche.

Invariable adjectives

A small number of adjectives do not change their ending: cool, chic, sympa, extra, marron, orange.

un garcon sympa → des garçons sympa

la musique cool; des lunettes de soleil cool

Il a les cheveux marron et porte des baskets orange.

Combination colours of two words are also invariable.

une jupe bleu marine *a navy blue skirt*

des chaussettes vert foncé *dark green socks*

Practice

Translate the following sentences into French.

(a) a good question

(b) a small garden

(c) a jealous friend (female)

(d) a light grey shirt

(e) an old object

Comparatives and superlatives

Comparatives compare two things, saying that one is more or less ... (adjective) than the other.

(5) Using *plus* and *moins*

In English, some comparatives end in -er (*faster*, *easier*): in French, use **plus** + adjective + **que**.

> Remember that the adjective must agree with the subject. **!**

Le train est plus cher que le bus. *The train is more expensive than the bus.*

L'Angleterre est plus grande que le pays de Galles. *England is bigger than Wales.*

Les exercices de français sont plus faciles que les devoirs d'anglais. *French exercises are easier than English homework.*

Use **moins** + adjective + **que** to say *less... than...*

L'escalade est moins dangereuse que le parapente. *Climbing is less dangerous than hang-gliding.*

Mon frère est moins patient que moi. *My brother is less patient than me.*

(2) Using *aussi ... que*

Use **aussi** + adjective + **que** to say *as... as*.

Elle est aussi grande que sa sœur. *She is as tall as her sister.*

Use **pas aussi** + adjective + **que** to say *not as... as*.

L'espagnol n'est pas aussi difficile que le chinois. *Spanish is not as difficult as Chinese.*

(5) Irregular comparatives

As in English, **bon** *good* and **mauvais** *bad* have irregular comparative forms.

	bon	**mauvais**
masc sing	meilleur	pire
fem sing	meilleure	pire
masc pl	meilleurs	pires
fem pl	meilleures	pires
English	better	worse

Ce film est meilleur que l'autre film. *This film is better than the other film.*

Les émissions de télé-réalité sont pires que les émissions de sport. *Reality TV programmes are worse than sports programmes.*

Les légumes sont meilleurs pour la santé que les gâteaux. *Vegetables are better for your health than cakes.*

(5) The superlative

In English, the superlative is often recognisable by the ending -est (*biggest / fastest / smallest*).

In French, use **le / la / les + plus / moins** + adjective.

The adjective must agree with the noun it is describing.

l'animal le plus dangereux *the most dangerous animal*

l'étudiant le moins sportif *the least sporty student*

les films les plus longs *the longest films*

Adjectives that go in front of the noun also go in front when used in the superlative form.

Elle est la plus belle fille. *She is the most beautiful girl.*

Le Mont Blanc est la plus haute montagne d'Europe. *Mont Blanc is the highest mountain **in** Europe.*

To say *the best* use: **le meilleur / la meilleure / les meilleur(e)s**. To say *the worst* use: **le / la pire / les pires**. They all go in front of the noun. **le meilleur acteur** *the best actor;* **le pire film** *the worst film*

(10) Practice

✎ Translate the following sentences into French.

(a) Horror films are more exciting than romantic films.

(b) Soap operas are more entertaining than the news.

(c) Sports programmes are as interesting as documentaries.

(d) *Amélie* is the funniest film.

(e) That is the most boring TV programme.

(f) Adele is the best singer.

(g) He is the worst actor.

(h) He chose the most expensive main course.

(i) I bought the least expensive souvenir.

(j) They are the most uncomfortable seats.

Possessive and demonstrative adjectives

Possessive and demonstrative adjectives in a sentence indicate ownership or reference to a specific thing.

⑩ Possessive adjectives

Possessive adjectives are words like *my*, *your* and *his*. They go in front of a noun to indicate to whom or what something belongs.

	masculine	feminine	plural
my	mon	ma	mes
your (sing)	ton	ta	tes
his / her / its	son	sa	ses
our	notre	notre	nos
your	votre	votre	vos
their	leur	leur	leurs

Possessive adjectives agree with the noun that follows them, not with the owner.

Je joue au tennis avec mon frère. (frère = m sing)
I play tennis with my brother.

Je joue au tennis avec ma sœur. (sœur = f sing)
I play tennis with my sister.

Je joue au tennis avec mes frères. (frères = m pl)
I play tennis with my brothers.

Je joue au tennis avec mes sœurs. (sœurs = f pl)
I play tennis with my sisters.

The possessive adjective of **on** is **notre / nos**.
On s'est promenés avec notre chien.

Mon, **ton** and **son** are used in front of a feminine noun that begins with a vowel or silent 'h'.

Mon émission préférée est *EastEnders*. (émission = f sing). *My favourite TV programme is EastEnders.*

Il va au cinéma avec son amie. (amie = f sing)
He is going to the cinema with his (female) friend.

Son, **sa** and **ses** can mean either *his*, *her* or *its* depending on the context of the sentence.

Robert et son frère *Robert and his brother*

Anne et son frère *Anne and her brother*

le chat et ses petits *the cat and its little ones*

② Possessives and parts of the body

Use the definite article rather than a possessive adjective when you are referring to parts of the body.

Je me lave les mains. *I wash my hands.*

Ils se brossent les dents. *They brush their teeth.*

Elle s'est coupé le doigt. *She cut her finger.*

Il s'est cassé la jambe. *He broke his leg.*

⑤ Demonstrative adjectives

Demonstrative adjectives are the words for *this*, *that*, *these* and *those*. The adjective changes its ending to agree with the noun it goes with.

	sing this / that	plural these / those
masc	ce / cet	ces
fem	cette	ces

There are two forms of the masculine singular adjective. **Cet** is used in front of a vowel or silent 'h'.

ce fromage *this / that cheese*; **cet œuf** *this / that egg*; **cette assiette** *this / that plate*; **ces plats** *these / those dishes*; **ces glaces** *these / those ice creams*

You can distinguish between *this* and *that* by adding **–ci** or **–là** after the noun.

ce restaurant-ci *this restaurant*; **ces magasins-ci** *these shops*; **ce café-là** *that café*; **ces pommes-là** *those apples*

⑤ Using demonstrative adjectives

When listing things, repeat the demonstrative adjective before each noun:

cet anorak, cette chemise, ces chaussures
this anorak, this shirt, these shoes

You can use demonstrative adjectives in front of adjectives and numbers.

cette belle robe *this beautiful dress*

ce joli tee-shirt *this pretty T-shirt*

ces chaussures noires *these black shoes*

ces trois personnes *these three people*

> Remember to use **rendre visite à** *to visit* a person. **Visiter** means *to visit* a place.

⑤ Practice

🖉 Translate the following sentences into French.

(a) My father lost his mobile phone in that shop.

(b) We visited our cousins.

(c) His parents and their friends stayed in that house.

(d) My friend (m) bought that souvenir for his sister.

Indefinite and interrogative adjectives

These adjectives are used to say *all*, *every* and *each*, and **quel** allows you to ask questions with *which* or *what*.

 Using *tout*

Tout can be used as an adjective to mean *all*, *the whole* or *every*. It has to agree with the noun that follows.

masculine singular	feminine singular	masculine plural	feminine plural
tout	toute	tous	toutes

tout le temps *all the time / the whole time*

toute la journée *all day*

tous les mercredis *every Wednesday*

toutes les chansons *all the songs*

 Using *chaque* and *quelques*

Chaque means *each* or *every* and is only used with singular nouns. It does not change.

chaque samedi *every Saturday*

chaque personne *each person*

Quelques means *some* or *a few*. It is only used with plural nouns.

il y a quelques mois *a few months ago*

 Interrogative adjectives

Interrogative adjectives are the words for *which* or *what*. The adjective agrees with the noun it goes with.

masculine singular	masculine plural
quel	quels

feminine singular	feminine plural
quelle	quelles

Quel temps fait-il? *What is the weather like?*

Quelle heure est-il? *What time is it?*

Vous désirez quelles chaussures? *Which shoes do you want?*

Vous prenez quel dessert? *Which dessert are you having?*

Sometimes **quel** is not next to the noun it goes with, but it still agrees with it.

Quelle est la date de ton anniversaire? *What is the date of your birthday?*

Quel est ton sport préféré? *What is your favourite sport?*

Quelles sont les meilleures émissions à la télé? *What are the best TV programmes?*

> **Quel / quelle** and a noun can also make an exclamation:
> **Quel dommage!** *What a pity!* **!**

 Practice

1 Fill in the gaps in the following phrases with the correct form of *tout*. What does each phrase mean?

(a) _____ les jours

(b) _____ les stations

(c) _____ la classe

(d) _____ le fromage

(e) _____ la famille

2 Translate the following phrases.

(a) every morning

(b) each student

(c) a few people

(d) a few words

(e) some time

3 Fill in the gaps with the correct form of *quel / quelle / quels / quelles*. What does each sentence mean?

(a) _____ boisson prends-tu?

(b) _____ taille voulez-vous?

(c) _____ sport aimes-tu?

(d) _____ genre de musique n'aimes-tu pas?

(e) _____ sont tes matières préférées?

(f) _____ est ton passe-temps préféré?

(g) Tu aimes _____ sorte de films?

(h) _____ sont les meilleurs feuilletons?

(i) _____ chance!

Adverbs

Adverbs are used to describe actions and to add meaning to a verb or an adjective.

 (5) Formation of adverbs

Adverbs tell you where, when or how an action is being done or taking place. They usually follow the verb.

Many adverbs in French are formed by adding -ment, to the feminine singular form of the adjective. This is the equivalent of the -ly ending in English.

adjective masc sing	adjective fem sing	adverb
heureux	heureuse	heureusement
immédiat	immédiate	immédiatement
franc	franche	franchement
doux	douce	doucement

If the adjective ends in a vowel just add –ment.

facile → facilement *easily*

vrai → vraiment *really*

absolu → absolument *absolutely*

Some adverbs add an accent: **énormément** *enormously*; **précisément** *precisely*.

Adjectives that end in –ant or –ent change to –amment or –emment (an exception is **lentement** = *slowly*).

courant → couramment *fluently*

évident → évidemment *evidently*

récent → récemment *recently*

A few adverbs are irregular:

gentil → gentiment *gently*; bref → brièvement *briefly*.

 (2) Adverbs of time and place A–Z

déjà *already*

de nouveau *again*

en retard *late*

tout de suite *immediately*

en bas / haut *downstairs / upstairs*

là bas *over there*

partout *everywhere*

Je viendrai tout de suite *I will come immediately*.

Mon frère est là bas *My brother is over there*.

 (2) Frequency adverbs A–Z

Frequency adverbs tell you how often an action takes place. Common frequency adverbs are:

de temps en temps *from time to time*

d'habitude *usually*

jamais *never*

normalement *normally*

quelquefois *sometimes*

rarement *rarely*

souvent *often*

toujours *always*

Nous allons souvent au cinéma le week-end. *We often go to the cinema at the weekend.*

 (10) Comparatives and superlatives

Adverbs form the comparative in the same way as adjectives, using **plus ... que, moins ... que, aussi ... que** and **pas si ... que**.

Ma grand-mère marche plus lentement que ma mère. *My grandmother walks more slowly than my mother.*

Mon frère travaille moins sérieusement que moi. *My brother works less seriously than me.*

The superlative is formed by using **le plus** or **le moins** + adverb

Il peut parler le plus couramment. *He can speak the most fluently.*

Le vin anglais coûte le moins cher. *English wine costs the least.*

VOCABULARY LINK PAGE **110**

Irregular comparatives and superlatives

bien *well*	mieux *better*	le mieux *best*
mal *badly*	plus mal *worse*	le plus mal *the worst*
beaucoup *a lot*	plus *more*	le plus *the most*
peu *little*	moins *less*	le moins *the least*

Ma sœur parle français mieux que mon frère. *My sister speaks French better than my brother.*

 (10) Practice

 Translate the following sentences into French.

(a) I usually leave the house early.

(b) Sometimes we go to the café.

(c) I play the piano better than my brother.

(d) He speaks more softly than me.

(e) Unfortunately the weather was bad.

Quantifiers and intensifiers

Quantifiers and intensifiers are words that can be used to add emphasis or meaning.

 Intensifiers

Intensifiers are used with adverbs and adjectives to add emphasis and meaning. Common intensifiers include:

assez *quite*

aussi *as*

de moins en moins *less and less*

de plus en plus *more and more*

pas du tout *not at all*

plutôt *rather*

presque *almost*

si *so*

tout à fait *utterly*

très *very*

trop *too*

un peu *a little*

Il n'est pas riche du tout. *He is not at all rich.*

Je devais parler de plus en plus lentement. *I had to speak more and more slowly.*

Les billets étaient trop chers. *The tickets were too expensive.*

 Adverbs of quantity

The following adverbs all refer to quantity. They are always followed by **de** + noun without an article:

beaucoup de *a lot of*

assez de *enough*

combien de *how many*

moins de *less / fewer*

pas mal de *quite a bit / lots of*

plein de *lots of / full of*

plus de *more*

tant de *so much / many*

trop de *too much*

Encore (*more*), **la moitié** (*half*), and **la plupart** (*most*) are followed by **du / de la / de l' / des** + noun.

Voulez-vous encore du pain?
Do you want some more bread?

La plupart des professeurs sont sympa.
Most teachers are nice.

la moitié du groupe *half the group*

 Vocabulary

Adverbs as intensifiers
Many adverbs that end in **-ment** can be used as intensifiers.

absolument *absolutely*

complètement *completely*

énormément *enormously*

extrêmement *extremely*

incroyablement *incredibly*

relativement *relatively*

strictement *strictly*

tellement *so*

vraiment *really*

 Aiming higher

Using a wide variety of intensifiers adds originality to your answers, and is a feature of the best answers.

C'est complètement stupide! *It's completely stupid!*

Ce n'est pas absolument nécessaire! *It's not absolutely necessary!*

 Expressions of quantity

Expressions of quantity are followed by **de** + noun without an article. Common expressions of quantity are:

un kilo de pommes *a kilo of apples*

une bouteille d'eau *a bottle of water*

un paquet de biscuits *a packet of biscuits*

une boîte de tomates *a tin of tomatoes*

un morceau de fromage *a piece of cheese*

une tranche de pain *a slice of bread*

 Practice

🖉 Translate the following sentences into French.

(a) There are a lot of trees in the garden.

(b) I ate too many cakes.

(c) You see so many homeless people on the streets.

(d) After a few days I had seen enough sights.

(e) My parents are so annoying.

 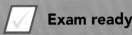

Subject and object pronouns

Pronouns are words like *she*, *they*, *it*, *him* and *them* and can be used in place of a noun or someone's name.

 Subject pronouns

Subject pronouns replace nouns that are doing an action: they are the subject of the verb. **Elle** can replace **ma sœur** in the phrase **Ma sœur aime les bananes.** → **Elle aime les bananes.** (*She likes bananas.*)

singular		plural	
je / j'	*I*	nous	*we*
tu	*you*	vous	*you*
il	*he / it*	ils	*they*
elle	*she / it*	elles	*they*
on	*one, we, you, they*		

- **On** can be used to refer to no one in particular, like *they*, *you* or *one* in English. It can also mean *we*: **Qu'est-ce qu'on fait ce soir?** *What are we doing this evening*?
- You need to know the gender of the word that the pronoun is replacing. As well as being used for people, **il** is used for masculine nouns and **elle** for feminine nouns: **le livre est** → **il est**; **la table est** → **elle est.**

 Object pronouns

Direct object pronouns replace nouns in a sentence when that noun is the object of a verb: I am reading a book → I am reading **it**; We are visiting our grandparents → We are visiting **them**.

singular		plural	
me	*me*	nous	*us*
te	*you*	vous	*you*
le	*him / it*	les	*them*
la	*her / it*		

- In French, the object pronoun goes in front of the verb: **Ça m'énerve!** *That annoys me!*

- In a negative sentence, **ne** goes in front of the pronoun, and the **pas** after the verb: **Je ne l'achète pas.**
- When there are two verbs in a sentence, the pronoun goes in front of the second verb in the infinitive: **Je vais le faire.** *I am going to do **it**.*
- The pronoun goes in front of the part of **avoir** and the past participle agrees with the pronoun:
  Je l'ai achetée (la pomme). *I bought **it.***
  Je l'ai vu (le film). *I saw **it**.*

 Indirect object pronouns

Indirect object pronouns are used when you want to say *to me, to him / her*, etc. They are used with many verbs followed by à, e.g. **donner à, dire à, parler à, offrir à, envoyer à, écrire à, demander à** and **répondre à.**

	indirect object pronoun
(to) me	me
(to) you (sing)	te
(to) him / her / it	lui
(to) us	nous
(to) you (pl)	vous
(to) them	leur

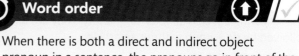 **Word order**

When there is both a direct and indirect object pronoun in a sentence, the pronouns go in front of the verb in the following order: **me, te, nous, vous le, la, les lui, leur.**

Il envoie le message à sa sœur. → **Il le lui envoie.** *He sends it to her.*

Je montre mes photos à mes copains. → **Je les leur montre.** *I show them to them.*

Il me le donne. *He is giving it to me.*

Using indefinite pronouns such as **quelqu'un** (*someone*) or **chacun** (*each one*) is also a feature of top grade answers.

Practice

🖉 Replace the underlined words with a pronoun.

(a) <u>Mes parents</u> donnent un vélo <u>à mon frère</u>.

(b) <u>Le professeur</u> a parlé <u>aux élèves</u>.

(c) <u>Ma sœur</u> est en train de lire <u>le livre</u>.

(d) <u>Mon frère et moi</u> voulons voir <u>le film</u>.

(e) J'ai acheté <u>les billets</u>.

Stressed and possessive pronouns

Stressed pronouns are words like **moi** meaning *me*, and **lui** meaning *him*. They are also known as emphatic or disjunctive pronouns.

 Stressed pronouns

singular		plural	
moi	*I / me*	nous	*we / us*
toi	*you*	vous	*you*
lui	*he / him*	eux	*they / them* (m)
elle	*she / her*	elles	*they / them* (f)
soi	*oneself*		

 Stressed pronouns and prepositions

Stressed pronouns are often used after prepositions like these:

avec *with*   selon *according to*

de *from / of*   chez *at home*

sans *without*   pas *not*

pour *for*

C'est pour toi. *It's for you;* selon lui *according to him*

 Using stressed pronouns

Stressed pronouns can be used in the following ways:

☑ to add emphasis to the subject pronoun:
Moi, je vais le faire. Lui, il a peur. *I am going to do it. **He** is afraid.*

☑ at the end of a sentence:
Tu aimes les escargots, toi? *Do **you** like snails?*
Je ne sais pas, moi. *I don't know.*

☑ after the verb to be:
C'est lui / elle. *It's **him** / **her**.*

☑ to show possession:
Ce vélo est à lui. *This bike is **his.***
C'est à moi. *It's **mine.***

☑ in comparisons:
Mon frère est plus grand que moi. *My brother is bigger than **me.***

 Possessive pronouns

Possessive pronouns in English are words like *mine, yours, his* and *theirs*. In French, they have to agree with the noun they replace. You need to be able to recognise these pronouns at Higher level.

	masculine singular	feminine singular	masculine plural	feminine plural
mine	le mien	la mienne	les miens	les miennes
yours (sing / familiar)	le tien	la tienne	les tiens	les tiennes
his, hers, its	le sien	la sienne	les siens	les siennes
ours	le nôtre	la nôtre	les nôtres	les nôtres
yours (plural / formal)	le vôtre	la vôtre	les vôtres	les vôtres
theirs	le leur	la leur	les leurs	les leurs

 Aiming higher

Use of possessive pronouns is a feature of top grade answers.

Voici mes chaussures. Où sont les tiennes?
Here are my shoes. Where are yours? (feminine plural to match les chaussures)

Ma sœur est plus grande que la sienne.
My sister is bigger than his / hers. (feminine singular to match ma sœur)

It should be clear from the context of a text whether **la sienne** means *his* or *hers*.

 Practice

👓 Translate the following sentences into English.

(a) Mes notes sont meilleures que les tiennes.

(b) Nos vacances étaient formidables. Comment étaient les vôtres?

(c) Tu as ton portable? Je ne peux pas trouver le mien.

(d) Il n'a pas de casquette? Il peut emprunter la mienne.

Relative and demonstrative pronouns

Relative pronouns, **qui**, **que** and **dont**, are used to link two parts of a sentence.

⑩ Relative pronouns

Relative pronouns are words like *who*, *that*, *which*, *where* and *whose* and are used to link two parts of a sentence.

Qui means *who* when referring to a person or *which*, when referring to a thing or a place. It is normally followed by a verb, and is the **subject** of that verb.

Qui cannot be shortened to **qu'**.

L'homme qui porte un pull lit le journal. *The man **who** is wearing a jumper is reading the newspaper.*

Que means *whom*, *that* or *which*. It is the **object** of the verb that follows it and it can be shortened to **qu'** if it comes before a vowel.

Le manteau que je porte est très à la mode.
*The coat **that** I am wearing is very fashionable.*

Les pommes qu'on a achetées étaient très bonnes.
*The apples **that** we bought were very good.*

> ❗ In the perfect tense the past participle (in this example, **achetées**) must agree with the noun to which **que** or **qu'** refers: **pommes** = feminine plural.

> ❗ **Ce qui** means *which* if it refers back to an idea and not a specific noun and is the subject in a sentence:
> **Il a oublié d'acheter du lait, ce qui l'a énervé.** *He forgot to buy milk, **which** annoyed him.*
> **Ce que** follows the same rules as **ce qui** but as the object of a sentence.
> **Elle a laissé son portable dans le train, ce qu'elle a regretté plus tard.** *She left her mobile on the train, **which** she regretted later.*

Dont can have various meanings: *whose*, *of which / whom* and *about which / whom*.

La femme dont le mari est mort vient nous voir.
*The woman **whose** husband died is coming to see us.*

It is often used with verbs followed by **de**.
Le livre dont j'ai besoin n'est pas disponible.
The book I need is not available. (avoir besoin de)

② Using *où*

Où links two parts of a sentence when referring to a place or a time. It means *where*, or may be omitted in English.

Le magasin où j'ai trouvé mon tee-shirt. *The shop where I found my T-shirt.*

Le jour où nous sommes arrivés... *The day we arrived...*

⑤ Demonstrative pronouns

Demonstrative pronouns are used when you want to say *the one* or *the ones*. The pronoun agrees with the noun to which it is referring.

	masc	fem	English
singular	celui	celle	*this / that / the one*
plural	ceux	celles	*these / those ones*

On a vu beaucoup de pulls au marché. Celui que j'ai acheté n'était pas cher. *We saw lots of jumpers in the market. **The one** I bought wasn't expensive.*

Quelles pommes voulez-vous? Celles qui sont moins chères. *Which apples do you want? **The ones** that are less expensive.*

② This one / that one

Add **-ci** (*this / these*) or **-là** (*that / those*) to be more specific.
Je voudrais celui-ci (m sing). *I would like this one.*
Ceux-là sont très bons (m pl). *Those are very good.*

> ❗ **Ceci** means *this*, and **cela** (**ça** for short) means *that*, when referring to something general or unspecified, e.g.
> **Ça (Cela) m'étonne**. *That surprises me.*
> **Ceci est difficile**. *This is difficult.*

② Showing possession

Celui, **celle**, **ceux** and **celles** can be used with **de** to show something belonging to someone / something.

Mes notes sont meilleures que celles de mon frère.
My marks are better than those of my brother.

Les fromages français ont un meilleur goût que ceux d'Espagne. *French cheeses taste better than Spanish ones.*

⑤ Practice

 Translate the following sentences into English.

(a) Le magasin qui se trouve à côté du musée est fermé.

(b) L'homme que j'ai vu portait un pull noir.

(c) Les enfants dont je m'occupe sont mignons.

 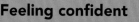

Pronouns y and *en*

Y means *there* and en means *some* or *any*. They are two common pronouns that go in front of the verb.

About the pronoun *en*

En means *some* or *any* and replaces nouns preceded by du, de la, de l' and des.

Est-ce qu'il y a du pain? *Is there **any** bread?*

Oui, il y en a. *Yes, there is **some**.*

Non, il n'y en a pas. *No, there isn't **any**.*

En and expressions of quantity

En means *of it* or *of them* when referring to expressions of quantity, often in response to combien?

Combien de pommes de terre as-tu acheté? *How many potatoes did you buy?*
J'en ai acheté un kilo. *I bought a kilo (of them).*

Vous avez de l'argent? *Do you have any money?*

Oui, mais je n'en ai pas assez. *Yes, but I don't have enough (of it).*

Oui, j'en ai beaucoup. *Yes, I have a lot (of it).*

En and verbs followed by *de*

En is used to replace phrases introduced by de. This occurs with verbs that use de to link to an infinitive or to a noun.

avoir envie de:
Vous avez envie de venir? Oui, j'en ai envie. *Do you want to come? Yes, I want to.*

être capable de:
Est-ce que tu es capable d'effectuer cette tâche? Non, je n'en suis pas capable. *Are you capable of doing this task? No, I am not capable **of it**.*

En can be used with the following common verbs:

rentrer de *to return from / be back from*; se souvenir de *to remember*; arriver de *to arrive*

Il est rentré du collège. → Il en est rentré. *He's back from school. → He's back from it.*

Je me souviens de mon anniversaire.
→ Je m'en souviens. *I remember my birthday. →
I remember **it**.*

When **y** and **en** appear together, **y** always goes before **en**.

About the pronoun *y*

Y replaces a phrase referring to a place (à or en + place) and means *there* or *here* depending on the context.

We went **to the cinema**. → *We went **there**.*

It goes in front of the verb, regardless of the tense.
Je vais au cinéma. → J'y vais.

With the immediate future tense it goes in front of the infinitive.

On va aller au cinéma. → On va y aller.

Y and verbs followed by *à*

Y is used to replace phrases introduced by à (referring to something, rather than someone). This occurs with verbs that use à to link to an infinitive or to a noun.

réussir à: Tu as réussi à répondre aux questions?
-Oui, j'y ai réussi. *Did you manage to answer the question? Yes I managed.*

répondre à: Est-ce que tu as répondu à son e-mail? *Did you reply to his email?*
-Oui, j'y ai répondu. *Yes, I replied **to it**.*
-Non, je n'y ai pas répondu. *No, I haven't replied **to it**.*

Vocabulary

Common expressions with *en*
Je n'en sais rien. *I don't know anything (about it).*
J'en ai marre. *I'm fed up (with it).*
J'en ai assez. *I've had enough (of it).*
Il n'y en a pas. *There isn't / aren't any left.*

Common expressions with *y*
il y a *there is / there **are***: Il y a un château et un parc. *There is a castle and a park.*
il y a + time phrase *ago*: il y a une semaine *a week ago*
Ça y est! *That's it!*
y compris *including*

Il y a trente personnes dans la salle de classe, y compris le professeur. *There are thirty people in the classroom, including the teacher.*

Practice

Translate the following sentences into French.

(a) Do you want some more salad?
(b) Yes, I want some.
(c) No, I don't want any.
(d) Do you need any money?
(e) Yes, I need some.
(f) He's back from the concert.→ He's back from it.
(g) I went to France.
(h) I went there.
(i) Are you thinking of coming?
(j) Yes, I am thinking about it.

Conjunctions and connectives

Conjunctions and connectives are words that link ideas together in a sentence or paragraph.

⑤ Coordinating conjunctions

Coordinating conjunctions are words that link together words or phrases of equal importance in a sentence. Common coordinating conjunctions are: **et** (*and*), **mais** (*but*), **ou** (*or*), **car** (*because*) and **donc** (*so / therefore*).

Il y a trop de déchets car on ne recycle pas assez.
There is too much rubbish because we don't recycle enough.

Je ne me suis pas levé de bonne heure, donc j'ai raté le bus.
I didn't get up early, so I missed the bus.

Ce jour-là, il pleuvait et il y avait du vent. *On that day, it was raining and it was windy.*

Je voudrais sortir ce soir mais mes parents ne le permettent pas. *I would like to go out this evening, but my parents won't allow it.*

On va aller au parc d'attractions ou à la fête foraine.
We are going to go to the theme park or to the funfair.

⑤ Time connectives

Connectives link ideas across two separate sentences or paragraphs. Use the following to describe a sequence of events across a period of time.

d'abord *first of all*
lorsque / quand *when*
ensuite / puis *then*
après que *after*
aussitôt que / dès que *as soon as*
tandis que / pendant que *while / whereas*
enfin / à la fin *finally / in the end*
avant de + infinitive *before (doing) something*

Quand nous sommes arrivés, nous avons fait la connaissance de nos partenaires. *When* we arrived we got to know our partners.

J'ai mis la table pendant que ma mère préparait le dîner. *I laid the table **while** my mother was preparing dinner.*

② Presenting an argument

Use the following connectives to looking at different sides of an argument, or the advantages and disadvantages of something:

à part *apart from*
cependant *however*
d'un côté *on the one hand*
d'un autre côté *on the other hand*
évidemment *evidently / obviously*
par contre *on the other hand*

c'est à dire *that is to say*
même si *even if*
pourtant *however*
par exemple *for example*
sans doute *without doubt / probably*
sinon *otherwise*
y compris *including*

② Reasons and consequences

Use the following connectives when you want to give a reason for something or to justify an opinion.

ainsi *so / therefore*
alors *so / therefore / then*
car *because / for*
donc *so / therefore*
puisque *since*
à cause de *because of*
lorsque *when*
par conséquent *as a result*

parce que *because*
si *if*
sinon *otherwise*
afin de + infinitive *in order to*
sans + infinitive *without + –ing, e.g. doing*
comme *as / like*

⑤ Exam focus

Pay attention to conjunctions in reading and listening texts, especially words like **mais**, **pourtant**, **cependant** and **par contre**. They can change the meaning of a sentence.

On dit que les films de guerre sont trop violents, pourtant, je ne suis pas d'accord car on pourrait dire que les films d'horreur sont pires.

*It is said that war films are too violent, **however** I disagree, because you could say that horror films are worse.*

This indicates that the speaker is about to disagree with the statement just made.

⑩ Practice

✎ Translate the following sentences into French.

(a) I hate living in town because there is too much pollution.

(b) We must stop the deforestation of our forests, otherwise we'll see more floods.

(c) You see a lot of homeless people on the streets because of the problems of unemployment and poverty.

(d) I think one should buy green products whereas my parents think that we must use less energy.

Made a start ✓ Feeling confident ✓ Exam ready

The present tense

Use this page to revise how to form and use the present tense.

 About the present tense

Use the present tense to describe what is happening now or what usually happens. In English, there are two forms of the present tense: *I play* and *I am playing*.
In French however, you use je joue for both.

It can sometimes be used with a future sense:
Je vais à Paris demain. *I am going to Paris tomorrow.*

Remember, in questions and negative statements you do not need an extra word for *do*:

Do I play? Je joue?; *I don't play.* Je ne joue pas.

 The present tense + *depuis*

When the present tense is used with depuis (*for / since*) it expresses how long something has been done for.

Je joue du violon depuis l'âge de sept ans.
I have been playing the violin since the age of seven.

> Verbs in the -er group make up about 80% of all French verbs. When new verbs are created from English words, they are -er verbs: for example, on social media you have tchatter, liker, bloguer.

 Verb patterns

When you look up a verb in the dictionary it is listed in the infinitive form, for example, ***to eat***, ***to start***, ***to sell***. Most verbs belong to one of three groups of regular verbs: -er, -ir or -re. In the present tense, these have the same endings depending on their group. Look at these examples of regular verbs for jouer (*to play*), finir (*to finish*) and descendre (*to go down*).
Faire (*to make / do*), venir (*to come*) and boire (*to drink*) are examples of irregular words.

	-er e.g. jouer	-ir e.g. finir	-re e.g. descendre
je / j'	joue	finis	descends
tu	joues	finis	descends
il / elle / on	joue	finit	descend
nous	jouons	finissons	descendons
vous	jouez	finissez	descendez
ils / elles	jouent	finissent	descendent

	faire to make / do	venir to come	boire to drink
je	fais	viens	bois
tu	fais	viens	bois
il / elle / on	fait	vient	boit
nous	faisons	venons	buvons
vous	faites	venez	buvez
ils / elles	font	viennent	boivent

 -er verbs with spelling changes

Some -er verbs make slight changes to their stem in the singular and third person plural of the present tense. Look out for other verbs that follow the same patterns as the examples.

	add grave accent	double consonant	y→i
infinitive	acheter	jeter	nettoyer
je	achète	jette	nettoie
tu	achètes	jettes	nettoies
il / elle / on	achète	jette	nettoie
nous	achetons	jetons	nettoyons
vous	achetez	jetez	nettoyez
ils / elles	achètent	jettent	nettoient

> **manger** and **commencer** make slight changes in the **nous** form: **nous mangeons** (add **e** before **-ons**)
> **nous commençons** (add cedilla to **c**)

The verb *faire*

The verb faire is used in a lot of common expressions.

faire des bêtises *to do something stupid*
faire la fête *to party*
faire les bagages *to pack*
faire la grève *to go on strike*
faire jour / nuit *to be daytime / nighttime*
ça ne fait rien *that doesn't matter*

 Practice

🖉 Translate the following sentences into **French**.

(a) I send text messages to my friends every day.

(b) We are reading some poems in class at the moment.

(c) We are going to the cinema today.

(d) I don't know him well.

(e) I have been learning French for five years.

Key verbs

Revise how to form and use the verbs avoir and être, and modal verbs.

 Auxiliary verbs

Avoir and être are auxiliary verbs. They are used in the formation of past tenses of all other verbs. The present tense of these two verbs is used to form the perfect tense, and their imperfect tense is used to form the pluperfect.

The verb *avoir*

The verb avoir means *to have*. It is used in a lot of common expressions as well in the formation of the perfect and pluperfect tenses.

	present	imperfect
j'	ai *have*	avais *had*
tu	as *have*	avais *had*
il / elle / on	a *has*	avait *had*
nous	avons *have*	avions *had*
vous	avez *have*	aviez *had*
ils / elles	ont *have*	avaient *had*

The verb *être*

The verb être means *to be*. It is used to form the perfect and pluperfect tense of reflexive verbs and certain other verbs.

	present	imperfect
je / j'	suis *am*	étais *was*
tu	es *are*	étais *were*
il / elle / on	est *is*	était *was*
nous	sommes *are*	étions *were*
vous	êtes *are*	étiez *were*
ils / elles	sont *are*	étaient *were*

 Modal verbs and the verb *aller*

Vouloir, devoir and pouvoir are modal verbs. They are followed by another verb in the infinitive. Aller is used to form the immediate future tense (see page 86).

	vouloir *to want*	pouvoir *to be able / can*	devoir *to have to / must*	aller *to go*
je	veux	peux	dois	vais
tu	veux	peux	dois	vas
il / elle / on	veut	peut	doit	va
nous	voulons	pouvons	devons	allons
vous	voulez	pouvez	devez	allez
ils / elles	veulent	peuvent	doivent	vont

Nous **voulons aller** à Londres ce week-end. We **want to go** to London this weekend.

Je ne **peux pas parler** couramment. I **can't speak** fluently.

On **doit faire** des efforts pour avoir de bonnes notes. You **have to make** an effort to get good marks.

Pendant les vacances scolaires, je **vais faire** du bénévolat. During the school holidays I **am going to do** some volunteering.

On **voulait aller** au cinéma. We **wanted to go** to the cinema.

Je **devais aider** mes parents. I **had to help** my parents.

Nous **devrions recycler** les sacs en plastique. We **ought to recycle** plastic bags.

Je ne **pouvais pas finir** l'exercice. I **couldn't (wasn't able to) finish** the exercise.

Pourrais-tu m'aider? **Could** you (**would** you **be able to**) **help** me?

 Modal verbs in other tenses

je voudrais *I would like to / I'd like to* (conditional)
je voulais *I wanted to* (imperfect)
je devrais *I ought to / I should* (conditional)
je devais *I had to* (imperfect)
je pourrais *I could / I would be able to* (conditional)
je pouvais *I could / I was able to* (imperfect)

 Practice

1 Translate the following common expressions using *avoir* into English.

(a) J'ai envie de sortir.

(b) Est-ce que tu as faim?

(c) On avait besoin d'aide.

(d) Ils ont soif.

(e) Nous n'avons pas eu de chance.

(f) Vous avez raison.

(g) Elle a peur des serpents.

2 Translate the following common expressions using *être* into English.

(a) Elle es ten train de faire la cuisine.

(b) Il est enrhumé depuis trois jours.

(c) On était obligés de partir avant la fin du concert.

(d) Je ne suis pas d'accord avec toi.

(e) Nous sommes sur le point de partir.

(f) Je suis de retour.

The perfect tense

The perfect tense is a past tense used for describing completed actions and is made up of two parts.

 About the perfect tense

The perfect tense is made up of two parts: auxiliary verb (present tense of avoir or être) + past participle.

Hier soir, j'ai regardé la télévision, mes parents ont écouté de la musique et mon frère a lu son livre.

*Yesterday evening I **watched** TV, my parents **listened** to music and my brother **read** his book.*

Regular verbs form the past participle in the following ways:

- er verbs: remove the r from the infinitive and add an acute accent to the *e*: jouer → joué
- ir verbs: remove the r from the infinitive: finir → fini
- re verbs: remove the re from the infinitive, add *u* to the stem: vendre → vendu

The perfect tense can be translated in a number of different ways: j'ai joué = *I played, I have played, I did play.*
Most verbs form the perfect tense with avoir. Reflexive verbs and some other verbs form the perfect tense with être.

 The perfect tense formed with *être*

Past participles formed with être agree with the subject.

je suis allé(e)	I went
tu es allé(e)	you went
il est allé	he went
elle est allée	she went
on est allé(e/s)	we went
nous sommes allé(e)s	we went
vous êtes allé(e/s)	you went (formal / pl)
ils sont allés	they went (m or mixed)
elles sont allées	they went (only f)

Verbs that take être: **MRS DR VANDERTRAMP**

verb	past participle
monter *to go up*	monté
rester *to stay*	resté
sortir *to go out*	sorti
descendre *to go down*	descendu
retourner *to return*	retourné
venir *to come*	venu
aller *to go*	allé
naître *to be born*	né
devenir *to become*	devenu
entrer *to enter*	entré
revenir *to come back*	revenu
tomber *to fall*	tombé
rentrer *to return*	rentré
arriver *to arrive*	arrivé
mourir *to die*	mort
partir *to leave*	parti

Ma sœur est allée à Paris avec ses copines. Elles sont parties de bonne heure, et elles y sont arrivées à midi.
My sister went to Paris with her friends. They left early and arrived there at midday.

 Common irregular verbs

All these verbs form the perfect tense with the present tense of avoir.

avoir *to have*	eu
boire *to drink*	bu
connaître *to know*	connu
croire *to believe*	cru
devoir *to have to*	dû
dire *to say*	dit
écrire *to write*	écrit
être *to be*	été
faire *to do / make*	fait
lire *to read*	lu
mettre *to put*	mis
ouvrir *to open*	ouvert
pouvoir *to be able to*	pu
prendre *to take*	pris
recevoir *to receive*	reçu
savoir *to know a fact*	su
voir *to see*	vu
vouloir *to want*	voulu

Remember to make the past participle *opened* agree with the direct object *presents*.

 Practice

✎ Translate the following message into French.

Yesterday I celebrated my birthday. My parents gave me a lot of presents that I opened in the morning. In the evening we had a party and a lot of my friends came. We drank cola and afterwards we danced. What did you do last weekend?

 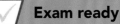

The imperfect tense

Revise how to form and use the imperfect tense.

About the imperfect tense

The imperfect tense is used to say:

- what things were like in the past:

  Il faisait chaud. *It was hot.*

  Le voyage était affreux. *The journey was awful.*

  Il y avait du monde. *There were a lot of people.*

- what used to happen:

  J'habitais à Lille *I lived / used to live in Lille.*

- what happened habitually or frequently:

  On rendait souvent visite à mes grands-parents. *We often visited my grandparents.*

- what someone was doing when an action was interrupted:

  Je regardais la télévision quand le téléphone a sonné. *I was watching television when the phone rang.*

Making suggestions

The imperfect tense can be used to make suggestions.

Si on allait au théâtre? *How about going to the theatre?*

Si on faisait une excursion? *Shall we go on an outing?*

Si on mangeait au restaurant? *How about eating in a restaurant?*

Venir + de

The imperfect tense of **venir + de** + infinitive is used to say something *had just* happened.

Il venait de finir son dîner quand quelqu'un a frappé à la porte. *He had just finished his dinner when someone knocked on the door.*

Forming the imperfect tense

To form the imperfect tense, take the **–ons** ending off the **nous** form of the present tense and add the imperfect endings shown in the table. The one exception to this rule is the verb **être** which simply adds the endings to the stem **ét-**.

	jouer *to play* (nous jouons)	finir *to finish* (nous finissons)	descendre *to go down* (nous descendons)
je	jouais	finissais	descendais
tu	jouais	finissais	descendais
il / elle / on	jouait	finissait	descendait
nous	jouions	finissions	descendions
vous	jouiez	finissiez	descendiez
ils / elles	jouaient	finissaient	descendaient

être	to be
j'étais	I was
tu étais	you were
il / elle / on était	he / she was
nous étions	we were
vous étiez	you were
ils / elles étaient	they were

Si + imperfect

  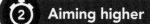

The imperfect is often combined with the conditional in sentences to say what you *would* do. See page 88.

Si j'étais riche, j'achèterais une belle maison.

If I were rich I would buy a nice house.

Si j'avais du temps, j'irais le voir.

If I had time I would go and see him.

Aiming higher

Use **depuis** followed by a verb in the imperfect tense to express for how long something *had been* done.

J'habitais à Londres depuis trois ans.
I had been living in London for three years.

J'habitais à Londres depuis septembre.
I had been living in London since September.

Practice

  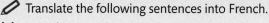

✎ Translate the following sentences into French.

(a) I was doing my homework when my mother asked me to go downstairs.

(b) I was in the middle of reading my book when someone knocked on the door.

(c) We were crossing the road when the accident happened.

(d) We had just arrived when it started to rain.

 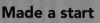 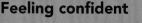

The pluperfect tense

The pluperfect tense is used to talk about events that happened further back in the past than those described using the perfect tense.

About the pluperfect tense

Use the pluperfect tense to say what you had done or what had happened.

Mes parents se fâchaient parce que je n'avais pas fait mes devoirs. *My parents were angry because I **hadn't done** my homework.*

Je n'étais jamais allé en France avant cette visite-là.
*I **had** never **been** to France before that visit.*

Regular verbs

The pluperfect tense is formed in an similar way to the perfect tense, but instead uses the imperfect tense of avoir or être before the past participle.

auxiliary	-er	-ir	-re
j'avais	joué	fini	vendu
tu avais	joué	fini	vendu
il / elle / on avait	joué	fini	vendu
nous avions	joué	fini	vendu
vous aviez	joué	fini	vendu
ils / elles avaient	joué	fini	vendu

J'avais fini mon dîner. *I **had finished** my dinner.*
Il avait vendu la maison. *He **had sold** the house.*
Elle avait mangé une glace. *She **had eaten** an ice cream.*

Verbs with *être*

Verbs that form the perfect tense using a present tense être auxiliary use an imperfect être auxiliary in the pluperfect tense. The verb and the subject have to agree.

j'étais allé(e)	I had been / gone
tu étais allé(e)	you had been / gone
il était allé	he had been / gone
elle était allée	she had been / gone
on était allé(e/s)	we had been / gone
nous étions allé(e)s	we had been / gone
vous étiez allé(e/s)	you had been / gone (formal / pl)
ils étaient allés	they had been / gone (m or mixed)
elles étaient allées	they had been / gone (only f)

Nous n'étions jamais allées à Paris. *We (f) had never been to Paris.*

Reported speech

Use the pluperfect tense to report speech.

Elle a dit qu'elle s'était bien amusée. *She said she had had a good time.*

Il a dit que son équipe n'avait pas gagné le match. *He said that his team hadn't won the match.*

Il a dit qu'il avait perdu son portable. *He said he had lost his mobile phone.*

Irregular verbs

For the past participles of irregular verbs see page 83, *The perfect tense.*

J'avais pris le train. *I had taken the train.*
Il avait mis son manteau. *He had put on his coat.*
Nous avions bu du thé. *We had drunk some tea.*
Ils avaient fait une erreur. *They had made a mistake.*
J'avais déjà lu ce livre. *I had already read that book.*
Elle lui avait écrit une lettre. *She had written a letter to him / her.*
On avait ouvert la fenêtre. *We had opened the window.*
Est-ce que tu l'avais vu auparavant? *Had you seen it / him before?*

Aiming higher

Sentences that contain examples of the pluperfect tense are characteristic of the top grade answers at Higher level.

J'ai reçu de bonnes notes parce que j'avais travaillé dur. *I got good marks because I had worked hard.*

Practice

Translate the following sentences into English.

(a) Mon frère était allé au café pour retrouver ses copains mais personne n'est venu.

(b) J'avais choisi mon repas avant d'aller au restaurant.

(c) Je n'avais jamais vu cette personne auparavant.

(d) Quand je suis arrivé au marché, j'ai remarqué que j'avais oublié mon porte-monnaie.

(e) Nous étions partis de bonne heure mais nous sommes arrivés tard à notre hôtel.

The immediate future tense

The immediate future tense is used to say what is going to happen, and is formed using the verb **aller**.

About the immediate future tense

Use the immediate future tense to talk about events that will happen soon. It is the equivalent of the English *going to...* and is formed by using the present tense of the verb **aller** + the infinitive. It can also be used to talk about future plans.

Je vais lire ce livre. *I**'m going to read** this book.*

Qu'est-ce que tu vas faire? *What **are** you **going to do**?*

On va manger en ville. *We **are going to eat** in town.*

Nous allons louer des vélos. *We **are going to hire** some bikes.*

Est-ce que vous allez voir ce film? Are *you **going to see** this film?*

Ils vont regarder la télé. *They **are going to watch** television.*

Other future expressions

You can use:

- the present tense with a future time phrase:

  Il part dans deux heures. *He is leaving in two hours.*

  Mes parents rentrent tard ce soir. *My parents are coming home late this evening.*

- **être sur le point de** *to be on the point of / about to do something*

  Nous sommes sur le point de partir. *We are about to leave.*

Aiming higher

If you use a reflexive verb in the immediate future, you need to make the reflexive pronoun agree with the subject.

Je vais me lever de bonne heure.
I am going to get up early.

Est-ce que tu vas t'habiller avant de prendre le petit-déjeuner?
Are you going to get dressed before having breakfast?

Il va s'échauffer avant de faire de l'exercice.
He's going to warm up before exercising.

Nous allons nous / On va se balader dans le parc cet après-midi. *We are going to go for a stroll in the park this afternoon.*

Est-ce que vous allez vous reposer?
Are you going to have a rest?

Ils vont se détendre en écoutant de la musique.
They are going to relax by listening to music.

Future time phrases

après-demain *the day after tomorrow*
bientôt *soon*
ce soir *tonight / this evening*
à l'avenir *in the future*
dans deux jours *in two days*
demain *tomorrow*
demain matin *tomorrow morning*
l'été prochain *next summer*
la semaine prochaine *next week*
le mois prochain *next month*
le week-end prochain *next weekend*
l'année prochaine *next year*
lundi prochain *next Monday*
pendant les vacances *during the holidays*
plus tard *later*

VOCABULARY LINK PAGE 97

Il va pleuvoir.

Practice

✏ Translate the following sentences into French.

(a) We are going to visit a museum during the exchange.

(b) They are going to see a film this evening.

(c) It is going to be windy.

(d) I hope it is going to snow soon.

(e) France is going to win the match.

The future tense

The future tense is used to say what will happen in the future.

(5) Forming the future tense

For verbs ending -er and -ir, you add the future endings to the infinitive.

person	ending
je / j'	-ai
tu	-as
il / elle / on	-a
nous	-ons
vous	-ez
ils / elles	-ont

-er verbs that add an accent or double a consonant in the present tense make similar changes to their stem in the future tense.

J'appellerai mon copain. *I will call my friend.*

Elle achètera des provisions. *She will buy food.*

Some -er verbs with y in their stem change to i.

nettoyer (*to clean*), employer (*to employ*), essuyer (*to wipe*).

Nous nettoierons la cuisine. *We will clean the kitchen.*

(5) Verbs ending in -re

Verbs that end in -re drop the e at the end of the infinitive before adding the endings.

Je prendrai la soupe à l'oignon. *I'll have the onion soup.*

Est-ce que tu boiras de l'eau? *Will you drink water?*

Il ne dira rien. *He won't say anything.*

Nous écrirons des lettres. *We'll write some letters.*

Est-ce que vous mettrez vos baskets? *Are you wearing your trainers?*

Ils vivront en France. *They will live in France.*

(5) Future tense with *si* and *quand*

Use the future tense in sentences where the other half is si + present tense.

S'il fait beau demain, on fera un pique-nique.

If it is fine tomorrow, we will have a picnic.

Si j'ai de la chance, je gagnerai à la lotterie.

If I'm lucky, I will win the lottery.

Use the future tense after quand if the verb describes what will happen in the future. Take care with this as it's different from what happens in English.

Quand j'aurai trente ans, je me marierai.

When I am thirty I will get married.

(5) Common irregular future forms

A number of common verbs use an irregular stem, to which the future tense endings are added.

aller *to go*	ir-	pouvoir *to be able to*	pourr-
avoir *to have*	aur-	recevoir *to receive*	recevr-
courir *to run*	courr-	savoir *to know*	saur-
devoir *to have to*	devr-	venir *to come*	viendr-
envoyer *to send*	enverr-	voir *to see*	verr-
être *to be*	ser-	vouloir *to want*	voudr-
faire *to do*	fer-		

devenir (*to become*), tenir (*to hold*) and revenir (*to come back*) follow this pattern.

mourir (*to die*) follows this pattern.

Impersonal verbs such as pleuvoir (*to rain*), falloir (*to be necessary*) and valoir (*to be worth*) are all irregular.

il faudra *it will be necessary;* il pleuvra *it will rain;* il vaudra *it will be worth*

(2) Aiming higher

The best answers will include a variety of verbs in a range of tenses. Include examples of the future tense, especially irregular verbs.

À la fin de ma scolarité, je prendrai une année sabbatique et j'irai à l'étranger pour faire du bénévolat.

At the end of my schooling, I will take a gap year and I will go abroad to volunteer.

(10) Practice

Translate the following sentences into French.

(a) I will see him tomorrow.

(b) We will have to take the bus.

(c) She will be twenty years old.

(d) Will you (sing) go cycling tomorrow?

(e) How will he be coming?

(f) We will go to the theatre.

(g) He won't buy anything.

(h) What will you (pl) eat?

(i) When will you (sing) go out?

(j) I won't have a starter.

The conditional

The conditional is used to say what would or could happen.

 Forming the conditional

The conditional is formed in a similar way to the future tense. The conditional endings are the same as the imperfect endings and are added to the infinitive of -er and -ir verbs.

person	ending
je / j'	-ais
tu	-ais
il / elle / on	-ait
nous	-ions
vous	-iez
ils / elles	-aient

jouer → je jouerais *I would play*

finir → je finirais *I would finish*

For -re verbs, take off the final *e* of the infinitive and add the conditional endings.

vendre → je vendrais *I would sell*

 Using the conditional with *si*

If a si clause uses the imperfect, the second part of the sentence should be in the conditional. (This follows the same pattern as in English.)

- Si mes parents ne se fâchaient pas, je serais plus heureux.
  If my parents didn't get angry, I would be happier.
- S'il avait de l'argent, il achèterait un nouveau portable.
  If he had the money, he would buy a new mobile phone.
- Si j'étais riche, j'aurais une belle maison.
  If I were rich, I would have a nice house.
- Si on recyclait plus, il y aurait moins de gaspillage.
  If we recycled more, there would be less waste.
- Si nous allions en France, nous pourrions perfectionner notre français
  If we went to France, we could improve our French.
- Si j'avais le choix, j'habiterais dans un pays chaud.
  If I had the choice, I would live in a warm country.

Use **la tour Eiffel**.

Use the verb **fonctionner**.

Use **en** in front of the verb *to buy*.

 Irregular verbs in the conditional

Verbs that have irregular stems in the future tense (see page 87) use the same stem to form the conditional.

aller *to go*	ir-
avoir *to have*	aur-
courir *to run*	courr-
devoir *to have to*	devr-
envoyer *to send*	enverr-
être *to be*	ser-
faire *to do*	fer-
pouvoir *to be able*	pourr-
recevoir *to receive*	recevr-
savoir *to know*	saur-
venir *to come*	viendr-
voir *to see*	verr-
vouloir *to want*	voudr-

j'aurais *I would have*
je serais *I would be*

 Polite requests and statements

Using the conditional form makes requests sound even more polite.

Pourriez-vous m'aider?
Could you help me?

Pourriez-vous répéter la question, s'il vous plaît?
Could you repeat the question?

Est-ce qu'il serait possible de venir demain?
Would it be possible to come tomorrow?

Est-ce que je pourrais vous poser une question?
Could I ask you a question?

Je voudrais savoir si... *I would like to know if...*

J'aimerais mieux partir demain.
I would prefer to leave tomorrow.

 Practice

✎ Translate the following sentences into French.

(a) If he was rich he wouldn't work.

(b) I would prefer to go to Spain.

(c) If I went to Paris I could go up the Eiffel Tower.

(d) If my mobile phone no longer worked I would buy a new one.

(e) If I had no money I would find a job.

 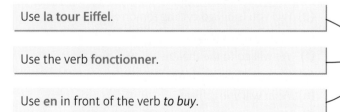

Negative forms

Revise how to make a sentence negative, using ne ... pas and other negative expressions with verbs.

⑤ Formation of the negative

The negative is made up of two parts: ne and pas, which you put either side of the verb.

Je ne joue pas au tennis. *I don't play tennis.*

ne shortens to n' in front of a vowel or silent *h*.

Ils n'aiment pas les films de guerre. *They don't like war films.*

Elle n'habite pas au centre-ville. *She doesn't live in the centre of town.*

② Pas / plus + de

After pas or plus, just use de or d' instead of du, de la, de l' and des.

Je n'ai pas de frères. *I don't have any brothers.*

On n'a pas d'argent. *We don't have any money.*

② Word order with pronouns

Je ne l'aime pas. *I don't like it.*

Il n'en mange pas. *He doesn't eat any of it.*

Le prof ne leur donne pas de devoirs. *The teacher doesn't give them any homework.*

② Word order in the perfect tense

In the perfect tense, ne and pas go around the auxiliary être / avoir verb.

Je n'ai pas fait mes devoirs. *I haven't done my homework.*

Ils ne sont pas allés au cinéma. *They didn't go to the cinema.*

② Word order with two verbs

When two verbs are used together, the ne and pas go around the first verb, not around the infinitive.

Je ne vais pas voir ce film. *I am not going to see this film.*

Ils ne veulent pas aider à la maison. *They don't want to help at home.*

To contradict a negative statement or question you use si, meaning *yes*.

Il n'y a plus de lait. *There's no more milk.*

-Si, il y en a. *Yes, there is some.*

Tu n'aimes pas les bananes? *You don't like bananas?*

-Si, je les aime. *Yes, I do like them.*

② Other negative forms

ne ... plus *no longer / not any more*

ne ... jamais *never / not ever*

ne ... rien *nothing / not anything*

ne ... personne *no one / not anyone*

ne ... que *only / nothing but*

ne ... ni ... ni ... *neither ... nor*

ne ... guère *hardly / scarcely*

ne ... nulle part *nowhere*

ne ... pas encore *not yet*

VOCABULARY LINK PAGE 101

These work in the same way as ne ... pas.

Il ne travaille plus. *He doesn't work anymore.*

Personne and que are slightly different from other negatives, in that they go after the complete verb in the perfect tense, rather than just after the auxiliary.

Je n'ai vu personne ce soir. *I didn't see anyone this evening.*

On n'a acheté que deux pizzas. *We only bought two pizzas.*

② Negative imperatives

With imperatives, put ne and pas (or other negation) around the verb.

Ne cours pas! *Don't run!*

Ne fumez pas! *Don't smoke!*

Ne soyez jamais impoli(s)! *Never be rude!*

⑤ Negative questions

In questions where the subject and verb are inverted (Veux-tu...?), put ne and pas round the whole structure.

Ne veux-tu pas sortir ce soir? *Don't you want to go out this evening?*

N'aimes-tu pas cette musique? *Don't you like this music?*

N'a-t-il pas de portable? *Hasn't he got a mobile phone?*

⑩ Practice

✏ Translate the following sentences into French.

(a) There is no butter left.

(b) I have never been to France.

(c) We didn't go to the cinema.

(d) We are not going there.

(e) He didn't talk to anyone.

Reflexive verbs

Reflexive verbs have an extra pronoun between the subject and verb.

About reflexive verbs

Reflexive verbs are listed with **se** in front of them in the dictionary: **se lever** *to get up*; **se dépêcher** *to hurry*.

The reflexive pronoun changes depending on who or what the subject is and always comes immediately before the verb. The verb endings are as they would normally be.

Negative form of reflexive verbs

To make a reflexive verb negative, the **ne** goes in front of the reflexive pronoun.

Elle ne s'est pas dépêchée. *She didn't hurry.*

Je ne me couche pas. *I didn't go to bed.*

The present tense of reflexive verbs

Many reflexive verbs are –er verbs with regular endings.

se réveiller	to wake up
je **me** réveille	I wake up
tu **te** réveilles	you wake up
il / elle / on **se** réveille	he / she / it / one wakes up
nous **nous** réveillons	we wake up
vous **vous** réveillez	you wake up
ils / elles **se** réveillent	they wake up

me, **te** and **se** become **m'**, **t'** and **s'** in front of a vowel or a silent 'h': **je m'appelle, tu t'ennuies, il s'habille**.

Reflexive verbs used in the infinitive

The reflexive pronoun changes to agree with the subject when a reflexive verb is used in the infinitive, after verbs such as **vouloir**, **devoir**, **pouvoir** and **aller**.

Je vais me coucher de bonne heure.
I am going to go to bed early.

Voulez-vous vous asseoir là-bas?
Do you want to sit down over there?

Se and **nous** can sometimes mean *each other*, for example:

On doit se revoir bientôt.
*We must see **each other** again soon.*

Perfect tense of reflexive verbs

Reflexive verbs form the perfect tense with the verb **être**. The past participle must agree with the subject.

je me suis réveillé(e)	I woke up	nous nous sommes réveillé(e)s	we woke up
tu t'es réveillé(e)	you woke up	vous vous êtes réveillé(e/s)	you woke up
il s'est réveillé	he woke up	ils se sont réveillés	they woke up (m)
elle s'est réveillée	she woke up	elles se sont réveillées	they woke up (f)
on s'est réveillé(e/s)	one / we / you woke up		

Reflexive verbs and parts of the body

Reflexive verbs are often used with parts of the body.

se brosser les dents *to brush one's teeth*

se laver les mains *to wash one's hands*

When a reflexive verb is used with a part of the body in the perfect tense, the past participle does not agree.

Elle s'est coupé le doigt. *She cut her finger.*

Reflexive verbs and the imperative

In the imperative, the pronoun follows the verb.
Te changes to **toi**.

Lève-toi, levez-vous! *Get up!*

Levons-nous. *Let's get up.*

Assieds-toi, asseyez-vous! *Sit down!*

Asseyons-nous. *Let's sit down.*

Practice

✏ Translate the following sentences into French.

(a) I don't get up early.

(b) They never argue.

(c) They washed their hands.

(d) We want to have a good time.

 Made a start **Feeling confident** **Exam ready**

The imperative

You can use the imperative form of a verb to give instructions, orders and advice or to make a request.

(5) Forming the imperative

There are three forms of the imperative, used for addressing *you* (familiar), *you* (polite) and *us*. These are simply the **tu**, **nous** and **vous** forms of the present tense of the verb, but without the pronoun.

(For **-er** verbs, drop the **-s** in the **tu** form, except when followed by **y** or **en.**)

	travailler *to work*	choisir *to choose*	attendre *to wait*
tu	travaille	choisis	attends
nous	travaillons	choisissons	attendons
vous	travaillez	choisissez	attendez

Travaillez plus dur. *Work harder.*

Choisis ton entrée. *Choose your starter.*

Attendons le bus là-bas. *Let's wait for the bus over there.*

Manges-en! *Eat some!*

Faites vos devoirs. *Do your homework.*

> The verb **aller** drops the **-s** in the **tu** form except when followed by **y.**
> **Va chez le médecin.** *Go to the doctor.*
> **Vas-y.** *Go (on).*

> The verb **ouvrir,** which takes **-er** endings in the present tense, drops the **-s** in the **tu** form.
> **Ouvre la porte!** *Open the door!*

(2) Irregular imperatives

The following verbs have irregular imperative forms.
être (*to be*): sois, soyons, soyez
avoir (*to have*): aie, ayons, ayez
savoir (*to know*): sache, sachons, sachez
vouloir (*to want*): veuille, veuillons, veuillez

(5) Reflexive verbs and imperatives

Réveille-toi! *Wake up!*

Réveillez-vous! *Wake up!*

Réveillons-nous à sept heures. *Let's wake up at seven o'clock.*

In a negative sentence, the reflexive pronoun comes before the imperative.

Ne t'inquiète pas! *Don't worry!*

Ne vous inquiétez pas! *Don't worry!*

Ne nous inquiétons pas! *Let's not worry!*

(2) Using the imperative

The imperative is often used in the following contexts:

- advice for a healthy lifestyle
- school rules
- instructions for how to do something: a recipe or an exercise
- giving directions
- rubrics on the exam paper.

(2) Negative imperatives

Put **ne** and **pas** (or other negation) around the verb.

N'aie pas peur. *Don't be afraid.*

Ne soyez jamais impolis. *Never be rude.*

Ne portez pas de maquillage. *Don't wear make-up.*

(10) Practice

1 Your friend has left some directions for you in a voicemail. Listen to the instructions and write the correct letter in each box.

A	Continue straight ahead.
B	Cross the square.
C	Cross the bridge.
D	Go as far as the traffic lights.
E	Go towards the river.
F	Go up to the crossroads.
G	Turn left.
H	Turn right.

1	On leaving the station, ...	
2	At the traffic lights, ...	
3	After 200 metres, ...	
4	At the end of the rue Victor Hugo, ...	

2 Translate the following sentences into English.

(a) Pour une vie saine...

(b) ... buvez huit verres d'eau par jour.

(c) ... mangez au moins cinq portions de fruits et de légumes par jour.

(d) ... ne fumez pas.

(e) ... évitez les aliments riches en matières grasses.

(f) ... faites de l'exercice régulièrement.

(g) ... ne restez pas assis trop longtemps.

Impersonal verbs

Impersonal verbs are used to make general statements. They are only used in the **il** form of the verb.

⑤ Il y a

- **Il y a** means *there is* or *there are*.
  Il y a des magasins près de chez moi. *There are some shops near my home.*
- **Il y avait** means *there was* or *there were* (imperfect).
  Il y avait du brouillard. *It was foggy.*
  Il y avait une trentaine d'invités. *There were about thirty guests.*
- **Il y aura** means *there will be* (future).
  Il y aura du monde. *There will be a lot of people.*
  il y a + period of time = *ago*
  il y a un an = *a year ago*

② Il faut

Il faut comes from the verb **falloir** *(to be necessary)*. Use it as an alternative to **devoir**. It can be followed by an infinitive or by **que** + subjunctive (see page 96).

It can be translated in different ways, depending on the context.

Il faut partir de bonne heure. *You / we have to leave early.*

You might see it used in other tenses, such as imperfect (**il fallait**) and future (**il faudra**).

Il faudra trouver un emplacement. *We will have to find a camping spot.*

⑤ Weather expressions

Il fait is used for a lot of common weather phrases.
Il fait beau / mauvais. *It is fine / bad weather.*
Il faisait chaud / froid. *It was hot / cold.*
Il fera beau. *It will be nice weather.*

present	imperfect	future
il pleut *it's raining*	il pleuvait *it was raining*	il pleuvra *it will rain*
il neige *it's snowing*	il neigeait *it was snowing*	il neigera *it will snow*
il gèle *it's freezing*	il gelait *it was freezing*	il gèlera *it will be freezing*

② Other impersonal verbs

il reste *there is / are ... left*
Il reste des places. *There are some seats left.*
il manque *it is missing / lacking*
Il manque du pain. *The bread is missing / There is no bread left.*
Il manque de personnel. *There is a lack of staff.*
il vaut mieux *it's better / it would be better / best.*
Il vaut mieux venir maintenant. *It's best to come now.*

② Impersonal phrases with *être*

Il est facile de trouver de l'information. *It's easy to find some information.*

Il est difficile de comprendre ce texte. *It is difficult to understand this text.*

Il est possible de trouver des solutions. *It's possible to find some solutions.*

Il est défendu de fumer. *It is forbidden to smoke.*

> Use **C'est...** if you are using an adjective only:
> **C'est facile.** *It's easy.*
> **C'est incroyable.** *It's incredible.*

⑤ Aiming higher

Use impersonal verbs to expand and develop your answers.
il s'agit de *it's about / it's a question of*
Il s'agit d'un garçon et d'une fille... *It's about a boy and a girl...*
il suffit de *it's enough to / you just have to*
Il suffit d'acheter un billet. *You just need to buy a ticket.*
Il semble qu'il va arriver en retard. *It seems that he is going to arrive late.*

⑩ Practice

1 Translate the following sentences into French.
- ✏ **(a)** There is some money left.
- **(b)** It was windy.
- **(c)** There is a lack of information.
- **(d)** It was about a true story.

2 Translate the following sentences into English.
- ✏ **(a)** À cause de la grève, il fallait aller au collège à pied.
- **(b)** Il suffit de parler avec lui.
- **(c)** Il est interdit de marcher sur la pelouse.

The infinitive

The infinitive is the form of the verb you will find first in the dictionary.

About the infinitive

In English, the infinitive has *to* in front of the verb: *to do; to eat*. In French, the infinitive form of the verb ends in -er, -ir or -re: **jouer, choisir, attendre**.

The infinitive is used after a number of common verbs such as: **aimer, adorer, détester** and **préférer**.
With these verbs, the infinitive is often translated into English by *-ing*: **J'aime jouer du piano.** *I like playing the piano.*

Verbs followed by the infinitive

Common verbs that are followed by another verb in the infinitive (without **de** or **à**) are:

- **Modal verbs**: **vouloir, pouvoir** and **devoir**
  Peux-tu venir ce soir? *Can you come this evening?*
  Je veux voir ce film. *I want to see this film.*
  Nous devons porter un uniforme. *We have to wear a uniform.*
- **Aller** to form the immediate future tense:
  Je vais étudier le français. *I am going to study French.*
- Verbs such as **aimer, détester, espérer, préférer** and **savoir**.
  J'espère prendre une année sabbatique. *I hope to take a gap year.*

Aiming higher

Include verbs that are followed by the preposition **à** + infinitive of another verb.

s'amuser à *to enjoy oneself (doing);* **apprendre à** *to learn;*
commencer à *to begin;* **continuer à** *to continue;*
hésiter à *to hesitate;* **inviter à** *to invite;*
se mettre à *to start*
Il a commencé à pleuvoir. *It started to rain.*
J'ai appris à faire du ski. *I learnt how to ski.*

Include verbs that are followed by the preposition **de** + infinitive of another verb.

décider de *to decide;* **essayer de** *to try;*
oublier de *to forget;* **refuser de** *to refuse;*
s'arrêter de *to stop*
Il a oublié d'acheter le pain. *He forgot to buy the bread.*

> **venir de** + infinitive means *to have just done something.*
> **Je viens de visiter la France.** *I have just visited France.*

Prepositions + infinitive

Use the infinitive after the following prepositions: **pour** (*for*), **sans** (*without*), **au lieu de** (*instead of*) and **avant de** (*before*).

Je prends le petit-déjeuner avant d'aller au collège.
I have breakfast before going to school.

J'ai lu mon livre au lieu de regarder la télé.
I read my book instead of watching television.

Je vais en ville pour acheter des provisions.
I am going to town to buy some food.

Perfect infinitive

The perfect infinitive is **avoir** or **être** + the past participle of the verb: **avoir mangé; être arrivé(e/s)**.

It is often used after **après** to mean *after having done something*.

Après avoir fait mes devoirs, j'ai regardé la télé.
After having done my homework, I watched TV.

Après être rentrées chez elles, les filles ont bu un chocolat chaud.
After having returned home, the girls drank a hot chocolate.

> The past participle **rentrées** has to agree with the subject to which it refers.

Practice

1 Translate the following sentences into French.
- **(a)** He hates doing his homework.
- **(b)** She loves listening to music.
- **(c)** I tried to learn the new words.
- **(d)** I can (know how to) speak Chinese.

2 Translate the following sentences into English.
- **(a)** On nous a invités à participer à un sondage.
- **(b)** Après avoir mangé, on est allés au cinéma.
- **(c)** Ils ont décidé de partir de bonne heure.
- **(d)** Il est parti sans dire un mot.

The present participle

The present participle ends in **-ant** in French and is the equivalent of *-ing* in English.

About the present participle

The present participle is used to show that two things are happening at the same time and can be translated by *while –ing* something.

Il a fait ses devoirs en écoutant de la musique.
He did his homework while listening to music.

Elle a parlé avec ses copines en attendant le car de ramassage.
She talked to her friends while waiting for the school bus.

Formation of the present participle

The present participle is formed by removing the **-ons** ending from the **nous** form of the present tense, and adding **-ant**.

nous écrivons → écrivant

nous choisissons → choisissant

The present participle follows **en**:

en écrivant; en choisissant

The following verbs have irregular present participles:

être → étant

avoir → ayant

savoir → sachant.

Aiming higher

Using the present participle to convey the idea of *while* or *on doing* something is a feature of higher level answers.

Elle avait perdu son portable en faisant de la voile.
She lost her mobile phone while sailing.

Il a fait du repassage en regardant la télévision.
He did the ironing while watching TV.

En faisant ses devoirs de français, elle a appris tout son vocabulaire.
While doing her French homework, she learnt all her vocabulary.

En rentrant du collège, il a allumé la télévision. *On returning home from school, he switched on the TV.*

By –ing...

Nicole a amélioré son français...
Nicole improved her French...

... en apprenant beaucoup de mots.
... by learning a lot of words.

... en écoutant des podcasts.
... by listening to podcasts.

... en faisant des exercices de grammaire.
... by doing grammar exercises.

... en lisant des textes en ligne.
... by reading texts on line.

As a noun

The present participle is sometimes used as a noun. In this case it has masculine and feminine forms and the noun rarely contains *–ing*.

un étudiant / une étudiante *student*

un participant / une participante *participant*

un enseignant / une enseignante *teacher*

un assistant / une assistante *assistant*

As an adjective

The present participle can often be used as an adjective. It has to agree with the noun or pronoun it corresponds with.

une ville charmante *a charming town*

une histoire fascinante *a fascinating story*

des voitures polluantes *polluting cars*

un sport fatigant *a tiring sport*

Practice

🖉 Translate the following sentences into English.

(a) Ayant peur de la violence, elle n'est pas allée voir ce film de guerre.

(b) En épargnant son argent de poche, il a pu acheter un nouveau vélo.

(c) Il s'est trouvé en difficulté en nageant.

(d) Je me suis coupé le doigt en préparant le dîner.

(e) En entendant le bruit, nous nous sommes réveillés.

 Made a start **Feeling confident** **Exam ready**

The passive voice

The passive form is when the subject has something done to it, rather than actively doing whatever is expressed in the verb.

About the passive

In a passive sentence, the subject is not doing the action, but having something done to it.

The boy broke the window. (active)

The window was broken by the boy. (passive)

The passive is formed by using an **être** auxiliary (tense dependent on context) + past participle. The past participle has to agree with the subject.

La fenêtre a été cassée par le garçon.

> This agrees with **fenêtre** (feminine singular).

Le dîner est servi.

Forming the passive

The passive can have different tenses, by using different tenses of the verb **être**.

Present: **Les bouteilles sont recyclées.** *The bottles are recycled.*

Perfect: **Les bouteilles ont été recyclées.** *The bottles were recycled.*

Pluperfect: **Les bouteilles avaient été recyclées.** *The bottles had been recycled.*

Future: **Les bouteilles seront recyclées.** *The bottles will be recycled.*

Use of the passive

The passive is often used to describe processes.

Les plantes sont cultivées dans des pays tropicaux. *The plants are cultivated in tropical countries.*

Les grains de café sont cueillis par des ouvriers. *The coffee beans are picked by the workers.*

Ils sont transportés en bateau vers les pays européens. *They are transported by boat to European countries.*

Le café est mis en paquet dans des usines, et il est vendu partout. *The coffee is packaged in factories and is sold all over.*

Avoiding the passive

It is often more natural in French to use other constructions and avoid the passive. The sentence can use **on** instead (note that the English translation might still use a passive form if appropriate).

On a construit l'église au douzième siècle. *The church was built in the twelfth century.*

On a réduit les prix. *Prices have been reduced.*

On a organisé des excursions. *Outings were organised. / They organised outings.*

On m'a invité au mariage. *I was invited to the wedding.*

A verb can sometimes be made reflexive to avoid the passive.

Comment ça s'écrit? *How is that written?*

Aiming higher

Although you are not expected to be able to use the passive at GCSE level, if you feel confident you could include an example, such as: **Il a été invité.** (*He was invited*). You are expected to recognise the use of the passive at Higher level in your French GCSE.

Practice

✏ Translate the following sentences into English

(a) Le château a été construit au seizième siècle.

(b) La rue est bloquée par un arbre.

(c) Les bâtiments ont été détruits par le tremblement de terre.

(d) Les voleurs ont été arrêtés.

(e) Les prix seront réduits.

The subjunctive mood

The subjunctive mood is a form of the verb that is used in certain circumstances, such as expressing uncertainty.

⑤ About the subjunctive

The subjunctive mood has four different tenses: present, imperfect, perfect and pluperfect. However, at Higher level GCSE you will only be expected to recognise some common expressions in the present tense form.

The subjunctive is usually introduced by a verb that expresses an opinion, attitude or emotion, followed by **que**.

Je veux qu'il vienne à ma fête. *I want him to come to my party.*

Je suis désolé que tu sois malade. *I am sorry that you are ill.*

It is also used after expressions such as:

- **il faut que** *it is necessary that*
- **bien que** *although*
- **quoique** *although*
- **pour que** *so that*
- **afin que** *so that*
- **jusqu'à ce que** *until.*

⑤ Using the subjunctive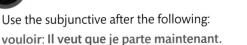

Use the subjunctive after the following:

vouloir: Il veut que je parte maintenant.
He wants me to leave now.

préférer: Je préfère qu'elle s'en aille maintenant.
I'd prefer that she go away now. / I'd prefer her to go away now.

croire + negative: Je ne crois pas que vous ayez raison.
I don't think that you are right.

regretter: Je regrette qu'ils soient en retard.
I regret that they are late.

Il est important que vous compreniez.
It's important that you understand.

Il faut qu'on boive de l'eau.
We must drink some water.

⑤ Common irregular forms

faire → Il faut que je le fasse. *I must do it.*

pouvoir → Il est important que tu puisses venir.
It's important that you are able to come.

savoir → Je veux que tu saches la vérité.
I want you to know the truth.

The verbs **être, avoir** and **aller** are also irregular:

être: sois, sois, soit, soyons, soyez, soient

avoir: aie, aies, aie, ayons, ayez, aient

aller: aille, ailles, aille, allions, alliez, aillent.

Vive la France!

Vive la France! is a patriotic expression that uses the subjunctive of **vivre.** It means *Long live France!* People say it at sporting events, national holidays and political rallies. You might also hear **Vive la liberté!** (*Long live liberty!*), **Vive l'égalité!** (*Long live equality!*) and **Vive la fraternité!** (*Long live fraternity!*)

⑤ Formation of present subjunctive

As a general rule the present subjunctive is formed by removing the **-ent** ending from the **ils / elles** form of the present tense and adding the subjunctive endings: -e, -es, -e, -ions, -iez, -ent .

	ils jouent	ils finissent	ils vendent
je	joue	finisse	vende
tu	joues	finisses	vendes
il / elle / on	joue	finisse	vende
nous	jouions	finissions	vendions
vous	jouiez	finissiez	vendiez
ils / elles	jouent	finissent	vendent

- The **nous** and **vous** forms are the same as the imperfect tense.
- For –**er** verbs, the singular and **ils / elles** forms are the same as the present tense.
- For –**ir** and –**re** verbs, the **ils / elles** form is the same as the present tense.

⑩ Practice

✏ Translate the following sentences into English.

(a) Je préfère aller à pied, bien que j'aie une voiture.

(b) Je lui ai envoyé un e-mail afin qu'il sache l'heure du rendez-vous.

(c) Je resterai près du téléphone jusqu'à ce qu'il revienne.

(d) Bien qu'il soit riche, il n'est pas généreux.

General vocabulary

Time expressions

à la fois	at the same time
à l'avenir	in the future
à l'heure	on time
an (m)	year
année (f)	year
après	after
après-demain	the day after tomorrow
après-midi	afternoon
aujourd'hui	today
auparavant	formerly, in the past
avant	before
avant-hier	the day before yesterday
bientôt	soon
d'abord	at first, firstly
d'habitude	usually
de bonne heure	early
début (m)	start
demain	tomorrow
dernier / dernière	last
de temps en temps	from time to time
déjà	already
de nouveau	again
en attendant	whilst waiting (for), meanwhile
en avance	in advance
en ce moment	at the moment
en retard	late
en même temps	at the same time
encore une fois	once more, again
enfin	at last, finally
environ	about, approximately
fin (f)	end
hier	yesterday
il y a	ago
jour (m)	day
journée (f)	day
lendemain (m)	the next day
longtemps	a long time
maintenant	now

matin (m)	morning
mois (m)	month
normalement	normally
nuit (f)	night
parfois	sometimes
passé (m)	past
pendant	during
plus tard	later
presque	almost, nearly
prochain	next
quelquefois	sometimes
rarement	rarely
récemment	recently
semaine (f)	week
seulement	only
siècle (m)	century
soir (m)	evening
soudain	suddenly
souvent	often
suivant	following
tard	late
tôt	early
toujours	always, still
tous les jours	every day
tout à coup	suddenly, all of a sudden
tout de suite	immediately
vite	quickly

Seasons

printemps (m)	spring
été (m)	summer
automne (m)	autumn
hiver (m)	winter

Weather

averse (f)	shower
briller	to shine
brouillard (m)	fog
brume (f)	mist
chaleur (f)	heat
ciel (m)	sky
climat (m)	climate

couvert	overcast
doux	mild
éclair (m)	lightning
éclaircie (f)	bright spell
ensoleillé	sunny
faire beau	to be fine (weather)
faire mauvais	to be bad (weather)
geler	to freeze
glace (f)	ice
humide	humid, wet
météo (f)	weather forecast
mouillé	wet
neiger	to snow
nuage (m)	cloud
nuageux	cloudy
ombre (f)	shade, shadow
orage (m)	storm
orageux	stormy
pleuvoir	to rain
pluie (f)	rain
sec / sèche	dry
tempête (f)	storm
temps (m)	weather
tonnerre (m)	thunder
tremper	to soak
vent (m)	wind

Greetings and exclamations

à bientôt	see you soon
à demain	see you tomorrow
à tout à l'heure	see you soon / later
allô	hello (on phone)
amitiés	best wishes
au secours	help
bien sûr	of course, certainly
bienvenue	welcome
bon anniversaire	happy birthday
bon appétit	enjoy your meal
bon voyage	have a good trip
bonne année	happy new year
bonne chance	good luck
bonne idée	good idea
bonne nuit	good night

 Made a start   **Feeling confident**   ☑ **Exam ready**

bonnes vacances	have a good holiday	franchement	frankly	marrant	funny
bonsoir	good evening	généralement	generally	mauvais	bad
d'accord	ok	(s')intéresser à	to be interested in	merveilleux / merveilleuse	marvellous
de rien	don't mention it	marre (en avoir)	(to be) fed up	mignon / mignonne	cute
désolé(e)	sorry	(moi) non plus	nor me neither, nor do I	moche	ugly
excusez-moi	excuse me	penser	to think	nouveau	new
félicitations	congratulations	peut-être	perhaps	nul	rubbish
joyeux Noël	Merry Christmas	préférer	to prefer	parfait	perfect
meilleurs voeux	best wishes	promettre	to promise	passionnant	exciting
pardon	excuse me	sembler	to seem	pratique	practical
quel dommage	what a pity	supporter	to put up with	ridicule	ridiculous
salut	hi	vouloir	to wish, want	rigolo	funny
santé	cheers	vraiment	really, truly	sage	well behaved
s'il te / vous plaît	please			sensass	sensational
				utile	useful

Expressing opinions

Opinions: adjectives

Questions

absolument	absolutely	affreux	awful	à quelle heure?	at what time?
avis (m)	opinion	agréable	pleasant	ça s'écrit comment?	how is that written?
à mon avis	in my opinion	amusant	funny	c'est combien?	how much is it?
bien entendu	of course	barbant	boring	c'est quelle date?	what is the date?
bien sûr	of course	casse-pieds	annoying	c'est quel jour?	what day is it?
ça dépend	that depends	cher	dear, expensive	de quelle couleur?	what colour?
ça m'énerve	it gets on my nerves	chouette	great	d'où?	from where?
ça me fait rire	it makes me laugh	compliqué	complicated	où?	where?
ça me plaît	I like it	content	happy	pour combien de temps?	for how long?
ça m'est égal	it's all the same to me	désagréable	unpleasant	pourquoi?	why?
ça ne me dit rien	it means nothing to me / I don't fancy that / I don't feel like it	drôle	funny	quand?	when?
		embêtant	annoying	que?	what?
ça suffit	that's enough	enchanté	delighted	que veut dire...?	what does...mean?
certainement	certainly	ennuyeux	boring	quel / quelle?	which?
comme ci comme ça	so-so	étonné	astonished, amazed	quelle heure est-il?	what time is it?
croire	to believe	facile	easy	qu'est-ce que?	what?
désirer	to want	faible	weak	qu'est-ce qui?	what?
détester	to hate	formidable	great	qu'est-ce que c'est?	what is it?
dire	to say	génial	great	qui?	who?
en général	in general	grave	serious	quoi?	what?
espérer	to hope	habile	clever		
évidemment	obviously	injuste	unfair		
		intéressant	interesting		
		inutile	useless		
		incroyable	incredible		
		inquiet / inquiète	worried		

Conjunctions and connectives

à cause de	because of
à part	apart from
ainsi	so, therefore
alors	so, therefore, then
aussi	also
car	because
cependant	however
c'est-à-dire	that is to say, ie
comme	as, like
d'un côté / de l'autre côté	on the one hand / on the other hand
donc	so, therefore
ensuite	next
mais	but
même si	even if
ou	or
par contre	on the other hand
par exemple	for example
pendant que	while
pourtant	however
puis	then
puisque	seeing that, since
quand	when
sans doute	undoubtedly, without doubt, probably
si	if
y compris	including

Location and distance

à droite	on / to the right
à gauche	on / to the left
banlieue (f)	suburb
centre-ville (m)	town centre
campagne (f)	countryside
chez	at the house of
de chaque côté	from each side
de l'autre côté	from the other side
en bas	down(stairs)
en haut	up(stairs)
est (m)	east
ici	here

là	there
là-bas	over there
loin de	far from
nord (m)	north
nulle part	nowhere
ouest (m)	west
par	by
partout	everywhere
quelque part	somewhere
situé(e)	situated
sud (m)	south
tout droit	straight ahead
tout près	very near
toutes directions	all directions
ville (f)	town

Colours

blanc / blanche	white
bleu	blue
brun	brown (of hair)
châtain	light brown
clair	light
foncé	dark
gris	grey
marron	brown
noir	black
noisette	hazel
violet	purple
rose	pink
rouge	red
roux	ginger
vert	green

Weights and measures

assez	enough, quite
bas	low
boîte (f)	box, tin, can
bouteille (f)	bottle
court	short
demi (m)	half
encore de	more
étroit	narrow
haut	high

large	wide
moitié (f)	half
morceau (m)	piece
nombre (m)	number
paquet (m)	packet
pas mal de	lots of
peser	to weigh
peu	little
un peu de	a little
plein de	full of, lots of
plus de	more
pointure (f)	size (for shoes)
suffisamment	sufficiently
taille (f)	size (for clothes)
tranche (f)	slice
trop	too (much)

Shape

carré	square
rond	round

Access

complet / complète	full
entrée (f)	entry, entrance
libre	free, vacant, unoccupied
fermer	to close
interdit	forbidden, not allowed
occupé	taken, occupied, engaged
ouvert	open
ouvrir	to open
sortie (f)	exit

Correctness

avoir raison	to be right
avoir tort	to be wrong
corriger	to correct
erreur (f)	error, mistake
faute (f)	fault, mistake
faux / fausse	false
il (me) faut	you (I) must

juste	correct	annuler	to cancel	frapper	to knock / hit
obligatoire	compulsory	appeler	to call	habiter	to live
parfait	perfect	s'appeler	to be called	(s')habituer à	to get used to
sûr	certain, sure	arriver	to arrive	informer	to inform
se tromper	to make a mistake	s'asseoir	to sit down	introduire	to introduce
vrai	true	attendre	to wait (for)	inviter	to invite
		atterrir	to land	lever	to lift

Materials

argent (m)	silver	avoir	to have	manger	to eat
béton (m)	concrete	bavarder	to chat	marcher	to walk
bois (m)	wood	casser	to break	mériter	to deserve
cuir (m)	leather	changer	to change	monter	to climb / go up
fer (m)	iron	charger	to load / charge	monter dans	to get on / in
laine (f)	wool	coller	to stick	montrer	to show
or (m)	gold	connaître	to know (be familiar with)	noter	to note
soie (f)	silk			s'occuper de	to look after
verre (m)	glass	conseiller	to advise	offrir	to give (presents)
		contacter	to contact	organiser	to organise

Comparatives and superlatives

		décider	to decide	ouvrir	to open
plus / moins	more / less	décrire	to describe	pardonner	to forgive
plus que / moins que	more than / less than	se dépêcher	to hurry	parler	to speak
		descendre	to go down	passer	to pass (by)
bon / meilleur / le meilleur	good / better / best	désirer	to want / desire	perdre	to lose
		détester	to hate	pleurer	to cry
mauvais / pire / le pire	bad / worse / worst	dire	to say, tell	poser	to put down
		se disputer	to argue	poser une question	to ask a question
bien / mieux / le mieux	well / better / best	donner	to give		
		durer	to last	pousser	to push
mal / plus mal / le plus mal	badly / worse / worst	s'échapper	to escape	pouvoir	to be able
		écouter	to listen	préférer	to prefer
beaucoup / plus / le plus	lots / more / the most	écrire	to write	présenter	to present
		emprunter	to borrow	se présenter	to introduce oneself
peu / moins / le moins	few, little / less / the least	entendre	to hear	prêter	to lend
		en train de (faire...)	(to be) doing	prévenir	to warn
		entrer	to enter / go in	se promener	to go for a walk

General verbs

		s'ennuyer	to be bored	quitter	to leave (a place)
accepter	to accept	être	to be	raconter	to tell
accompagner	to accompany	expliquer	to explain	se rappeler	to remember
adorer	to love	se fâcher	to get angry	rater	to miss / mess up
s'adresser à	to speak to	faire la connaissance	to get to know	rechercher	to research
aimer	to like			recommander	to recommend
ajouter	to add	fermer	to close / switch off	regretter	to regret / be sorry
s'amuser	to enjoy oneself	finir	to finish / end	rembourser	to refund

  Made a start **Feeling confident** ✓ **Exam ready**

remettre	to put back
remplacer	to replace
rendre visite à	to visit (a person)
rentrer	to return
réparer	to repair
répondre	to answer / reply
ressembler à	to look like / resemble
réviser	to revise
rire	to laugh
rouler	to go along (in a car)
sauter	to jump
sembler	to seem
servir	to serve
se servir de	to use
signer	to sign
sonner	to ring
souhaiter	to wish
sourire	to smile
se souvenir de	to remember
stationner	to park
sur le point de (être)	(to be) about to
se taire	to be quiet
taper	to type
téléphoner	to phone
tenir	to hold
se terminer	to end
tirer	to pull
tomber	to fall
toucher	to touch
tourner	to turn
se trouver	to be located
venir	to come
vérifier	to check
visiter	to visit (a place)
vivre	to live
vouloir	to want

Higher tier

se débrouiller	to get by, to cope
déranger	to disturb
donner sur	to overlook
manquer	to miss
paraître	to seem
plaire	to please
traduire	to translate

Common abbreviations

CDI centre de documentation et d'information (m)	resource centre
CES collège d'enseignement secondaire (m)	secondary school
EPS éducation physique et sportive (f)	PE (physical education)
HLM habitation à loyer modéré (f)	council / social housing accommodation
SAMU service d'aide médicale d'urgence (m)	emergency medical services
SDF sans domicile fixe (m/f)	homeless person
SNCF société nationale des chemins de fer français (f)	National Rail Service
TGV train à grande vitesse (m)	high-speed train
TVA taxe sur la valeur ajoutée (f)	VAT (Value Added Tax)
VTT vélo tout terrain (m)	mountain bike

Negatives

ne...jamais	never
ne...pas	not
ne...personne	nobody, no-one
ne...plus	no more, no longer
ne...que	only, nothing but
ne...rien	nothing
ni...ni	neither...nor
pas encore	not yet

Prepositions

à	to, at
à côté de	next to
à travers	across, through
au bord de	at the side / edge of
au bout de	at the end of (ie length, rather than time)
au-dessous de	beneath, below
au-dessus de	above, over
au fond de	at the back of, at the bottom of
au lieu de	instead of
au milieu de	in the middle of
autour de	around
contre	against
de	of, from
depuis	since, for
derrière	behind
devant	in front of
en	in, within (time)
en dehors de	outside (of)
en face de	opposite
entre	between
jusqu'à	up to, until
malgré	despite, in spite of
parmi	amongst
pour	for, in order to
près de	near
sans	without
selon	according to
sous	under
sur	on
vers	towards

Lifestyle

Describing appearance

barbe (f)	*beard*
beau / bel / belle	*beautiful*
bouclé	*curly*
cheveux (m pl)	*hair*
court	*short*
frisé	*curly*
gros / grosse	*fat*
jeune	*young*
joli	*pretty*
laid	*ugly*
long / longue	*long*
lunettes (f pl)	*glasses*
maigre	*skinny, thin*
mince	*slim, thin*
mi-long	*medium length*
moyen / moyenne	*medium, average*
raide	*straight*
de taille moyenne	*medium height*
vieux / vieil / vieille	*old*
yeux (m pl)	*eyes*

Higher tier

bouton (m)	*spot, pimple*
ondulé	*wavy*

Describing personality

aimable	*kind*
aîné	*elder*
s'appeler	*to be called*
avoir...ans	*to be...years old*
bavard	*chatty / talkative*
bête	*stupid, silly*
célèbre	*famous*
égoïste	*selfish*
fâché	*angry*
généreux / généreuse	*generous*
gentil / gentille	*kind, nice*
heureux / heureuse	*happy*
méchant	*naughty*

paresseux / paresseuse	*lazy*
pénible	*annoying*
sens de l'humour (m)	*sense of humour*
sportif / sportive	*sporty*
sympa	*kind, nice*
timide	*shy*
tranquille	*quiet, calm*
travailleur / travailleuse	*hard-working*
triste	*sad*

Higher tier

compréhensif / compréhensive	*understanding*
confiance (f)	*trust*
de mauvaise humeur	*bad tempered*
esprit (m)	*mind*
étonnant	*amazing*
étrange	*strange*
fier / fière	*proud*
fou / folle	*mad, crazy*
gêner	*to annoy*
jaloux / jalouse	*jealous*
marre (en avoir)	*(to be) fed up*
mépriser	*to despise*
se mettre en colère	*to get angry*
vif / vive	*lively*

Relationships

amour (m)	*love*
beau-père (m)	*step-father*
belle-mère (f)	*step-mother*
célibataire	*single*
copain (m) / copine (f)	*friend, mate*
demi-frère (m)	*half-brother*
demi-sœur (f)	*half-sister*
se disputer	*to argue*
ensemble	*together*
s'entendre (avec)	*to get on (with)*
se faire des amis	*to make friends*
femme (f)	*wife / woman*

fille (f)	*daughter / girl*
fils (m)	*son*
grand-mère (f)	*grandmother*
grand-père (m)	*grandfather*
grands-parents (m pl)	*grandparents*
mari (m)	*husband*
se marier	*to get married, marry*
mort	*dead*
naissance (f)	*birth*
né(e) le...	*born on the...*
nom (m)	*name*
partager	*to share*
partenaire (m/f)	*partner*
petit ami (m)	*boyfriend*
petite amie (f)	*girlfriend*
petite-fille (f)	*granddaughter*
petit-fils (m)	*grandson*
prénom (m)	*first name*
rapports (m pl)	*relationships*
séparé	*separated*
sortir	*to go out*
tante (f)	*aunt*
unique	*only*

Higher tier

bague (f)	*ring*
connaître	*to know (a person)*
épouser	*to marry*
fiançailles (f pl)	*engagement*
gâter	*to spoil*
jumeau (m) / jumelle (f)	*twin*
jeunesse (f)	*youth*
mourir	*to die*
naître	*to be born*
neveu (m)	*nephew*
noces (f pl)	*wedding*
se rendre compte	*to realise*
(se) séparer	*to separate*

Healthy living

aller bien	*to be well*
aller mieux	*to be better*

  Made a start **Feeling confident** **Exam ready**

bonheur (m)	happiness		
se détendre	to relax		
dormir	to sleep		
en bonne forme	fit		
en bonne santé	in good health		
équilibré	balanced		
faible	weak		
faire un régime	to be on a diet		
fatigué	tired		
forme (f)	fitness		
fort	strong		
fumer	to smoke		
garder	to look after		
gras	fatty		
habitude (f)	habit		
laver	to wash		
(se) laver	to get washed		
lentement	slowly		
malade	ill, sick		
maladie (f)	illness		
malsain	unhealthy		
matières grasses (f pl)	fats		
médecin (m)	doctor		
médicament (m)	medicine		
obésité (f)	obesity		
odeur (f)	smell		
pressé	in a hurry, rushed / squeezed		
se relaxer	to relax		
sain	healthy		
santé (f)	health		
(se) sentir	to feel		
sommeil (m)	sleep		
tabac (m)	tobacco		
vomir	to be sick		

Higher tier

avoir sommeil	to be sleepy
cancer (des poumons) (m)	(lung) cancer
crise cardiaque (f)	heart attack
dégoûtant	disgusting
déprimé	depressed
désintoxiquer	to detox
douleur (f)	pain
épuiser	to exhaust
s'entraîner	to train
essoufflé	breathless
foie (m)	liver
hors d'haleine	out of breath
musculation (f)	weight training
peau (f)	skin
quotidien(ne)	daily
respirer	to breathe
soigner	to care for
soin (m)	care
tousser	to cough
valoir mieux	to be better, preferable
voix (f)	voice

Social issues

alcool (m)	alcohol
(s')arrêter	to stop
association caritative (f)	charity
combattre	to combat
devenir	to become
drogue (f)	drug
se droguer	to take drugs
eau potable (f)	drinking water
égalité (f)	equality
espace vert (m)	green area

éviter	to avoid
réussir	to succeed
suivre	to follow
travail bénévole (m)	voluntary work
tuer	to kill
vide	empty

Higher tier

accro	addicted
agir (il s'agit de)	to act (it's a question of)
alcoolique	alcoholic
avertir	to warn
cacher	to hide
coupable	guilty
conseil (m)	advice
consommation (f)	consumption, usage
dette (f)	debt
s'enivrer	to get drunk
enquête (f)	enquiry
entraînement (m)	training
ivre	drunk
mannequin (m)	model
mener	to lead
personnes défavorisées (f pl)	disadvantaged people
renoncer	to give up
sida (m)	AIDS
surveiller	to watch
tabagisme (m)	addiction to smoking
tatouage (m)	tattooing
tenter	to attempt
toxicomane (m/f)	drug addict

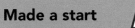

Leisure and the media

Free time

actualités (f pl)	news
argent (m)	money
club des jeunes (m)	youth club
commencer	to start
coûter	to cost
débuter	to begin
essayer	to try
fana de (m)	a fan of
s'intéresser à	to be interested in
passe-temps (m)	hobby
passer du temps	to spend time
payer	to pay (for)
pêche (f)	fishing / peach
prendre	to take
randonnée (f)	walk, hike
rencontrer	to meet
temps libre (m)	free time
vouloir	to wish, want

Higher tier

s'abonner	to subscribe
ado (m/f)	adolescent
chorale (f)	choir
distractions (f pl)	things to do
échecs (m pl)	chess
lieu (m) (avoir lieu)	place (to take place)

Music, cinema and television

billet (m)	ticket
chanter	to sing
chanteur (m) / chanteuse (f)	singer
chanson (f)	song
dessin animé (m)	cartoon
feuilleton (m)	soap opera
film de guerre (m)	war film
film policier (m)	detective film
jeu télévisé (m)	game show
publicité (f)	adverts
série (f)	series
télé réalité (f)	reality television

vedette (f)	film star
voir	to see

Higher tier

effets spéciaux (m pl)	special effects
espèce (f)	type, kind
séance (f)	performance
tournée (f)	tour

Eating out

assiette (f)	plate / dish
boire	to drink
carte (f)	menu
choisir	to choose
commander	to order
goûter	to taste
hors d'œuvre (m)	starter
plat principal (m)	main meal / dish
pourboire (m)	tip
serveur (m) / serveuse (f)	waiter, waitress

Food

alimentation (f)	food
agneau (m)	lamb
beurre (m)	butter
bière (f)	beer
bœuf (m)	beef
boisson (f)	drink
bonbon (m)	sweet
canard (m)	duck
chocolat (m)	chocolate
cerise (f)	cherry
champignon (m)	mushroom
chou (m)	cabbage
chou-fleur (m)	cauliflower
citron (m)	lemon
confiture (f)	jam
crêpe (f)	pancake
crudités (f pl)	raw chopped vegetables
déjeuner (m)	lunch
dîner (m)	evening meal

dinde (f)	turkey
eau (minérale) (f)	(mineral) water
escargot (m)	snail
fraise (f)	strawberry
framboise (f)	raspberry
fruits de mer (m pl)	seafood
glace (f)	ice cream
haricots verts (m pl)	green beans
jambon (m)	ham
lait (m)	milk
légumes (m pl)	vegetables
nourriture (f)	food
œuf (m)	egg
oignon (m)	onion
pâtes (f pl)	pasta
pêche (f)	fishing / peach
petit-déjeuner (m)	breakfast
petits pois (m pl)	peas
poire (f)	pear
poisson (m)	fish
poivre (m)	pepper
pomme (f)	apple
pomme de terre (f)	potato
potage (m)	soup
poulet (m)	chicken
raisins (m pl)	grapes
repas (m)	meal
riz (m)	rice
saucisse (f)	sausage
saumon (m)	salmon
sel (m)	salt
steak haché (m)	burger
sucre (m)	sugar
sucré	sugary
tasse (f)	cup
thé (m)	tea
thon (m)	tuna
truite (f)	trout
viande (f)	meat
yaourt (m)	yoghurt

Higher tier

ail (m)	garlic
amer / amère	sour
ananas (m)	pineapple
bien cuit	well cooked
casse-croûte (m)	snack
épicé	spicy
noix (f)	nut
nourriture bio (f)	organic food
pamplemousse (m)	grapefruit
piquant	spicy
prune (f)	plum
salé	salty
veau (m)	veal

Sport

cheval (m)	horse
basket (m)	basketball
centre sportif (m)	sports centre
courir	to run
équitation (f)	horse riding
escalade (f)	rock climbing
natation (f)	swimming
patin à glace (m)	ice skating
patinoire (f)	ice rink
pêche (f)	fishing / peach
planche à voile (f)	windsurfing
piscine (f)	swimming pool
promenade (f)	walk
skate (m)	skateboarding
ski (nautique) (m)	(water) skiing
sports d'hiver (m pl)	winter sports
stade (m)	stadium
voile (f)	sailing
volley (m)	volleyball

Higher tier

concours (m)	competition
course (f)	race
féliciter	to congratulate

marquer un but / un essai	to score a goal / try
plongée sous-marine (f)	underwater diving
tournoi (m)	tournament

Travel and tourism

accueil (m)	welcome
agence de voyages (f)	travel agency
Alpes (f pl)	Alps
arrivée (f)	arrival
aventure (f)	adventure
bagages (m pl)	luggage
(se) baigner	to bathe, swim
bord de la mer (m)	seaside
bronzer	to sunbathe
carte (f)	map
carte postale (f)	postcard
colonie de vacances (f)	holiday / summer camp
crème solaire (f)	sun cream
départ (m)	departure
Douvres	Dover
échange (m)	exchange
à l'étranger	abroad
étranger (m)	stranger / foreigner
faire du camping	to go camping
Londres	London
lunettes de soleil (f pl)	sun glasses
maillot de bain (m)	swimming costume
Manche (f)	English Channel
nager	to swim
parc d'attractions (m)	theme park
sable (m)	sand
sac de couchage (m)	sleeping bag
spectacle (m)	show
tourisme (m)	tourism
vacances (f pl)	holidays
valise (f)	suitcase

voyager	to travel
vue de mer (f)	sea view

Higher tier

foire (f)	fair
station balnéaire (f)	seaside resort
tour (f)	tower, tour
trajet (m)	journey
traversée (f)	crossing

Countries, nationalities and languages

Afrique (f) / africain	Africa / African
Algérie (f) / algérien	Algeria / Algerian
Allemagne (f) / allemand	Germany / German
Angleterre (f) / anglais	England / English
Belgique (f) / belge	Belgium / Belgian
Chine (f) / chinois	China / Chinese
Ecosse (f) / écossais	Scotland / Scottish
Espagne (f) / espagnol	Spain / Spanish
Etats-Unis (m pl)	USA
Grande-Bretagne (f) / britannique	Great Britain / British
Maroc (m) / marocain	Morocco / Moroccan
Méditerranée (f)	Mediterranean
Pays de Galles (m) / gallois	Wales / Welsh
Suisse (f) / suisse	Switzerland / Swiss
Tunisie (f) / tunisien	Tunisia / Tunisian

Transport

aéroport (m)	airport
auto (f)	car
autobus (m)	bus
autoroute (f)	motorway

avion (m)	plane	propriétaire (m/f)	owner	lecteur MP3 (m)	MP3 player
bateau (m)	boat	rendez-vous (m)	meeting	en ligne	online
car (m)	coach	remercier	to thank	mettre	to put
conduire	to drive	renseignements (m pl)	information	mettre en ligne	to upload
essence (f)	petrol			mot de passe (m)	password
(se) garer	to park	réserver	to book, reserve	ordinateur (m)	computer
moto (f)	motor bike	rester	to stay	ordinateur portable (m)	laptop
route (f)	road, way	retour (m)	return		
voiture (f)	car	retourner	to return	tablette (f)	tablet
vol (m)	flight	revenir	to come back	portable (m)	mobile (phone)
voler	to fly	séjour (m)	stay, visit	recevoir	to receive

Higher tier

atterrir	to land
chemin (m)	way, path
chemin de fer (m)	railway
décoller	to take off
permis de conduire (m)	driving licence
se mettre en route	to set off

tarif (m)	price list / rate
visite (f) (guidée)	(guided) visit

Higher tier

chambre d'hôte (f)	bed and breakfast
climatisation (f)	air conditioning
dresser	to put up (tent)
emplacement (m)	pitch (tent)
événement (m)	event
frontière (f)	border, frontier
héberger	to lodge, accommodate
jumelé	twinned
lavabo (m)	wash basin
lits superposés (m pl)	bunk beds
logement (m)	accommodation
voyage organisé (m)	package holiday

réseau social (m)	social network
rester en contact	to stay in contact
site internet / web (m)	website
souris (f)	mouse
surfer sur Internet	to surf the internet
taper	to type
tchatter	to talk online
télécharger	to download
texto (m)	text
touche (f)	key

Higher tier

bloggeur (m)	blogger
caméscope (m)	camcorder
compte (m)	account
console de jeux (f)	games console
courrier électronique (m)	email
écran tactile (m)	touch screen
effacer	to delete
enregistrer	to record
fichier (m)	file
genre (m)	type, kind
imprimer	to print
internaute (m)	internet user
logiciel (m)	software
moniteur (m)	monitor
numérique	digital
page d'accueil (f)	welcome page
pile (f)	battery
remplir	to fill (in)
sauvegarder	to save
traitement de texte (m)	word processing

Planning and reservations

ascenseur (m)	lift
auberge de jeunesse (f)	youth hostel
chambre familiale (f)	family room
chercher	to look for
clé (f)	key
demi-pension (f)	half board
dortoir (m)	dormitory
horaire (m)	timetable
laisser	to leave
location de voitures (f)	car rental
logement (m)	accommodation
loger	to stay, lodge
loisir (m)	free time (activity)
louer	to hire, rent
partir	to leave
pension complète (f)	full board
pièce d'identité (f)	means of identification
plan de ville (m)	town plan
projet (m)	plan

Everyday technology

acheter	to buy
avantage (m)	advantage
clavier (m)	keyboard
cliquer	to click
dangereux	dangerous
désavantage (m)	disadvantage
écran (m)	screen
envoyer	to send
faire des achats	to shop
forum (m)	chat room
imprimante (f)	printer
inconvénient (m)	disadvantage, drawback
jeu (m)	game
lecteur DVD (m)	DVD player

 Made a start   Feeling confident   ✓ Exam ready

Home and the environment

Describing your home

armoire (f)	wardrobe
bain (m)	bath
bâtiment (m)	building
cave (f)	cellar
se coucher	to go to bed
cuisine (f)	kitchen / cooking
déménager	to move house
douche (f)	shower
escalier (m)	staircase
étage (m)	floor, storey
faire la grasse matinée	to lie in, sleep in
fenêtre (f)	window
jardinage (m)	gardening
immeuble (m)	block of flats
(se) lever	to get up
lit (m)	bed
maison (f) (individuelle / jumelée / mitoyenne)	house (detached / semi-detached / terraced)
meubles (m pl)	furniture
mur (m)	wall
pièce (f)	room
propre	clean, tidy
ranger	to tidy
(se) réveiller	to wake up
rez-de-chaussée (m)	ground floor
sale	dirty
salle à manger (f)	dining room
salle de bains (f)	bathroom
salle de séjour (f)	lounge
salon (m)	living room, lounge
sous-sol (m)	basement

Higher tier

bricolage (m)	DIY (do it yourself)
four (m)	oven
foyer (m)	home
loyer (m)	rent
lumière (f)	light
moquette (f)	carpet
pelouse (f)	lawn

Neighbourhood and town

animé	lively
bibliothèque (f)	library
boucherie (f)	butcher's shop
boulangerie (f)	bakery
bijouterie (f)	jeweller's shop
bruit (m)	noise
bureau (m)	office, study
bruyant	noisy
calme	quiet
centre commercial (m)	shopping centre
charcuterie (f)	delicatessen
circulation (f)	traffic
commerces (m pl)	shops
commissariat (m)	police station
gare (f)	railway station
gare routière (f)	bus station
gens (m pl)	people
grand magasin (m)	department store
habitant (m)	inhabitant
hôtel de ville (m)	town hall
librairie (f)	bookshop
mairie (f)	town hall
marché (m)	market
musée (m)	museum
parc (m)	park
pâtisserie (f)	cake shop
place (f)	square
poste (f)	post office
quartier (m)	quarter, area
station-service (f)	service station
tabac (m)	newsagent's
transport en commun (m)	public transport
se trouver	to be situated
usine (f)	factory
voisin (m)	neighbour
zone piétonne (f)	pedestrian zone

Higher tier

aire de jeux (f)	play area
embouteillage (m)	traffic jam
endroit (m)	place

fermeture (f)	closure
grande surface (f)	superstore
jardin zoologique / zoo (m)	zoo
surchargé	overcrowded

Shopping

aider	to help
besoin (m) (avoir besoin de)	need (to need)
bon marché	cheap
caisse (f)	till
carte bancaire (f)	bank card
choix (m)	choice
chose (f)	thing
démodé	old-fashioned
dépenser	to spend (money)
devoir	to have to
économiser	to save
essayer	to try on
gratuit	free (of charge)
livrer	to deliver
parfum (m)	perfume
pauvre	poor
portefeuille (m)	wallet
porte-monnaie (m)	purse
prix (m)	price
réduire	to reduce
réduit	reduced
soldes (m pl)	sale
vendeur (m) / vendeuse (f)	shop assistant
vendre	to sell
ville (f)	town
vitrine (f)	shop window

Higher tier

lèche-vitrine (m) (faire du)	window shopping (to go window shopping)
marque (f)	make, label, brand
rayon (m)	department
rembourser	to reimburse

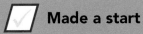

Clothing

baskets (f pl)	trainers
bijou (m)	jewel, jewellery
blouson (m)	coat / jacket
ceinture (f)	belt
chapeau (m)	hat
chaussette (f)	sock
chaussure (f)	shoe
chemise (f)	shirt
cravate (f)	tie
gilet (m)	waistcoat
jupe (f)	skirt
manteau (m)	overcoat
mode (f)	fashion
nettoyer	to clean (clothes)
pantalon (m)	trousers
pull (m)	jumper
robe (f)	dress
veste (f)	jacket
vêtements (m pl)	clothes

Higher tier

écharpe (f)	scarf
foulard (m)	scarf
pull à capuche (m)	hoodie

The environment

arbre (m)	tree
campagne (f)	countryside
champ (m)	field
colline (f)	hill
en plein air	in the open air
environnement (m)	environment
ferme (f)	farm
fleur (f)	flower
île (f)	island
lac (m)	lake
monde (m)	world
montagne (f)	mountain
(à la) montagne (f)	(in the) mountain(s)
paysage (m)	countryside / landscape
plage (f)	beach
rivière (f)	river

sécurité (f)	safety

Higher tier

herbe (f)	grass

Global issues

allumer	to switch on
boîte (f) (en carton)	(cardboard) box
centre de recyclage (m)	recycling centre
chômage (m)	unemployment
chauffage central (m)	central heating
cultiver	to grow
en danger	in danger
déchets (m pl)	rubbish
détruire	to destroy
disparaître	to disappear
éteindre	to switch off
faire du recyclage	to recycle
gaspiller	to waste
inondation (f)	flood
jeter	to throw (away)
ordures (f pl)	rubbish
pauvreté (f)	poverty
pétrole (m)	oil
piste cyclable (f)	cycle lane
pollué	polluted
poubelle (f)	dustbin
protéger	to protect
réchauffement de la Terre (m)	global warming
risque (m)	risk
robinet (m)	tap
sac en plastique (m)	plastic bag
sans-abri (m)	homeless person
sauver	to save
utiliser	to use
vie (f)	life

Higher tier

agresser	to attack
améliorer	to improve
attaque (f)	attack
augmenter	to increase

bande (f)	gang
campagne (f)	campaign
charbon (m)	coal
couche d'ozone (f)	ozone layer
croire	to believe
déboisement (m)	deforestation
effet de serre (m)	greenhouse effect
effrayant	frightening
égal	equal
emballage (m)	packaging
empêcher	to prevent
endommager	to damage
énergie renouvelable (f)	renewable energy
ennui (m)	problem, worry
entouré	surrounded
état (m)	state
gaz carbonique (m)	carbon dioxide
gaz d'échappement (m)	exhaust fumes
guerre (f)	war
harceler	to bully, harass
harcèlement (m)	bullying, harassment
immigré (m)	immigrant
incendie (m)	fire
inconnu	unknown
inonder	to flood
s'inquiéter	to worry
lourd	heavy, serious
lutter	to struggle
manifestation (f)	demonstration
marée (f)	tide
mentir	to lie
mondial	worldwide
niveau (m)	level
paix (f)	peace
perte (f)	loss
(se) plaindre	to complain
produire	to provide
produits bio (m pl)	green products
ramasser	to pick up
reconnaissant	grateful
réfugié (m)	refugee

 Made a start   **Feeling confident**   ✓ **Exam ready**

Work and education

My studies

allemand (m)	German
anglais (m)	English
théâtre (m)	drama
biologie (f)	biology
chimie (f)	chemistry
dessin (m)	art
EPS (f)	PE (physical education)
espagnol (m)	Spanish
études des médias (f pl)	media studies
français (m)	French
géographie (f)	geography
histoire (f)	history
informatique (f)	IT (information technology)
instituteur (m)	primary school teacher (male)
institutrice (f)	primary school teacher (female)
langue (f)	language
mathématiques / maths (f)	maths
matière (f)	subject
musique (f)	music
physique (f)	physics
professeur (m)	teacher
religion (f)	religious studies
sciences (f pl)	sciences

Higher tier

couture (f)	sewing
langues vivantes (f pl)	modern languages
instruction civique (f)	citizenship
proviseur (m)	head teacher

School life

apprendre	to learn
calculette (f)	calculator
collège (m)	secondary school
comprendre	to understand
cours (m)	lesson
demander	to ask
devoirs (m pl)	homework
difficulté (f)	difficulty
diplôme (m)	qualification
directeur (m)	headmaster
directrice (f)	headmistress
discuter	to discuss
distribuer	to give out

droit (m)	right
école (f) (primaire / secondaire)	(primary / secondary) school
élève (m/f)	pupil
emploi du temps (m)	timetable
en seconde	in year 11
études (f pl)	studies
étudiant (m)	student
examen (m)	examination
faire attention	to pay attention
leçon (f)	lesson
lecture (f)	reading
lire	to read
maquillage (m)	make up
note (f)	mark
oublier	to forget
passer un examen	to sit an exam
pause (f)	break, pause
penser	to think
permettre	to allow, permit
porter	to wear, carry
pression (f)	pressure
récré(ation) (f)	break
règle (f)	rule
règlement (m)	school rules
rentrée (f)	return to school
répéter	to repeat
réponse (f)	reply
résultat (m)	result
réussir un examen	to pass an exam
salle de classe (f)	classroom
savoir	to know
scolaire	school (adj)
tableau (m)	board
terrain de sport (m)	sports ground
trimestre (m)	term
trouver	to find

Higher tier

bien équipé	well equipped
bulletin scolaire (m)	school report
car de ramassage (m)	school bus
couloir (m)	corridor
doué	gifted
échouer	to fail
enseigner	to teach

incivilités (f pl)	rudeness	croisière (f)	cruise
injure (f)	insult	débouché (m)	prospect / job prospect / opportunity
mal équipé	badly equipped		
maternelle (f)	nursery school	debout	standing
redoubler	to repeat the year	dessinateur de mode (m); dessinatrice de mode (f)	fashion designer
retenue (f)	detention		

Jobs and careers

		disponible	available
agent de police (m/f)	police officer	élargir	to widen
à temps partiel	part-time	entreprise (f)	firm, enterprise
boucher (m) / bouchère (f)	butcher	entretien (m)	interview
boulanger (m) / boulangère (f)	baker	enrichissant	enriching, rewarding
		interprète (m)	interpreter
boulot (m)	job	outil (m)	tool
candidat(e) (m/f)	candidate	tâche (f)	task
coiffeur (m) / coiffeuse (f)	hairdresser	venir de	to have just
compter (sur)	to count (on)		

Ambitions

employé(e) (m/f)	employee	avenir (m)	future
employeur (m) / employeuse (f)	employer	espérer	to hope
		prêt	ready
facteur (m) / factrice (f)	post officer	rêve (m)	dream
fermier (m) / fermière (f)	farmer	rêver	to dream
gagner	to earn, win		

Higher tier

idée (f)	idea	espoir (m)	hope
infirmier (m) / infirmière (f)	nurse		
informaticien(ne) (m/f)	IT worker		

Education post-16

ingénieur(e) (m/f)	engineer	année sabbatique (f)	gap year
journal (m)	newspaper	apprenti(e) (m/f)	apprentice
livre (f) (sterling)	pound (sterling)	avoir envie de	to want to
maçon(ne) (m/f)	builder	avoir l'intention (de)	to intend (to)
mécanicien(ne) (m/f)	mechanic	bac(alauréat) (m)	A-level(s)
mettre de l'argent de côté	to save money	en première	in year 12
patron(ne) (m/f)	boss	en terminale	in year 13
petit job (m)	part-time job	étudier	to study
plombier (m) / plombière (f)	plumber	laisser tomber	to drop
policier (m) / policière (f)	police officer	liberté (f)	freedom
recevoir	to receive	lycée (m)	sixth form college, grammar school
travailler	to work		
varié	varied		

Higher tier

vétérinaire (m/f)	vet	conseiller d'orientation (m)	careers adviser

Higher tier

à peine	scarcely	épreuve (f)	test
assis	sitting	établissement (m)	establishment
avocat(e) (m/f)	lawyer	faculté (f)	university, faculty
comptable (m/f)	accountant	former	to train
		licence (f)	degree

 Made a start   **Feeling confident**   **Exam ready**

French life and culture

Customs

église (f)	church
juif / juive	Jewish
mosquée (f)	Mosque
musulman	Muslim
religieux / religieuse	religious

Higher tier

défilé (m)	procession
jour férié (m)	public holiday
messe (f)	mass
réunion (f)	meeting

Festivals and celebrations

cadeau (m)	present
fête (f)	festival, celebration, party

fête des mères (f)	Mother's Day
fête des rois (f)	Twelfth Night / Epiphany
fête du travail (f)	May Day
fêter	to celebrate
feux d'artifice (m pl)	fireworks
Jour de l'An (m)	New Year's Day
Pâques	Easter
poisson d'avril	April Fools' Day, April Fool!
Saint-Sylvestre (f)	New Year's Eve
Saint Valentin (f)	St. Valentine's Day
Toussaint (f)	All Saints' Day
réveillon de Noël (m)	Christmas Eve

Higher tier

Pentecôte (f)	Whitsuntide

Transcripts

Page v Paper 1: Listening
Exam explainer

1 Le six janvier, douze jours après Noël, on fête la visite des trois rois à l'enfant Jésus. On mange un gâteau spécial qui s'appelle la galette des Rois.

2 À la grande fête médiévale, on peut assister à la reconstitution de la bataille de Crécy en 1346.

3 Les Francofolies, le grand festival de la chanson francophone actuelle, ont lieu chaque année en juillet à la Rochelle. Au festival, des artistes font parfois filmer leur concert pour un DVD.

4 Plusieurs étapes du tour de France ont lieu dans les Pyrénées. Les montagnes présentent un défi énorme pour les cyclistes.

Page 1 Numbers
Practice

1 37% des Français aiment aller sur des réseaux sociaux.

2 Regarder la télé est l'activité préférée de 84% des gens.

3 63% vont au cinéma pendant leur temps libre.

4 75% préfèrent écouter la radio.

Page 2 The French alphabet
Practice

1 Nous avons réservé nos places sur le TGV.

2 Le soir, je m'occupe des SDFs en travaillant chez les Restos du Coeur.

3 J'ai trouvé ce livre au CDI du collège.

4 Ce que j'adore c'est l'EPS, surtout en été.

5 Le collège se trouve en face de l'HLM.

Page 3 Dates
Practice

1 Le premier jour de la Fête des lumières à Lyon est le huit décembre.

2 Le dernier jour du festival de Cannes est le vingt-huit mai.

3 Le dernier jour de la Fête du Citron à Menton est le premier mars.

4 La Fête de la musique a lieu le vingt et un juin chaque année.

Page 4 Telling the time
Practice

1 - Quand est-ce que le train arrive?

- Le soir, à six heures moins le quart.

2 L'exposition est ouverte de neuf heures à dix-huit heures trente.

3 Ce soir, on va au concert. Il commence à vingt heures quinze.

4 Je me couche tard, vers onze heures du soir.

Page 5 Seasons and weather
Practice

Exemple: Ma saison préférée est l'hiver car j'adore la neige. J'aime faire du ski.

1 J'adore la chaleur d'été parce que je peux me bronzer au soleil.

2 Pour moi, les beaux jours de printemps quand il fait doux sont idéals parce que j'aime faire des promenades à la campagne.

Page 6 Greetings
Practice

1 Bon voyage, prends beaucoup de belles photos!

2 Bon appétit à tous!

3 Je vous souhaite meilleurs voeux pour le Nouvel An!

4 Bonne nuit, dors bien!

Page 9 Describing people
Practice

1 Pour moi, cela n'a aucune importance si elle est grande ou petite. Je cherche tout simplement quelqu'un qui me fait rire.

2 Mon copain idéal serait quelqu'un d'aimable qui prend soin de moi.

3 Les filles qui bavardent tout le temps ne m'intéressent pas. J'aime plutôt les filles qui sont un peu timides.

4 J'aimerais un copain qui est mince et bien taillé. Il serait beau, bien sûr, et il aurait les cheveux bruns.

Page 13 Food
Practice

Voici mes conseils pour une alimentation équilibrée. Au petit-déjeuner, vous pouvez manger 100 grammes de fruit et 50 grammes de pain.

Pour le déjeuner, il faut choisir entre 100 grammes de viande ou 150 grammes de poisson.

Vous devriez consommer au moins 200 grammes de légumes. Cependant, si vous mangez des pommes de terre, il faut limiter votre consommation à 125 grammes.

Le soir, on devrait manger seulement 50 grammes de viande.

Page 15 Feeling unwell

Worked example

Exemple: Michelle a mal aux dents. Elle doit aller chez le dentiste.

Alors, Daniel a la grippe en ce moment et il doit rester au lit.

Carole est tombée en faisant de la gymnastique et elle s'est cassé le bras. Elle ne peut pas écrire en ce moment.

Henri s'est blessé le genou pendant un match de foot. Il a des difficultés à marcher maintenant.

Fatima a mal à l'estomac. Son médecin lui a dit de rester à la maison.

Page 17 Social issues

Practice

1 Depuis un an, je souffre de dépression et c'est ça la cause de tous mes problèmes.

2 Tout allait bien, mais il y a six mois j'ai perdu mon emploi. La vie est vraiment difficile quand on est au chômage.

3 Pourquoi je suis sans-abri? C'est tout simplement le manque de logement à prix raisonnable.

4 Je suis sans-abri parce que ma vie familiale était devenue insupportable. Je me disputais tout le temps avec mes parents, j'ai quitté la maison et me voilà à la rue.

Page 18 Charity and voluntary work

Practice

1 En ce moment, je m'entraîne pour une course sponsorisée de 5km qui aura lieu le week-end prochain.

2 J'adore faire de la pâtisserie. Je suis en train de faire des gâteaux pour une vente de gâteaux.

3 À mon avis, la façon la plus facile d'amasser des fonds est d'utiliser les réseaux sociaux pour informer les autres de nos activités.

Page 20 Cinema

Practice

Avant de lire les critiques enthousiastes, mes copains m'avaient déjà parlé de ce film et ont dit que c'est une super production à ne pas manquer. Au début du film, les vues aériennes qui font la comparaison entre l'Australie et l'Inde sont à couper le souffle. Mais ce sont les scènes tournées sur le train et à la gare où le petit garçon se perd qui vous font pleurer, ainsi que la réunion entre le jeune homme et sa mère naturelle.

Page 24 Travel and transport

Practice

Exemple: Quand je suis arrivé, j'ai pris un taxi qui était rapide, mais cher.

1 Le pire, c'était que le train avait trois heures de retard.

2 On a passé deux jours en bateau et j'avais le mal de mer.

3 Le voyage en avion était confortable, mais on a perdu nos bagages.

4 Le car n'était pas cher, mais il y avait trop de circulation sur l'autoroute.

Page 26 Reservations

Practice

1 On ne pourrait pas trouver un meilleur hôtel, c'était vraiment luxueux avec tout confort.

2 La chambre avait une belle vue sur la rivière et elle n'était pas chère. Cependant, j'étais déçu par la piscine qui n'était pas chauffée.

3 Je ne logerais plus jamais dans cet établissement. Ma chambre était bruyante et sale et les employés étaient impolis.

4 J'avais lu de mauvaises critiques de cet hôtel, mais en fait, je les ai trouvées injustes. Je n'hésiterais pas à y retourner.

Page 27 Describing your holiday

Practice

1 Un jour, on a fait une visite guidée du château le plus historique dans la région, mais le guide ne savait rien!

2 Au grand marché, j'ai trouvé un joli vase, mais j'ai dû négocier, car au début, le prix était trop élevé.

3 Quand je suis arrivé à l'aéroport, je me suis rendu compte que j'avais oublié mon passeport, alors j'ai dû rentrer chez moi pour aller le chercher. Quel idiot!

4 On était allés à un concert en plein air où il y avait une foule de personnes. Quand je suis rentré à l'auberge, j'ai découvert que mon porte-monnaie n'était plus dans mon sac.

Page 28 Social media

Practice

1 On voit des gens assis au café qui ne se parlent pas parce qu'ils passent tout leur temps en ligne. C'est complètement débile.

2 Pour moi les réseaux sociaux me permettent de rester en contact avec ma famille et mes copains que je ne vois pas régulièrement.

3 Il faut faire attention à ce qu'on poste sur les réseaux sociaux. Une photo qui semble amusante aujourd'hui pourrait te compromettre dans l'avenir.

4 Les réseaux sociaux me sont indispensables et m'aident à organiser ma vie. D'ailleurs, je ne suis pas du tout d'accord qu'ils soient une perte de temps.

5 À mon avis, trop de jeunes ne se méfient pas des dangers d'avoir leur identité volée par les criminels. Cependant, on peut bien s'amuser sur les réseaux sociaux.

Page 32 Shopping
Practice

Oui, il y a certainement beaucoup de choix, mais le plus important est que c'est moins cher en ligne. Cependant, ça m'embête quand il faut renvoyer un article qui n'est pas de la bonne taille.

Page 33 Town and region
Worked example

1 Avant, j'habitais une ville industrielle, mais il y a six mois nous avons déménagé dans une maison située dans un petit village à la campagne. La vie ici est beaucoup plus tranquille mais il y a peu de magasins.

2 Depuis quatre ans, j'habite au centre d'une grande ville. On peut y profiter d'une vie culturelle, riche et variée, mais le samedi soir, c'est trop bruyant.

3 Le pire de vivre dans une grande ville est sans doute les embouteillages aux heures de pointe quand les gens vont au travail le matin et rentrent chez eux le soir. Cependant, les transports en commun sont meilleurs qu'à la campagne.

4 Ce que j'apprécie le plus est l'absence de la pollution, mais j'ai un trajet plus long pour aller au collège.

Page 34 The environment
Practice

1 À mon avis, il faut absolument arrêter le gaspillage alimentaire. Tant de gens achètent trop de fruits ou de légumes ou d'autres aliments qu'ils jettent parce qu'ils deviennent pourris.

2 Certes, le développement des sources d'énergie renouvelables est important, mais je pense que nous devons plutôt faire des efforts pour réduire notre consommation d'énergie en éteignant les lumières et les appareils électriques quand nous ne les utilisons pas.

3 Je ne comprends pas pourquoi les producteurs utilisent tant d'emballage pour leurs produits. Nous devrions refuser d'acheter des produits emballés en plastique et carton.

4 L'eau est un bien précieux. Alors il faut éviter le gaspillage autant que possible en prenant des douches au lieu d'un bain et en faisant plus attention à la manière dont nous utilisons cette ressource.

Page 35 Global issues
Practice

1 À mon avis, il faut absolument arrêter la destruction des forêts tropicales car elles sont les poumons de la planète. Sans elles, le réchauffement de la Terre deviendra de plus en plus sévère.

2 Notre dépendance au charbon et pétrole n'est plus durable. Il faut trouver des alternatives en utilisant le vent, le soleil et les vagues.

3 Dans les grandes cités du monde on ne peut plus bien respirer. On ne voit que du brouillard créé par des gaz d'échappement.

4 On ne peut pas éviter des catastrophes comme les tremblements de terre ou l'éruption d'un volcan. Cependant, la protection des animaux et des plantes qui sont en train de disparaître devrait être notre priorité et nous devons les sauver!

Page 36 My studies
Practice

Ma passion, c'est les langues, surtout l'anglais. Le prof rend les cours vraiment intéressants. Il y a plusieurs matières que je n'aime pas, les maths par exemple, car je trouve ça difficile et le prof nous donne trop de devoirs. Cependant, le pire, c'est l'instruction civique, car c'est une perte de temps. En plus, le prof est toujours de mauvaise humeur et il nous critique tout le temps.

Page 37 Your school
Practice

1 Dans mon collège, on manque d'installations modernes technologiques. Pourtant, les profs font toujours des efforts pour nous donner des cours stimulants.

2 Pour ceux qui ne sont pas très scolaires, ce n'est pas le collège pour eux. Il y a trop de redoublements.

3 Le collège nous permet d'être indépendant et d'avoir du succès, même si ce n'est pas du succès scolaire.

4 On nous offre un grand choix d'activités périscolaires, comme des activités sportives, musicales, créatives et culturelles. C'est vraiment inclusif car tout le monde peut y participer selon ses intérêts.

Page 39 Ambitions
Worked example

Quand j'étais tout petit, je voulais devenir astronaute. Cependant, au cours de ma scolarité, je me suis rendu compte que je ne suis pas assez fort en sciences. Ensuite, j'ai développé une passion pour les langues, surtout pour celles qui utilisent les alphabets différents comme le chinois et le russe. Je n'ai pas encore décidé si je prendrai une année sabbatique, bien qu'il y ait plein d'avantages à passer un an à voyager dans le monde et à faire la connaissance d'autres gens et de cultures.

Page 41 Francophone countries
Practice

Le Cameroun, un pays francophone de l'Afrique de l'Ouest, est un des pays les plus pauvres au monde. Dans le domaine de l'éducation, 91% des écoles primaires au Cameroun n'ont pas d'électricité. Parfois les cours doivent être annulés parce que les salles sont mal éclairées.

Un autre problème pour les élèves dans 69% des écoles primaires et dans 73% des collèges au Cameroun est le manque d'accès à l'eau potable.

Encore plus grave, c'est l'absence de toilettes dans 59% des écoles primaires. C'est pour cette raison que beaucoup de filles abandonnent leurs études scolaires.

Page 42 French customs
Practice

1. La gastronomie fait partie du patrimoine culturel de la France. Pour un vrai repas gastronomique, il faut plusieurs jours de préparation.

2. On fait une blague à ses copains ou aux membres de sa famille en leur accrochant un poisson en papier dans le dos en criant 'Poisson d'avril'!.

3. Le jour de la Toussaint, on apporte des fleurs au cimetière et on les laisse sur les tombes à la mémoire des membres de la famille décédés.

4. Les anniversaires, comme celui de la naissance ainsi que celui du mariage, sont une occasion pour se réunir et être ensemble.

Page 47 General conversation
Practice

1. Quelles matières n'aimes-tu pas à l'école?

2. Quelles sont les matières les plus importantes?

3. Qu'est-ce que tu penses des installations sportives dans ton école?

4. Décris un voyage scolaire que tu as fait récemment.

5. Qu'est-ce que tu changerais dans ton école si tu étais le directeur ou la directrice?

6. Comment serait ton ami(e) idéal(e)?

7. Qu'est-ce que tu as fait avec tes ami(e)s récemment?

8. Qu'est-ce que tu penses des réseaux sociaux?

9. Quels sont les dangers d'Internet?

10. Quels sont tes projets pour le week-end prochain?

Page 51 Listening strategies
Practice

Il n'y a pas de doute que les Jeux Olympiques apportent une activité économique importante en attirant plein de visiteurs au pays, mais il ne faut jamais oublier que créer une infrastructure pour les Jeux coûte vraiment cher. Il existe beaucoup de pays endettés à cause des Jeux.

Page 52 Listening
Worked example

1. Depuis le dix-neuvième siècle, la Fête des Lumières a lieu chaque année à Lyon du sept au dix décembre. Cette fête sert à remercier la Vierge Marie, la mère de Jésus Christ, qui aurait libéré la ville de la peste au seizième siècle. Pendant la fête, les façades des monuments et des bâtiments publics, tout comme celle de la cathédrale, sont illuminées avec des couleurs différentes chaque soir. Traditionnellement, les Lyonnais illuminent aussi leurs fenêtres et leurs balcons avec des bougies, placées dans des verres colorés.

2. La ville de Menton, sur la Côte d'Azur, devient un spectacle en jaune et orange pendant la saison du carnaval chaque février. La Fête du Citron attire plus de 230 000 visiteurs qui viennent admirer les défilés avec leurs grands véhicules décorés de citrons et d'oranges, ainsi que les sculptures géantes créées avec ces fruits dans les jardins publics. Quelques-unes de ces structures font plus de dix mètres de haut.

Practice

Suite à une collision entre quatre véhicules sur le boulevard périphérique parisien près de la Porte d'Orléans, un homme est décédé et deux blessés ont été transportés à l'hôpital.

Page 53 Listening: Finding reasons
Worked example 1

1. - Florence, vous portez un uniforme scolaire. Ça vous plaît?
   - Mes amis se plaignent que nous devons porter un uniforme scolaire, mais je le trouve pratique parce que je n'ai pas besoin de passer du temps à décider de ce que je vais mettre chaque matin. Cependant, la veste est assez chère et n'est pas très élégante.

2. - Et vous, Didier. Qu'est-ce que vous en pensez?
   - Pour moi, les vêtements sont un moyen d'exprimer ma personnalité et ils font partie de mon identité. Alors l'uniforme scolaire m'empêche de faire ça. D'autre part, les profs disent que notre comportement en classe est meilleur quand nous portons un uniforme que quand nous mettons nos propres vêtements.

Worked example 2

- Gérard, tu paies en espèces quand tu achètes un café?
- Non, pas du tout. Je n'ai jamais de pièces de monnaie, alors j'utilise ma carte sans contact, c'est plus pratique!

Practice 1

(Interviewer) - Que penses-tu du mariage, Claire?

(Claire) - J'aime bien l'idée de passer ma vie avec une seule personne qui devient mon compagnon constant. D'autre part je ne voudrais pas me marier trop jeune parce que je ne veux pas perdre la liberté de faire ce que je veux.

(Interviewer) - Merci Claire, et maintenant, Hubert?

(Hubert) - Quand on veut fonder une famille je pense que le mariage offre normalement de la stabilité aux enfants. Cependant, la fête elle-même peut devenir incroyablement chère!

Practice 2

1 C'était affreux, nous nous attendions à une belle vue sur la mer, mais notre appartement donnait sur un chantier de construction. On s'est plaint et le propriétaire nous a promis de rembourser la moitié de la location.

2 Quand nous nous sommes installés dans l'hôtel nous avons remarqué que la douche ne fonctionnait pas, alors nous avons dû changer de chambre.

Page 91 The imperative

Practice 1

1 Quand vous arrivez, sortez de la gare et tournez à gauche.

2 Allez tout droit jusqu'aux feux, puis tournez à droite.

3 Prenez la rue Saint Martin. Après deux cents mètres, vous arriverez à la place de la Victoire. Traversez la place.

4 À l'hôtel de ville, descendez la rue Victor Hugo en direction de la rivière et traversez le pont.

Answers

Page x Understanding rubrics

1 Write P+N for a positive and negative opinion.

2 Beware! You can use the same letter more than once.

3 Choose two sentences that are true.

4 Fill in the blanks.

5 Identify the correct person.

6 What is the correct answer?

7 Write the correct letter in the box.

Page 1 Numbers

37% B; 63% A; 75% C; 84% F

Page 2 The French alphabet

1 **1** D; **2** E; **3** F; **4** G; **5** B

2 *Answers will vary.*

Page 3 Dates

1 F **2** D **3** A **4** E

Page 4 Telling the time

1 5:45 p.m. / 17:45

2 6:30 p.m. / 18:30

3 8:15 p.m. / 20:15

4 11 p.m. / 23:00

Page 5 Seasons and weather

1 hot weather / sunbathing

2 mild weather / walks in the countryside

Page 6 Greetings

1 B **2** A **3** D **4** E

Page 7 Opinions

| @noah_K | **P** | @karim | **P/N** |
| @selim_O | **P** | @Loulou | **N** |

Page 8 Asking questions

Model answers:

- Heure du concert (at a box office)
  - *À quelle heure est-ce que le concert commence / finit?*
- Végétarien (in a restaurant with the waiter)
  - *Qu'est-ce qu'il y a sur le menu pour les végétariens?*
  - *Quels plats végétariens avez-vous sur le menu?*
- Projets pour les vacances (talking to a friend)
  - *Qu'est-ce que tu vas faire pendant les vacances?*
  - *Quels sont tes projets pour les vacances?*
- Tarifs pour les étudiants (museum entry)
  - *C'est combien pour les étudiants?*
  - *Est-ce qu'il y a un tarif spécial pour les étudiants?*

Page 9 Describing yourself and others

1 E **2** C **3** F **4** B

Page 10 Family

Model answer:

- Normalement, on reste à la maison le samedi parce que je dois faire mes devoirs et mes parents font des tâches ménagères. S'il fait beau le dimanche, nous sortons pour faire une promenade, mais s'il fait mauvais nous allons peut-être au cinéma. Cependant, le week-end dernier, nous sommes allés voir mes grands-parents qui habitent à Londres. Nous y sommes allés en train car c'est plus pratique et confortable. Nous sommes arrivés vers midi et après avoir déjeuné je leur ai montré des photos de nos vacances récentes.

- À mon avis, il y a plein d'avantages à faire partie d'une famille nombreuse. On peut bien s'amuser ensemble et quand on a beaucoup de frères et de soeurs, on n'est jamais seul car on a toujours quelqu'un avec qui on peut jouer ou parler. Cependant si on se dispute, par exemple, sur ce qu'on regarde à la télé ou on ne s'entend pas bien, ça peut être désagréable.

Page 11 Friends and relationships

1 D **2** D+M **3** D+M

Page 12 Marriage and partnership

Model answers:

- Tu rêves de te marier?

  Je voudrais me marier un jour, mais pas trop tôt, de toute façon pas avant l'âge de trente ans. J'aimerais célébrer mon mariage dans un bel endroit avec ma famille et mes copains.

- Est-ce que tu es allé(e) à un mariage récemment?

  Non, pas récemment, mais il y a deux ans, ma cousine s'est mariée en Écosse. Le mariage a eu lieu dans une vieille église et ensuite, nous sommes allés dans un grand château pour la fête. Une centaine d'invités sont venus et après le repas de noces, on a dansé toute la soirée.

- Est-ce que le mariage est nécessaire à ton avis?

  Je sais qu'il y a des gens qui disent que le mariage est démodé et qu'on peut tout simplement vivre ensemble, mais à mon avis, c'est le mode de vie idéal, surtout si on veut avoir des enfants.

- Est-ce que tu utiliserais Internet pour trouver un partenaire?

  Ça, c'est une question intéressante! J'utiliserais Internet si je ne pouvais pas trouver un partenaire autrement. Il y a peut-être des dangers, mais mon frère aîné a rencontré sa petite amie sur un site Internet et ils vont se marier l'année prochaine.

Page 13 Food

1 50 **2** 150 **3** 200 **4** 50

Page 14 Meals
Model answers:

• Quel est ton repas préféré? Pourquoi?

Mon repas préféré est le dîner parce que chez nous, c'est un repas chaud. J'aime les aliments savoureux mais pas trop épicés. Hier, on a mangé des pâtes avec une sauce à la tomate. C'était délicieux!

• Est-ce qu'il est important de bien manger au petit-déjeuner?

À mon avis, le petit-déjeuner est très important parce qu'il vous donne de l'énergie au début de la journée. Cependant, il faut manger un petit-déjeuner équilibré: des céréales ou du pain avec des produits laitiers et des fruits.

• Quel repas est le plus important, à ton avis? Pourquoi?

Ça, c'est une question difficile. Je pense que tous les repas sont importants, à part le goûter parce qu'on mange souvent trop d'aliments sucrés et plein de matières grasses comme les gâteaux et les biscuits. Pour moi, il est important que je mange sainement. Au déjeuner, par exemple, je prends souvent une salade et un fruit.

Page 15 Feeling unwell
B; D; E

Page 16 Healthy and unhealthy living
Model answers:

• Qu'est-ce qui est mauvais pour la santé?

Il y a plein de choses qui sont mauvaises pour la santé. Le tabagisme, par exemple, est non seulement la cause du cancer du poumon et de problèmes respiratoires, mais aussi de maladies cardio-vasculaires. Je n'ai jamais fumé de cigarette et je n'ai aucune intention d'essayer. À part le tabagisme, je pense que les gens qui consomment des drogues sont bêtes et risquent leurs vies.

• Qu'est-ce que tu feras ce week-end pour rester en forme?

Ce week-end, j'irai à la salle de gym où je participerai à un cours de fitness. Je fais ce cours depuis trois mois et maintenant, je peux monter l'escalier facilement sans être essoufflé. S'il fait beau, je ferai aussi du vélo avec ma mère.

Page 17 Social issues
1 D **2** F **3** A **4** C

Page 18 Charity and voluntary work
1 C **2** A **3** E

Page 19 Music
Model answer:
Moi, j'adore toutes sortes de musiques, mais celle que je préfère est la pop parce que je trouve que les mélodies sont toujours très rythmiques. Il y a quelques années, j'ai entendu la musique d'Ed Sheeran pour la première fois. À mon avis, il est le meilleur chanteur en ce moment, car il écrit des chansons dont les paroles et la musique sont inoubliables. Récemment, j'ai téléchargé toutes ses chansons sur mon portable et je l'ai vu en concert sur Internet. Si j'ai de la chance, j'achèterai des billets pour son prochain concert. Ça serait génial!

Page 20 Cinema
1 His friends had talked about it.
2 They are striking (breathtaking) aerial shots.
3 He was moved to tears / he cried. (He felt emotional.)

Page 21 Television
Model answers:

• Quelles émissions est-ce que tu regardes régulièrement?

Je regarde les actualités chaque soir parce que je pense que c'est important de s'informer de ce qui se passe dans le monde.

• Quels sont les avantages de regarder un film à la télé?

À mon avis, le plus grand avantage de regarder un film à la télé c'est qu'on ne doit pas sortir et on peut s'installer confortablement sur le canapé! Ce qui m'embête au cinéma c'est d'avoir des gens très grands assis devant moi qui me bloquent la vue. Je déteste aussi les gens qui mangent du pop-corn pendant tout le film. D'autre part, c'est vraiment génial de voir un film sur grand écran.

• Voudrais-tu participer à une émission de télé-réalité?

Ça dépend de l'émission. Cela pourrait être intéressant de passer une semaine à vivre comme les gens des années cinquante, mais en général, je pense que les émissions de télé-réalité sont débiles, alors je dirais non!

• Qu'est-ce que tu as vu à la télé hier?

Je m'intéresse beaucoup aux animaux et hier, j'ai vu un documentaire très informatif sur les animaux qui habitent en Afrique. On a expliqué que plusieurs espèces sont menacées.

Page 22 Eating out
1 19% **2** 20% **3** 11% **4** 22%

Page 23 Sport
Model answers:

• Qu'est-ce qu'il y a sur la photo?

Sur la photo, on voit des gens qui courent. Je pense qu'ils participent à une course, peut-être à un marathon. Les gens au premier plan semblent très heureux. Je pense qu'ils viennent de traverser la ligne d'arrivée.

• Qu'est-ce que tu fais normalement pour rester en forme?

Je joue au basketball et je m'entraîne deux fois par semaine. Je suis dans l'équipe du collège et il y aura un match samedi matin, ici au collège. J'espère que nous gagnerons!

• Parle-moi d'un événement sportif que tu as vu récemment.

Récemment, j'ai vu un match de rugby à la télévision. C'était l'Angleterre contre la France et l'Angleterre a gagné dix-neuf points à seize. À mon avis, c'était un match très passionnant et j'espère que l'Angleterre va gagner le championnat!

• Est-ce que les événements sportifs internationaux sont importants, à ton avis?

Ça, c'est une question intéressante! J'aime bien regarder les événements sportifs comme les Jeux Olympiques ou la

Coupe du Monde, car je trouve l'ambiance vraiment géniale et on peut admirer les efforts des sportifs. Cependant, je pense aussi que ces événements coûtent très cher et c'est difficile pour les athlètes des pays pauvres d'y participer.

Page 24 Travel and transport

	Transport	Problem
1	train	three hours late
2	boat	seasick
3	plane	luggage lost
4	coach	too much traffic on the motorway

Model answers:

- Comment vas-tu au collège?

  Normalement, j'y vais à pied, mais hier, j'y suis allé(e) en bus parce qu'il pleuvait.

- Quel est ton moyen de transport préféré? Pourquoi?

  Je préfère voyager en train parce que c'est plus écolo que les autres moyens de transport et je peux lire ou travailler pendant mon voyage.

- Est-ce que tu es allé(e) en France? Décris ton voyage.

  Oui, j'y suis allé(e) en échange scolaire l'année dernière. Le voyage était assez fatigant car nous devions nous lever tôt pour arriver à l'aéroport deux heures avant le départ du vol. L'avion a décollé à l'heure et nous sommes arrivés en France vers dix heures.

- Comment voyagerais-tu si tu avais le choix?

  À mon avis, la voiture est le moyen de transport le plus pratique parce qu'elle vous donne la liberté d'aller où vous voulez, quand vous voulez.

Page 25 Planning a holiday
Model answers:

- Est-ce que tu préfères les vacances d'été ou les vacances d'hiver?

  Je préfère les vacances d'hiver parce que j'adore la neige et j'aime faire du ski. Cependant, mes parents aiment le soleil, alors nous passons normalement les vacances dans un pays chaud comme la Grèce ou l'Espagne.

- Comment seraient tes vacances idéales?

  Je passerai mes vacances idéales dans un endroit isolé où je pourrais apprécier le paysage et la nature. Je pourrais me détendre en faisant des randonnées et en prenant de belles photos.

- Selon toi, est-ce que les vacances sont importantes? Pourquoi / pourquoi pas?

  À mon avis, les vacances sont importantes car il est essentiel de se détendre et de récupérer un peu; on ne devrait pas travailler tout le temps. Si on ne peut pas partir en vacances, on pourrait se relaxer chez soi et faire des excursions locales.

- Quel type de vacances préfères-tu et pourquoi?

  Je préfère des vacances actives ou culturelles. Je n'aime pas m'allonger sur une plage et ne rien faire. Je pense que les vacances vous donnent la chance de voir le monde.

Page 26 Reservations
1 P **2** P/N **3** N **4** P

Page 27 Describing your holiday
1 Advantage – visited a lot of interesting places / all meals included / could exercise on board

Disadvantage – was sometimes seasick

2 (Listening) **1** E **2** D **3** F **4** B

Page 28 Social media
1 N **2** P **3** N **4** P **5** P/N

Page 29 Mobile technology
Fatima: F; Léon: E; Nora: D; Guy: B

Page 30 My home
Model answers:

- Que penses-tu de ta maison?

  J'aime ma maison, surtout l'emplacement car elle se trouve non loin du collège et du centre-ville. Elle est assez moderne et tout fonctionne bien. Nous avons une grande cuisine et un salon au rez-de-chaussée, ce qui est bien quand mes copains sont chez moi, mais ma chambre est assez petite. Cependant, c'est une chambre très lumineuse car il y a une grande fenêtre qui donne sur le jardin.

- Comment serait ta maison idéale?

  Ma maison idéale se trouverait au bord d'une rivière avec vue sur les collines. Elle ne serait ni grande ni petite et il y aurait une grande cuisine. Elle serait en briques rouges et elle aurait une porte verte et des fenêtres énormes. J'adore lire, alors la maison aurait une salle de lecture avec beaucoup de livres et un fauteuil confortable, où je passerais tout mon temps libre. De plus, j'aime organiser des soirées donc il faudrait que la maison ait une grande salle à manger et au moins deux chambres d'amis.

Page 31 The neighbourhood
Model answer:

J'habite à Exeter. C'est une assez grande ville dans le sud-ouest de l'Angleterre. Dans le passé, la ville était plus petite qu'aujourd'hui, mais elle avait de l'importance grâce à sa cathédrale qui domine encore la cité. Le centre-ville médiéval a été détruit par des bombes pendant la Deuxième Guerre mondiale, mais on a construit de nouveaux magasins et immeubles à la place des anciens bâtiments.

Pour les habitants d'Exeter, la vie est très agréable. Il y a quand même des inconvénients qu'on retrouve dans toutes les grandes villes, surtout les problèmes de pollution car il y a beaucoup de voitures. Cependant, on ne doit pas oublier les avantages de vivre en ville, car on y trouve quelque chose pour tout le monde: des cinémas et des théâtres ainsi que des restaurants et des centres sportifs. Pour une vie active et culturelle avec de bons transports en commun, il vaut mieux vivre en ville.

Page 32 Shopping
1 Things are cheaper.

2 You have to send something back if it is the wrong size.

Page 33 Town and region

Model answer (Translation):

J'habite dans une ferme à la campagne depuis trois ans. J'aime vivre ici parce que je peux faire des promenades dans les champs avec mon chien. Cependant, mon frère déteste le village parce que c'est trop petit. Il voudrait habiter une grande ville. L'année dernière, il a passé six mois dans une famille aux États-Unis.

Model answers (Speaking):

- Qu'est-ce qu'on peut faire dans ta région?

  J'habite dans le sud-ouest de l'Angleterre. C'est une région très pittoresque où on peut faire des randonnées à la campagne ou au bord de la mer. En été, beaucoup de gens passent leurs vacances dans une des stations balnéaires le long de la côte. On peut y faire des sports nautiques, se bronzer sur les plages ou nager dans la mer. Pour les touristes, il y a quelques vieux châteaux ainsi que des villes intéressantes.

- Où voudrais-tu habiter à l'avenir?

  À l'avenir, je voudrais habiter à la campagne parce que j'aime faire des activités de plein air. Je pourrais faire de l'équitation ainsi que de la pêche. En plus, il y a moins de pollution et la vie est moins stressante. Pourtant, il y aurait des inconvénients parce que je n'ai pas le permis de conduire et il faudrait prendre les transports en commun pour aller en ville.

- Tu aimes habiter dans ta région?

  J'adore habiter dans une grande ville parce qu'il y a tant de choses à faire! On peut se déplacer facilement si on veut rencontrer des amis ou aller au cinéma. C'est une ville très historique et il y a beaucoup de choses intéressantes à voir pour les touristes comme la cathédrale médiévale et le vieux quartier. Récemment, j'ai vu une exposition sur les origines de la ville qui était vraiment informative.

- Tu voudrais vivre à l'étranger? Pourquoi / pourquoi pas?

  Je voudrais vivre à l'étranger parce que ça m'intéresse de rencontrer de nouvelles personnes et de découvrir d'autres cultures. Cependant, je ne voudrais pas vivre dans un pays tropical car je n'aime pas tellement la chaleur. D'un autre côté, mes parents aimeraient bien vivre en Espagne parce qu'il y fait plus chaud qu'ici, mais ils ne parlent pas espagnol, alors ça serait difficile pour eux.

Page 34 The environment

1 C **2** F **3** A **4** E

Page 35 Global issues

1 C **2** A **3** E **4** B

Page 36 My studies

1 English

2 The teacher makes it interesting.

3 Citizenship

4 The speaker thinks it's a waste of time; the teacher is always in a bad mood; the teacher criticizes them all the time. (any **two**)

Page 37 Your school

1 **1** P+N; **2** N; **3** P; **4** P

2 Model answers:

- Que penses-tu de la journée scolaire? Pourquoi?

  À mon avis, la journée scolaire est trop longue parce les horaires sont de huit heures et demie jusqu'à quatre heures. Si on veut faire des activités périscolaires, il ne reste pas assez de temps pour faire les devoirs.

- Que penses-tu du règlement scolaire?

  Généralement, je trouve que le règlement scolaire est raisonnable, par exemple, on ne doit pas courir dans les couloirs et on doit être poli, mais les règles en ce qui concerne le maquillage et l'uniforme sont bêtes.

- Comment était ton école primaire?

  Mon école primaire se trouvait assez près de chez moi et elle était petite. Il y avait un jardin à côté de la cour de récréation où nous cultivions des fleurs et des légumes.

- À ton avis, quelles sont les pressions pour les élèves dans ton collège?

  À mon avis, nous travaillons toujours sous pression, car il faut réussir aux examens. Tout le monde s'y attend, les parents et les profs!

- Qu'est-ce que tu as fait au collège hier?

  Hier, j'avais cours toute la journée. C'était mercredi, mon jour préféré parce qu'on fait du sport l'après-midi. Hier, nous avons dû courir autour du terrain de sport avant de jouer au basket.

- Comment sont les repas à la cantine?

  En fait, je ne sais pas parce que j'apporte des sandwichs de chez moi pour le déjeuner. Cependant, mes copains disent que les repas sont assez bons et pas chers.

Page 38 Jobs and careers

B, C, D, F

Page 39 Ambitions

Model answers :

- Tu veux aller à l'université ou trouver un emploi? Pourquoi?

  Je voudrais aller à l'université avant de trouver un emploi parce que je voudrais continuer à faire des études et je pense que je trouverai un meilleur emploi si j'ai un diplôme. En plus, je ne sais pas encore ce que je voudrais faire comme travail.

- Est-ce que tu voudrais étudier à l'université à l'étranger à l'avenir? Pourquoi / pourquoi pas?

  À l'avenir, je voudrais étudier à l'université à l'étranger parce que je pense qu'on peut gagner de nouvelles expériences et améliorer ses compétences linguistiques, surtout si on étudie à une université dans un pays européen.

- Tu voudrais prendre une année sabbatique à l'avenir? Pourquoi / pourquoi pas?

  Je n'ai pas encore décidé parce que je pense qu'on doit avoir une bonne idée de ce qu'on voudrait faire pendant cette année, par exemple voyager à l'étranger ou faire du bénévolat, sinon

on pourrait gaspiller du temps. Pour le moment, j'ai l'intention d'aller à l'université après avoir passé mon bac.

- Quel emploi est-ce que tu voulais faire quand tu étais plus jeune?

Quand j'étais jeune, je rêvais d'être médecin car ma mère faisait ce métier. Malheureusement, il faut avoir de bonnes notes en sciences et je suis très faible dans cette matière. L'important pour moi maintenant est de faire quelque chose d'intéressant.

Page 40 Education post-16

(a) En septembre j'étudierai les matières qui m'intéressent le plus.

(b) Je suis content de laisser tomber la géographie parce que c'est ennuyeux.

(c) La plupart de mes amis ont l'intention d'aller à l'université.

(d) Je pense qu'on peut trouver un meilleur emploi si on a fait des études universitaires.

(e) Je voudrais trouver un emploi ou un apprentissage.

Page 41 Francophone countries

1 dark; there is no electricity

2 thirsty; there is no (drinking) water

3 toilets; girls leaving school

Page 42 French customs

1 1 D   2 F   3 G   4 C

2 Model answers:

- Qu'est-ce qu'il y a sur la photo?

Sur la photo, on voit plusieurs personnes qui fêtent peut-être un anniversaire. Ils sont assis à une table dans un jardin ou un parc. Sur la table, il y a la nourriture et les boissons. Ils sont tous très heureux car ils rient.

- Quel est ton cadeau d'anniversaire idéal?

Mon cadeau d'anniversaire idéal c'est de l'argent parce que je voudrais une tablette et j'économise en ce moment pour en acheter une.

- Qu'est-ce que tu as fait pour fêter ton anniversaire l'année dernière?

L'année dernière, j'ai invité mes copains chez moi pour une fête. Ils m'ont offert des cadeaux et ils ont chanté «Joyeux anniversaire!». C'était super. Ma mère a fait un gâteau d'anniversaire au chocolat et on a bu du coca. On a dansé et écouté de la musique toute la soirée.

- Comment est-ce que tu fêtes le Nouvel An?

Quelquefois, on reste à la maison et on invite des copains chez nous, parfois on va chez des copains. À minuit, on regarde la télé et on dit «Bonne année!» L'année dernière, on est allés voir un feu d'artifice et après, tout le monde a chanté dans les rues.

- Est-ce que les fêtes en famille sont importantes?

Oui, je pense que les fêtes en famille sont très importantes, parce que c'est l'occasion de rassembler

toute la famille. L'année dernière, ma grand-mère a eu soixante-quinze ans et nous avons célébré son anniversaire dans un restaurant.

Page 43 French festivals
Model answers

- Que penses-tu des fêtes françaises?

À mon avis, les fêtes françaises sont intéressantes, surtout la fête nationale, parce qu'on peut aller voir un feu d'artifice le soir. J'adore les feux d'artifice et c'est formidable de voir le ciel illuminé comme ça.

- Tu es déjà allé(e) à une fête en France? C'était comment?

Non, je ne suis jamais allé(e) à une fête en France, mais notre prof nous a montré une vidéo d'un carnaval en France. C'est super parce qu'on peut danser et chanter dans les rues et partout on voit des gens déguisés. Je voudrais aller à un carnaval un jour.

Page 44 Pronunciation strategies
Access audio QR code on page for model examples.

Page 45 Speaking strategies
Model answers:

- Quels sont les effets du réchauffement de la Terre?

Je ne sais pas exactement, mais je pense que le changement climatique est un problème très grave. On voit de plus en plus de tempêtes tropicales tandis qu'en Afrique, il ne pleut pas.

- Qu'est-ce qu'on doit faire pour protéger l'environnement?

On pourrait faire beaucoup de choses. Moi, j'essaie de consommer moins d'énergie et d'utiliser les transports en commun.

Page 47 Exam skills: General conversation
Answers will vary.

Page 48 Exam skills: Using the photo card or picture stimulus
Model answers:
Sur la photo, on voit un jeune couple qui vient de se marier. La femme porte une robe blanche et un bouquet de fleurs orange, qui sont peut-être des roses. Ils sont dans un jardin avec leurs amis qui sont en train de les féliciter.

Page 49 Exam skills: Role-play (Foundation)
Model answers:
- *Je suis britannique / anglais(e) / écossais(e) / gallois(e) / irlandais(e).*
- *Je suis en France pour une semaine.*
- *Mon hotel est confortable et pas trop cher.*
- *J'adore la France, parce que la cuisine est délicieuse.*
- *Où est la gare, s'il vous plaît? / Pour aller à la gare, s'il vous plaît?*

Page 50 Exam skills: Role-play (Higher)
Model answers:
- *J'aime ta maison, parce qu'elle est très jolie / moderne / grande, etc.*
- *Le voyage était long et fatigant.*
- *J'aime les légumes, parce qu'ils sont bons pour la santé / J'adore les gateaux, parce que j'aime les aliments sucrés.*
- *Je voudrais faire du tourisme et manger dans un restaurant.*
- *Comment est-ce que tu utilises la technologie? / Est-ce que tu utilises un portable / un ordinateur / une tablette?*

Page 51 Listening strategies
- Olympic Games are good for the economy; the games attract more visitors / increase the number of visitors to the country.
- The cost of creating the infrastructure for the games is high; many countries are in debt as a result.

Page 52 Exam skills: Listening
C

Page 53 Exam skills: Listening: Finding reasons
1. Claire: avantage – on a un compagnon pour la vie; inconvénient – on perd sa liberté / on ne plus faire ce qu'on veut

   Hubert: avantage – stabilité pour les enfants / c'est bon pour fonder une famille; inconvénient – la fête est parfois très chère / coûte beaucoup d'argent
2. (a) Problem: Flat overlooked a building site / Flat didn't have a view of the sea. Solution: Owner will reimburse half the rent.
   (b) Problem: Shower (in hotel room) wasn't working. Solution: Changed rooms / Moved to a different room.

Page 55 Exam skills: Reading: Answering in English
1. You will eat smaller portions.
2. Use the stairs rather than the lift.
3. Memory and brain function.

Page 56 Exam skills: Reading: Answering in French
1. D, G, B, H, E
2. est honnête / dit la vérité

Page 57 Reading: Drawing conclusions
the (school) summer holidays

Page 58 Exam skills: Reading longer texts
1. A 2. A

Page 59 Exam skills: Translation into English
Model answers:
1. With a remote control, you/one/we can change TV programme without leaving your/one's/our chair or the sofa.

2. I went to the chemist/pharmacy with the prescription that the doctor had given me to get medicine.
3. I have just spent a week at the seaside/by the sea in this hotel. It has recently been refurbished with new furniture everywhere. On the ground floor, there is a beautiful dining room where dinner is served every evening/night. What I liked most was the heated swimming pool. I would like to go back there next year.

Page 60 Writing strategies
Model answer:
Il y a deux jours, c'était mon anniversaire et j'ai eu seize ans. Le matin, mes parents m'ont donné un nouveau portable comme cadeau et le soir, j'ai invité mes ami(e)s chez moi pour voir un film. Après avoir vu le film, on a mangé de la pizza. Mon anniversaire était super parce que j'ai reçu de beaux cadeaux. À Noël, nous nous réunissons en famille aussi, alors c'est une date importante. Heureusement, tout le monde s'entend vraiment bien dans ma famille. Le week-end prochain, on ira au théâtre à Londres pour voir la comédie musicale *Les Misérables*. J'adore la musique et je connais les paroles de toutes les chansons.

Page 61 Exam skills: Translation into French (Foundation)
Model answers:
1. Mon frère a treize ans.
2. Le matin, je prends mon petit-déjeuner dans la cuisine.
3. Il y a une bibliothèque en face du supermarché.
4. La semaine dernière, je suis allé(e) au théâtre avec ma famille.
5. Il y a quatre personnes dans ma famille.
6. Je n'aime pas faire mes devoirs.
7. Ma soeur joue/fait du piano le soir.

Page 62 Exam skills: Translation into French (Higher)
Model answers:
1. Pendant l'été, je suis allé(e) en vacances avec ma famille dans le sud de l'Espagne. L'hôtel était assez petit et ma chambre était sale. Mes parents aiment la nourriture espagnole mais je préfère les plats épicés. La semaine prochaine, c'est l'anniversaire de mon frère. Je lui achèterai des chaussettes blanches et un livre.
2. En février, j'ai fait/participé à un voyage scolaire en France. Le voyage était trop long et j'ai eu le mal de mer. À l'avenir, je préférerais voyager en avion. Je suis resté dans une famille sympa qui vit dans le centre-ville. L'année prochaine, mon ami(e) français(e) viendra chez moi et nous ferons du tourisme.

Page 63 Exam skills: Writing (Foundation)
Model answer:
En ce moment, je passe des vacances au bord de la mer dans le sud de la France. Il fait très beau et hier, nous avons nagé dans la piscine et nous sommes allés à la plage.

En France, il fait plus chaud qu'en Angleterre et on achète du pain frais tous les jours.

L'année prochaine, je voudrais aller à la montagne en Suisse parce que je préfère faire des randonnées ou du cyclisme.

À mon avis, les vacances sont très importantes parce qu'on doit se détendre, sinon on devient trop stressé.

Page 64 Exam skills: Writing (Higher)
Model answer:
Être un(e) bon(ne) ami(e) est très important car on a toujours besoin de copains en cas de problème. Récemment, une de mes meilleures amies a été victime d'harcèlement en ligne quand quelqu'un a mis sa photo sur un réseau social et a écrit des choses méchantes et fausses sur elle. J'ai dû la soutenir en passant des soirées avec elle pour la rassurer. Je lui ai conseillé de ne plus utiliser les réseaux sociaux et de changer son numéro de portable. J'étais très heureuse de l'aider car l'année dernière, quand j'avais des difficultés avec mes parents, elle était là pour moi.

Si je gagne les cent euros, j'inviterai mon amie à faire une sortie avec moi. Nous avons envie de passer la journée dans un parc d'attractions, mais ça coûte assez cher. Après y être allé(e)s, nous pourrons manger dans un restaurant italien s'il me reste encore un peu d'argent du prix du concours. À mon avis, ça serait une journée géniale!

Page 65 Articles
① **(a)** le **(b)** le **(c)** le **(d)** L'; les
(e) le **(f)** L'; l' **(g)** le; la **(h)** La; la; l'
(i) la **(j)** Le

② **(a)** Il a les cheveux gris et les yeux verts.
(b) Elle est infirmière et elle travaille dans un hôpital.
(c) Il y a des magasins dans le village.
(d) Nous mangeons le dîner dans la cuisine.
(e) J'ai visité l'Espagne l'été dernier.

Page 66 Prepositions
(a) *vers* la gare
(b) *contre* l'Angleterre
(c) *malgré* la pluie
(d) *parmi* mes amis
(e) *pour* mon anniversaire
(f) *chez* moi
(g) *sans* lait
(h) *sauf* le mardi
(i) *selon* un sondage

Page 67 The preposition à
① **(a)** au **(b)** aux **(c)** à l'
(d) à la **(e)** au

② **(a)** I would like a ham sandwich.
(b) It's the girl with blue eyes.

(c) My flat is on the third floor.
(d) I've got a stomach ache.
(e) They are playing volleyball.

③ **(a)** J'ai mal à l'oreille.
(b) C'est combien, la glace au café?
(c) Ils jouent aux cartes.
(d) J'adore la soupe à l'oignon.

Page 68 Partitives and preposition *de*
Model answers:
(a) J'ai acheté du lait, de la viande et des œufs.
(b) Il n'a pas de poisson.
(c) Le copain / Le petit ami de ma sœur est assez grand.
(d) Le parc est à côté du château.
(e) J'ai essayé de faire mes devoirs.

Page 69 Nouns
(a) mercredi (m) **(b)** pharmacienne (f)
(c) révolution (f) **(d)** chinois (m)
(e) rire (m) **(f)** serveuse (f)
(g) nourriture (f) **(h)** chou (m)

Page 70 Adjectives
(a) une bonne question
(b) un petit jardin
(c) une amie / copine jalouse
(d) une chemise gris clair
(e) un vieil objet

Page 71 Comparatives and superlatives
Model answers:
(a) Les films d'horreur sont plus passionnants que les films romantiques.
(b) Les feuilletons sont plus divertissants que les actualités.
(c) Les émissions de sport sont aussi intéressantes que les documentaires.
(d) *Amélie* est le film le plus amusant.
(e) C'est l'émission la plus ennuyeuse.
(f) Adele est la meilleure chanteuse.
(g) Il est le pire acteur.
(h) Il a choisi le plat principal le plus cher.
(i) J'ai acheté le souvenir le moins cher.
(j) Ce sont les places les plus inconfortables.

Page 72 Possessive and demonstrative adjectives
Model answers:
(a) Mon père a perdu son portable dans ce magasin-là.
(b) Nous avons rendu visite à nos cousins.
(c) Ses parents et leurs amis sont restés dans cette maison-là.
(d) Mon copain / ami a acheté ce souvenir pour sa sœur.

Page 73 Indefinite adjectives and using *quel*

1 **(a)** tous (every day)   **(b)** toutes (all the stations)

    (c) toute (the whole class)   **(d)** tout (all the cheese)

    (e) toute (all the family)

2 **(a)** chaque matin / tous les matins

    (b) chaque étudiant

    (c) quelques personnes

    (d) quelques mots

    (e) quelque temps

3 **(a)** Quelle (What drink do you want?)

    (b) Quelle (What size do you want?)

    (c) Quel (What sport do you like?)

    (d) Quel (What kind of music don't you like?)

    (e) Quelles (What are your favourite subjects?)

    (f) Quel (What is your favourite hobby?)

    (g) quelle (What kind of films do you like?)

    (h) Quel (Which are the best soap operas/TV dramas?)

    (i) Quelle (How lucky!)

Page 74 Adverbs

Model answers:

(a) D'habitude, je quitte la maison de bonne heure.

(b) Parfois / Quelquefois, nous allons / on va au café.

(c) Je joue du piano mieux que mon frère.

(d) Il parle plus doucement que moi.

(e) Malheureusement, il faisait mauvais temps.

Page 75 Quantifiers and intensifiers

Model answers:

(a) Il y a beaucoup d'arbres dans le jardin.

(b) J'ai mangé trop de gâteaux.

(c) On voit tant de sans-abri dans les rues.

(d) Après quelques jours, j'avais vu assez de monuments.

(e) Mes parents sont tellement embêtants / agaçants!

Page 76 Subject and object pronouns

(a) <u>Ils</u> <u>lui</u> donnent un vélo.

(b) <u>Il</u> <u>leur</u> a parlé.

(c) <u>Elle</u> est en train de <u>le</u> lire.

(d) <u>Nous</u> voulons <u>le</u> voir.

(e) <u>Je</u> <u>les</u> ai achetés.

Page 77 Stressed and possessive pronouns

Model answers:

(a) My marks are better than yours.

(b) Our holidays were great. What were yours like?

(c) Have you got your mobile phone? I can't find mine.

(d) He hasn't got a cap! He can borrow mine.

Page 78 Relative and demonstrative pronouns

Model answers:

(a) The shop which is next to the museum is closed.

(b) The man I saw was wearing a black pullover.

(c) The children I look after are sweet.

Page 79 Pronouns *y* and *en*

Model answers:

(a) Vous voulez encore de la salade?

(b) Oui, j'en veux.

(c) Non, je n'en veux pas.

(d) Avez-vous besoin d'argent?

(e) Oui, j'en ai besoin.

(f) Il rentre du concert. Il en rentre.

(g) Je suis allé en France.

(h) J'y suis allé.

(i) Tu penses venir?

(j) Oui, j'y pense!

Page 80 Conjunctions and connectives

Model answers:

(a) Je déteste habiter en ville parce qu'il y a trop de pollution.

(b) Nous devons arrêter le déboisement de nos forêts, sinon on verra plus d'inondations.

(c) On voit beaucoup de sans-abri dans les rues à cause des problèmes de chômage et de pauvreté.

(d) Je pense qu'on devrait acheter des produits verts tandis que me parents pensent que nous devons consommer moins d'énergie.

Page 81 The present tense

Model answers:

(a) J'envoie des textos / SMS à mes copains / amis tous les jours / chaque jour.

(b) Nous lisons des poèmes en classe, en ce moment.

(c) Nous allons au cinéma aujourd'hui.

(d) Je ne le connais pas bien.

(e) J'apprends le français depuis cinq ans.

Page 82 Key verbs

Model answers:

1 **(a)** I want to go out.   **(b)** Are you hungry?

    (c) We needed help.   **(d)** They are thirsty.

    (e) We were unlucky.   **(f)** You are right.

    (g) She is afraid of snakes.

2 **(a)** She is in the middle of / in the process of doing the cooking.

    (b) He has had a cold for three days.

    (c) We had to / were obliged to leave before the end of the concert.

    (d) I don't agree with you.

    (e) We are about to leave.

    (f) I am back.

Page 83 The perfect tense

Model answer:

Hier, j'ai fêté mon anniversaire. Mes parents m'ont donné beaucoup de cadeaux que j'ai ouverts le matin. Le soir, on a fait une fête et beaucoup de mes copains sont venus. Nous avons bu du coca et après, nous avons dansé. Qu'est-ce que tu as fait le week-end dernier?

Page 84 The imperfect tense

Model answers:

(a) Je faisais mes devoirs quand ma mère m'a demandé de descendre.

(b) J'étais en train de lire mon livre quand quelqu'un a frappé à la porte.

(c) Nous traversions la rue quand l'accident s'est passé.

(d) Nous venions d'arriver quand il a commencé à pleuvoir.

Page 85 The pluperfect tense

Model answers:

(a) My brother went to the café to meet his friends but no one came.

(b) I had chosen my meal before going to the restaurant.

(c) I had never seen this person before.

(d) When I arrived at the market I noticed that I had forgotten my purse.

(e) We had left early but arrived late at our hotel.

Page 86 The immediate future tense

Model answers:

(a) Nous allons visiter un musée pendant l'échange.

(b) Ils vont voir un film ce soir.

(c) Il va y avoir du vent.

(d) J'espère qu'il va neiger bientôt.

(e) La France va gagner le match.

Page 87 The future tense

Model answers:

(a) Je le verrai demain.

(b) Nous devrons prendre le bus.

(c) Elle aura vingt ans.

(d) Est-ce que tu feras du vélo demain?

(e) Comment est-ce qu'il viendra? / Comment viendra-t-il?

(f) Nous irons au théâtre.

(g) Il n'achètera rien.

(h) Qu'est-ce que vous mangerez?

(i) Quand est-ce que tu sortiras?

(j) Je ne prendrai pas d'entrée.

Page 88 The conditional

Model answers:

(a) S'il était riche, il ne travaillerait pas.

(b) Je préférerais aller en Espagne.

(c) Si j'allais à Paris, je pourrais monter sur la tour Eiffel.

(d) Si mon portable ne fonctionnait plus, j'en achèterais un nouveau.

(e) Si je n'avais pas d'argent, je trouverais un emploi.

Page 89 Negative forms

Model answers:

(a) Il n'y a plus de beurre.

(b) Je ne suis jamais allé(e) en France.

(c) Nous ne somme pas allé(e)s au cinéma.

(d) Nous n'y allons pas.

(e) Il n'a parlé à personne.

Page 90 Reflexive verbs

Model answers:

(a) Je ne me lève pas tôt / de bonne heure.

(b) Ils ne se disputent jamais.

(c) Ils se sont lavé les mains.

(d) Nous voulons bien nous amuser.

Page 91 The imperative

1 **1** G; **2** H; **3** B; **4** C

2 Model answers:

(a) For a healthy life …

(b) … drink eight glasses of water a day.

(c) … eat at least five portions of fruits and vegetables each day.

(d) … don't smoke.

(e) … avoid foods that are rich in fat.

(f) … exercise regularly.

(g) … don't stay sitting for too long.

Page 92 Impersonal verbs

Model answers:

1 **(a)** Il reste de l'argent.

(b) Il y avait du vent.

(c) Il manque des informations.

(d) Il s'agissait d'une histoire vraie.

2 **(a)** Because of the strike we / I / they had to walk to school.

(b) You just need to talk to him.

(c) It is forbidden to walk on the lawn.

Page 93 The infinitive

Model answers:

1 **(a)** Il déteste faire ses devoirs.

(b) Elle adore écouter de la musique.

(c) J'ai essayé d'apprendre les mots nouveaux.

(d) Je sais parler chinois.

2 **(a)** We were invited to participate in a survey.

(b) After having eaten we went to the cinema.

(c) They decided to leave early.

(d) He left without saying a word.

Page 94 The present participle

Model answers:

(a) Being afraid of violence, she didn't go to see that war film.

(b) He was able to buy a new bicycle by saving his pocket money.

(c) He found himself in trouble / difficulty while swimming.

(d) I cut my finger while preparing dinner.

(e) On hearing the noise, we woke up.

Page 95 The passive voice

Model answers:

(a) The castle was built in the sixteenth century.

(b) The road is blocked by a tree.

(c) The buildings have been destroyed by the earthquake.

(d) The thieves have been arrested.

(e) The prices will be reduced.

Page 96 The subjunctive mood

Model answers:

(a) I prefer to go on foot, although I have a car.

(b) I sent him an email so that he knows the time of the meeting.

(c) I will stay near the phone until he comes back.

(d) Although he is rich he is not generous.

Published by BBC Active, an imprint of Educational Publishers LLP, part of the Pearson Education Group, 80 Strand, London, WC2R 0RL.

www.pearsonschools.co.uk/BBCBitesize
© Educational Publishers LLP 2018
BBC logo © BBC 1996. BBC and BBC Active are trademarks of the British Broadcasting Corporation.

Typeset by Elektra Media Ltd
Produced and illustrated by Elektra Media Ltd
Cover design by Andrew Magee & Pearson Education Limited 2017
Cover illustration by Darren Lingard / Oxford Designers & Illustrators

The right of Liz Fotheringham to be identified as authors of this work have been asserted by her in accordance with the Copyright, Designs and Patents Act 1988.

First published 2018

21 20 19 18
10 9 8 7 6 5 4 3 2 1

British Library Cataloguing in Publication Data
A catalogue record for this book is available from the British Library.

ISBN 978 1 406 68592 3

Printed and bound in Slovakia by Neografia.
The Publisher's policy is to use paper manufactured from sustainable forests.

Note from the publisher
Pearson has robust editorial processes, including answer and fact checks, to ensure the accuracy of the content in this publication, and every effort is made to ensure this publication is free of errors. We are, however, only human, and occasionally errors do occur. Pearson is not liable for any misunderstandings that arise as a result of errors in this publication, but it is our priority to ensure that the content is accurate. If you spot an error, please do contact us at resourcescorrections@pearson.com so we can make sure it is corrected.

Acknowledgements
The authors and publisher would like to thank the following individuals and organisations for their kind permission to reproduce copyright material.

Photographs
(Key: b-bottom; c-centre; l-left; r-right; t-top)
123RF: Margouillat 43t, Jozef Polc 48b, **Alamy Stock Photo:** Louis-Paul st-onge Louis 10, Adrian Sherratt 18, DBURKE 23, Stefan Auth/imageBROKER 96, BananaStock: 63, **Getty Images:** Morsa Images/Taxi vi, Morsa Images/Taxi 48t, **Reuters:** Mal Langsdon 43b, **Shutterstock:** Monkey Business Images 14, 21, Syda Productions 42, Chris Pelle 71, Andrey Skutin 86, Rido 95.

All other images © Pearson Education

Websites
Pearson Education Limited is not responsible for the content of third-party websites.